Leia & Pense em
INGLÊS

Leia & Pense em INGLÊS

Dos editores da Revista *Think English!*

ALTA BOOKS
EDITORA
Rio de Janeiro, 2012

Leia & Pense em Inglês Copyright © 2011 da Starlin Alta Con. Com. Ltda.
ISBN 978-85-7608-564-5

Produção Editorial
Editora Alta Books

Gerência Editorial
Anderson da Silva Vieira

Supervisão de Produção
Angel Cabeza
Augusto Coutinho
Leonardo Portella

Equipe Editorial
Adalberto Taconi
Andréa Bellotti
Andreza Farias
Bruna Serrano
Cristiane Santos
Daniel Siqueira
Daniel Schilklaper
Deborah Marques
Gianna Campolina
Isis Batista
Jaciara Lima
Jéssica Vidal
Juliana de Paulo
Lara Gouvêa
Lícia Oliveira
Lorrane Martins
Marcelo Vieira
Heloisa Pereira
Otávio Brum
Patrícia Fadel
Rafael Surgek
Sergio Cabral
Sergio Souza
Thiê Alves
Taiana Ferreira
Vinicius Damasceno
Iuri Santos

Tradução
Rafael Bonelli

Revisão Gramatical
Zélia
José Mauro

Revisão Técnica
André Félix

Diagramação
Andréa Fiães

Fechamento
Andreza Farias

Marketing e Promoção
Vanessa Gomes
marketing@altabooks.com.br

Impresso no Brasil

Translated From Original: Read & Think English For McGraw-Hill ISBN: 978-0-07-149916-3

Original english language edition copyright © 2008 by Second Language Publishing. Published by Mc-Graw Hill. All rights reserved including the right of reproduction in whole or in part in any form. This translation published by arrangement with Wiley Publishing, Inc.

Portuguese language edition Copyright © 2011 da Starlin Alta Con. Com. Ltda. All rights reserved including the right of reproduction in whole or in part in any form. This translation published by arrangement with McGraw-Hill.

Todos os direitos reservados e protegidos pela Lei nº 9.610/98. Nenhuma parte deste livro, sem autorização prévia por escrito da editora, poderá ser reproduzida ou transmitida sejam quais forem os meios empregados: eletrônico, mecânico, fotográfico, gravação ou quaisquer outros.

Todo o esforço foi feito para fornecer a mais completa e adequada informação; contudo, a editora e o(s) autor(es) não assumem responsabilidade pelos resultados e usos da informação fornecida.

Erratas e atualizações: Sempre nos esforçamos para entregar ao leitor um livro livre de erros técnicos ou de conteúdo; porém, nem sempre isso é conseguido, seja por motivo de alteração de software, interpretação ou mesmo quando há alguns deslizes que constam na versão original de alguns livros que traduzimos. Sendo assim, criamos em nosso site, www.altabooks.com.br, a seção *Erratas*, onde relataremos, com a devida correção, qualquer erro encontrado em nossos livros.

Avisos e Renúncia de Direitos: Este livro é vendido como está, sem garantia de qualquer tipo, seja expressa ou implícita.

Marcas Registradas: Todos os termos mencionados e reconhecidos como Marca Registrada e/ou comercial são de responsabilidade de seus proprietários. A Editora informa não estar associada a nenhum produto e/ou fornecedor apresentado no livro. No decorrer da obra, imagens, nomes de produtos e fabricantes podem ter sido utilizados, e, desde, já a Editora informa que o uso é apenas ilustrativo e/ou educativo, não visando ao lucro, favorecimento ou desmerecimento do produto/fabricante.

Impresso no Brasil

O código de propriedade intelectual de 1º de julho de 1992 proíbe expressamente o uso coletivo sem autorização dos detentores do direito autoral da obra, bem como a cópia ilegal do original. Esta prática generalizada, nos estabelecimentos de ensino, provoca uma brutal baixa nas vendas dos livros a ponto de impossibilitar os autores de criarem novas obras.

Dados Internacionais de Catalogação na Publicação (CIP)

L525 Leia & pense em inglês / dos editores da Revista Think English! ; [tradução Isabella Nogueira]. – Rio de Janeiro, RJ: Alta Books, 2011.
220 p. : il. + 1 disco sonoro (70 min).
Inclui glossário bilíngue.
Tradução de: Read & Think English.
ISBN 978-85-7608-564-5

1 1. Língua inglesa - Estudo e ensino. 2. Língua inglesa - Leitura. 3. Língua inglesa - Fala. 4. Língua inglesa - Escrita. 5. Estados Unidos - História.

CDU 802.0
CDD 420.7

Índice para catálogo sistemático:
1. Língua inglesa : Estudo e ensino   802.0
(Bibliotecária responsável: Sabrina Leal Araujo – CRB 10/1507)

Rua Viúva Cláudio, 291 – Bairro Industrial do Jacaré
CEP: 20970-031 – Rio de Janeiro – Tels.: 21 3278-8069/8419 Fax: 21 3277-1253
www.altabooks.com.br – e-mail: altabooks@altabooks.com.br
www.facebook.com/altabooks – www.twitter.com/alta_books

Sumário

INTRODUÇÃO — X
GUIA PARA O SEU SUCESSO — XII

Culture

The American Dream	A imigração e o sonho americano	4
A Melting Pot	Um caldeirão de raças e culturas	5
The American Cowboy	O Caubói, um ícone americano	6
American Jazz	Música mais inovadora da América	8
Singing the Blues	As raízes e os sons do blues	10
Native American Culture	Os primeiros habitantes da América	11
African Heritage	Os afro-americanos, passado e presente	12
Early American Literature	A literatura norte-americana	14
Artistic Expression	A expressão artística	15
The Birthplace of Broadway	O berço de nascimento da Broadway	16
Cultural Values	Valores culturais norte-americanos	18
Test your comprehension	Teste sua compreensão	20

Travel

Camping Trips	Acampando por todo o país	24
Rafting the Grand Canyon	Praticando rafting no Grand Canyon	25
Down by the Boardwalk	Os melhores passeios marítimos	26
Tresure Islands	Explore as ilhas havaianas	28
The First National Park	O primeiro parque nacional	30
A Walking Tour of D.C	Uma caminhada para visitar monumentos	32
Unique Accommodations	Durma em um farol	34
Made in the USA	Visitas guiadas às fábricas	36
Home on the Range	Passe as férias com os caubóis	37
San Juan Orcas	Dando uma olhada nas orcas	38
Go to Jail!	Visite a famosa prisão de Alcatraz	39
Test your comprehension	Teste sua compreensão	40

Tradition

Choices in Education	Opções e práticas educativas	44
Prom and Homecoming	Festas escolares tradicionais	45
Tradidions for the New Year	Tradições do Ano Novo	46
Going to the Chapel	Tradições de casamento	48
April Fools!	Peguei você, primeiro de Abril!	49
An American Christmas	Celebrando o Natal nos Estados Unidos	50
Giving Thanks	Dando Graças	52
America's Favorite Sport	O esporte favorito dos norte-americanos	54
The National Pastime	Baseball, o esporte e suas tradições	56
The American Flag	A importância e o significado da bandeira	58
Trick or Treat	Doces ou travessuras	60
Remembrance and Honor	Dia festivo de recordação e honra	61
Test your comprehension	Teste sua compreensão	62

Celebration

Luck of the Irish	Dia de São Patrício	66
Groundhog Day	Uma marmota prevê o tempo	67
Powwows	Cerimônias dos indígenas norte-americanos	68
Seasonal Celebrations	Festivais e diversão durante a estação	70
Flavor of America	Festivais famosos de alimentos	72
Earth Day	O dia para cuidar da terra	74
Parents Appreciation Day	Dia do pai e da mãe	75
Season Of Merriment	Mardi Gras em Nova Orleans	76
A Salute to Spring	Tradições e crenças da Páscoa	78
Celebrating Workers	Comemorando o dia do trabalho	79
Shakespeare Festivals	Feiras para admiradores de Shakespeare	80
Martin Luther King Day	Em memória e honra	81
Ethnic Celebrations	Celebrações de diferentes culturas	82
Test your comprehension	Teste sua compreensão	84

People

Trail of Discovery	Descobrindo o Oeste norte-americano	88
Mother of Civil Rights	Mãe dos direitos civis	89
The Founding Fathers	Os pais fundadores dos Estados Unidos	90
The Best of Two Worlds	Entrevista com Pepe Stepensky	92
Frank Lloyd Wright	O arquiteto mais influente	94
Rags to Riches	A filantropia de Andrew Carnegie	95
America Takes Flight	Voando alto com os norte-americanos	96
Dr. Seuss	Divertindo-se com o Dr. Seuss	97
Author and Preservationist	Conservando a natureza	98
Dr. Jonas Salk	O milagroso Dr. Salk	99
Angel of the Battlefield	O anjo dos campos de batalha	100
Let There Be Light	Thomas Edison e a lâmpada elétrica	101
Hispanic American's Famous Firsts	Os primeiros famosos	102
Test your comprehension	Teste sua compreensão	104

Business

Introduction to Taxes	Tudo sobre impostos	108
Entrepreneurship	Montando um negócio	110
Banking in America	O setor bancário norte-americano	112
Negotiating Your Salary	Negociando seu salário	114
Retirement Plans	Aprendendo sobre planos de aposentadoria	116
Mastering the Interview	Dominando sua entrevista de trabalho	118
Test your comprehension	Teste sua compreensão	120

Empowerment

Citizenship	Cidadania norte-americana	124
Civic Participation	Participação cívica ativa	125
Empowerment with Education	Êxito na educação	126
Community Colleges	Universidades públicas	128
Helping Children Succeed	Seus filhos na escola	130
Maximizing Your Talents	Oportunidades profissionais para bilíngues	132
Legal Resources	Ajuda e recursos legais	134
Public Benefits	Seus direitos a benefícios	135
Owning Your Own Home	Comprando uma casa	136
Parent-Teacher Association	Associação de Pais e Mestres	137
You and Your Community	Explore sua comunidade	138
Hispanics in the Workplace	Hispânicos no mercado de trabalho	140
Test your comprehension	Teste sua compreensão	142

History

Independence Day	Dia da Independência	146
Stars and Stripes	A bandeira dos EUA — estrelas e listras	147
The Electoral College	Elegendo presidentes	148
Supreme Law of the Land	A lei suprema da nação	149
Divisions of Power	Leis do governo	150
History of the White House	A Casa Branca	152
The Bill of Rights	Direitos individuais	153
United States Presidency	A presidência dos Estados Unidos	154
The American Revolution	A revolução da nação	156
The Underground Railroad	Escravos encontram liberdade	158
A Time of Crisis	A Grande Depressão	159
Spanish-American War	Em guerra contra a Espanha	160
Women's Right to Vote	Direito de voto feminino	161
Test your comprehension	Teste sua compreensão	162

Geography

Wold Heritage Sites	Lugares interessantes	166
Majestic Mountains	Grandes e pequenas montanhas	168
North American Deserts	O clima e a vida dos desertos	170
The Great Lakes	Os cinco Grandes Lagos	172
Protecting Our Environment	Protegendo nosso meio ambiente	173
Land of Waterfalls	As incríveis cataratas	174
Tropical Rain Forests	As florestas tropicais do Havaí	176
Temperate Rain Forests	As florestas temperadas norte-americanas	177
Volcanoes of the United States	Os vulcões dos EUA	178
Test your comprehension	Teste sua compreensão	180

Gastronomy

American Apple Pie	Torta de maçã norte-americana	184
Taste of America	Deliciosa cozinha regional	186
Blue Plate Special	Restaurantes econômicos	188
Chocolate Chip Cookies	Biscoitos com gotas de chocolate	190
Buffalo Wings	Frango apimentado	192
Saltwater Taffy	Doce de praia	193
Waldorf Salad	Salada simples e famosa	194
Clam Chowder	A sopa favorita	195
Farmers's Markets	Mercado de agricultores	196
Soul Food	A comida do sul	197
American Barbecue	Churrasco norte-americano	198
Test your comprehension	Teste sua compreensão	200

RESPOSTAS 202

Introdução

Leia & Pense em Inglês apresenta uma abordagem inovadora e acessível à aprendizagem de uma língua estrangeira. É um método dinâmico de aprofundamento do idioma, projetado para ser usado em casa e aumentar seu domínio do inglês, através do estudo da vida e cultura dos Estados Unidos.

Criamos *Leia & Pense em Inglês* com o seguinte objetivo: facilitar o aperfeiçoamento e a fluidez de seu inglês, e aumentar seu conhecimento sobre a vida e a cultura norte-americana, para desta forma desenvolver as suas oportunidades de êxito nos Estados Unidos.

Nosso sistema de aprendizagem foi moldado para usar seus conhecimentos prévios de inglês e ampliá-los, apresentando os vocabulários e as frases em contextos relevantes e estimulantes, que também enfatizam as quatro habilidades da linguagem: leitura, escrita, fala e compreensão do idioma.

Leia & Pense em Inglês dá vida ao inglês! Leia sobre a história dos Estados Unidos e descubra as pessoas que contribuíram para sua formação. Explore as tradições e os costumes peculiares que são associados a este país. E não se esqueça de que enquanto desfruta dos fascinantes artigos, está aprendendo inglês.

Professores e estudantes de todas as idades usam *Leia & Pense em Inglês* para ter mais domínio da língua inglesa de uma maneira natural e eficaz. Os resultados são os mesmos, tanto sendo usado como complemento em sala de aula quanto no aprendizado autodidata. Você desenvolverá e melhorará seus conhecimentos de vocabulário e gramática.

A informação contida em cada capítulo facilita a melhor compreensão sobre a vida nos Estados Unidos e isto, por sua vez, instiga um maior interesse e êxito no aprendizado do inglês. Cada artigo é acompanhado de um glossário bilíngue, para que assim você possa ler e aprender sem ter que parar para pesquisar as palavras no dicionário ou em um manual de conversação.

Leia & Pense em Inglês **se ajusta a diferentes níveis de conhecimento, do iniciante ao avançado:**

> **Básico:** É recomendado que o nível de conhecimento de inglês do estudante seja equivalente ao do ensino médio ou do primeiro período universitário. Mesmo a sua experiência prévia com o inglês tendo sido através de estudos escolares ou pessoais, *Leia & Pense em Inglês* permitirá que você se aprofunde na língua e na cultura, e também aumentará sua compreensão sobre a estrutura da oração e o uso dos verbos.
>
> **Intermediário:** Como estudante de nível intermediário, você aprenderá mais vocabulários e frases novas, e notará um aumento em sua fluidez e capacidade de compreensão.
>
> **Avançado:** O estudante avançado continuará adquirindo informações valiosas e relevantes, já que o aprendizado de um idioma é um esforço para toda a vida.

Leia & Pense em Inglês é um método eficaz, divertido e acessível, não importando seu nível atual de conhecimento.

Experimente o entusiasmo e a satisfação que vêm do aprendizado de uma nova língua e descoberta de uma nova cultura. Leia, fale, aproveite... Pense em inglês.

Guia para o sucesso

O programa *Leia & Pense em Inglês* está dividido em capítulos que guiam o estudante através da vida nos Estados Unidos. Ao final de cada capítulo há uma seção chamada "Teste sua Compreensão". Esta seção estimula o desenvolvimento da compreensão da leitura e favorece o entendimento do inglês escrito.

Não é necessário ler a obra do começo ao fim, nem mesmo em uma ordem determinada. Você pode ler seguindo a ordem dos capítulos ou por determinado capítulo ou artigo que seja de seu interesse. Você pode completar as perguntas dos testes, artigo por artigo ou por capítulos. Esta flexibilidade permite que o usuário avance em seu próprio ritmo, lendo e relendo o material segundo sua necessidade. Os artigos, que são muito interessantes, fazem com que o estudo seja mais agradável e a leitura se torne estimulante.

> Em primeiro lugar, leia o artigo para ter uma ideia geral sobre o tema. Não se preocupe se, a princípio, não compreender todo o vocabulário.
>
> Após ter compreendido do que se trata o artigo, leia-o de novo, fixando-se no vocabulário que não conhece. Dê atenção especial ao contexto onde tal vocabulário é usado.
>
> Leia o texto em voz alta.
>
> Caso tenha acesso a algum sistema de gravação, pratique gravando os artigos ou peça a alguém para gravar. Depois, escute as gravações e perceba como sua compreensão auditiva vai melhorando com o tempo.

Repita, Repita, Repita! Isto é muito importante quando se está memorizando partes e formas das palavras que são relevantes. A repetição ativa é, algumas vezes, a única maneira de lembrar-se dos detalhes difíceis de serem retidos na memória. Estas repetições orais frequentes ajudam a fixar as formas em seu "ouvido interno". Esta dimensão auditiva o ajudará a lembrar das palavras mais adiante. Com *Leia & Pense em Inglês*, você tem a oportunidade de repetir diferentes processos de aprendizagem quantas vezes quiser e quantas vezes sejam necessárias. Leia, escute e fale repetidamente: isto lhe será de grande ajuda para alcançar seu objetivo de dominar a língua inglesa.

Glossário bilíngue sob medida

Ao lado de cada artigo é encontrado um glossário bilíngue correspondente e de fácil acesso. Então, como não é necessário interromper a leitura para usar um dicionário, a compreensão e a aquisição de vocabulário são feitas de uma maneira muito mais cômoda e rápida.

Cada artigo contém gramática, vocabulário e frases novas, assim como repetições de vocabulário e frases previamente estudadas. As repetições ao longo dos artigos servem para aumentar a compreensão da leitura e facilitar a memorização. Os artigos estão escritos a partir de diferentes perspectivas e ainda que a maioria esteja escrita na terceira pessoa, há também alguns na primeira pessoa. Esta mudança de pessoa ajuda o leitor a reconhecer a conjugação dos diferentes tempos verbais.

Muitos professores de inglês recomendam "criar uma imagem mental" das palavras estrangeiras ou associá-las a objetos e situações familiares para aumentar a memorização das mesmas. Entretanto, com *Leia & Pense em Inglês* você não precisa "criar" nenhuma imagem. As imagens são criadas automaticamente em sua imaginação com o desenvolvimento da história. Leia com calma e, ao ler, imagine a história da mesma forma que foi escrita e absorva o novo vocabulário. Caso uma palavra ou frase seja especialmente difícil, tente associá-la com a imagem que representa na história, enquanto a pronuncia em voz alta.

Os verbos estão incluídos no glossário, primeiro na forma conjugada conforme aparecem na história e, depois, no infinitivo. Por exemplo: **looking for/to look for**: procurando/procurar.

Teste sua compreensão

As perguntas dos testes no final de cada capítulo foram produzidas para que você continue desenvolvendo sua habilidade de compreensão da leitura e garantir seu êxito no estudo de inglês. Além disto, você aprenderá a usar o contexto para determinar os significados. Quando entendemos o contexto em geral, muitas vezes podemos "adivinhar" o significado das palavras desconhecidas com base no contexto de uma frase, parágrafo ou artigo. As respostas estão no final do livro.

Informações sobre a autora

Os artigos contidos neste livro foram escritos, coordenados e recompilados sob a direção de Kelly Garboden, Fundadora e Editora da Second Language Publishing (SLP), uma editora educativa que publica as revistas *Think Spanish Magazine* e *Think English Magazine*. A SLP é especializada na elaboração de produtos interessantes e informativos dedicados ao aprendizado de idiomas, e tais produtos têm como objetivo superar as barreiras de comunicação e fomentar o aprendizado do idioma e a integração cultural. Para obter mais informações sobre a Second Language Publishing e a *Think English Magazine* visite o site: www.thinkenglishmagazine.com

Um Agradecimento especial para:

Jean Garboden, Miguel Romá, Lucía Terra e LuciaTerra.com, Karen Young, Mesia Quatro e LatPro.com, Jessica Harrison, Ian Chaplin e Cleo Chaplin

Informações sobre sites

Alguns sites listados neste livro se encontram em inglês e podem ser alterados ou desativados a qualquer momento pelos seus mantenedores, sendo assim, a editora Alta Books não controla ou se responsabiliza por web sites ou qualquer conteúdo de terceiros.

Leia & Pense em
INGLÊS

I like to see a man proud of the place in which he lives.
I like to see a man live so that his place will
be proud of him.

Abraham Lincoln

Culture

often associated: muitas vezes associado
prosperity: prosperidade
freedom: liberdade
driven/to drive: levado/levar
viewed: visto
land of opportunity: terra da oportunidade
have settled/to settle: estabeleceram-se/estabelecer
fresh start: novo começo
new life: nova vida
promise: promessa
had begun/to begin: tinha começado/começar
to attract: atrair
looking for/to look for: procurando/procurar
hoped to escape: esperavam fugir
class boundaries: divisões classistas
helped shape: ajudou a moldar
creating/to create: criando/criar
thousands: milhares
development: desenvolvimento
big business: grandes negócios
standard of living: padrão de vida
tycoons: magnatas
willingness: vontade, disponibilidade
think/to think: pensam/pensar
implies/to imply: implica/implicar
financial security: segurança financeira
material comfort: conforto material
coined the term: cunhou o termo
broader meaning: significado mais amplo
land: terra
according: de acordo
ability: habilidade
wages: salários
merely: apenas
be able to attain: ser capaz de alcançar
fullest stature: desenvolvimento máximo
innately capable: naturalmente capazes
recognized: reconhecidos
birth: nascimento
position: posição
achieve/to achieve: realiza/realizar
answer: resposta
depends: depende
luckily: felizmente
living: vivendo
to choose from: para escolher

The American Dream

The American Dream is **often associated** with immigration. For years, the dream of **prosperity** and **freedom** has **driven** immigrants to the United States. America is **viewed** as the **land of opportunity** and immigrants from all over the world **have settled** in the U.S. with dreams of a **fresh start** and a **new life**.

By the 1900's, the **promise** of the American Dream **had begun to attract** large numbers of immigrants **looking for** work in large cities. With hard work and determination immigrants **hoped to escape** the **class boundaries** of their home countries.

The Industrial Revolution **helped shape** the American Dream by **creating thousands** of jobs. The **development** of **big business**, the Transcontinental Railroad, and the increase in oil production improved the American **standard of living**. "Rags to riches" stories of business **tycoons** led to the belief that if you had intelligence, and a **willingness** to work hard, you would have a successful life.

When people **think** of the American Dream they think of a successful and satisfying life. The term usually **implies financial security** and **material comfort**, but can also mean living a fulfilling life.

James Truslow Adams **coined the term** "American Dream" in his book *The Epic of America*. However, Truslow's coinage of the phrase had a **broader meaning**.

The American Dream is *"that dream of a **land** in which life should be better and richer and fuller for everyone, with opportunity for each **according** to **ability** or achievement. It is not a dream of motor cars and high **wages merely**, but a dream of social order in which each man and each woman shall **be able to attain** to the **fullest stature** of which they are **innately capable**, and be **recognized** by others for what they are, regardless of the fortuitous circumstances of **birth** or **position**."*

How do you **achieve** the American Dream? That **answer depends** upon your personal definition of the term. **Luckily** for us, **living** in America—the land of opportunity, there are many dreams **to choose from**!

4 culture

A Melting Pot

The **term** melting pot is **strongly associated with** the United States. The United States is a melting pot of **people** from different cultures and **races**. **Throughout** the country **you will notice differences** in the **way** people **live**, **eat** and **even talk**.

While American English is **generally standard**, American **speech** can **differ according to** what part of the **country** you are in.

Certain **traits** and **personalities** are **connected** with certain regions. Westerners are **known as** the **least** traditional of Americans, and the **most tolerant** of **change** and differences. Midwesterners are known for being **honest, straightforward** people of traditional **values**.

The southwest has had the least influence by European immigrants. Much of its culture **has been defined** by native Americans and by the Spanish.

Southerners are **probably** the most **distinctive** of all American groups, with more **relaxed attitudes** and traditional ways than their **neighbors** to the north. They are known for their **hospitality**.

The Northeast is well known for its culture with excellent theaters and **museums**. It is also **regarded** for its educational system with some of the most **highly rated** and **respected** universities in the country. This region is also known for its large **mix** of **ethnic groups**.

Every time we speak, we **say volumes** about where we are from; the **neutral tones** of the Midwest, the **rapid speech** of New York City, the **long drawl** that **characterizes** the South. If you say a **certain word** or **phrase**, people will **most likely** be able to **guess** where you are from.

term: termo
strongly: fortemente
associated with: associado com
people: pessoas
races: raças
throughout: por todo
you will notice: você perceberá
differences: diferenças
way: forma
live/to live: vivem/viver
eat/to eat: comem/comer
even: até mesmo
talk/to talk: falam/falar
while: ainda que
generally: geralmente
standard: padrão
speech: fala
differ: diferenciar-se
according to: de acordo com
country: país
traits: características
personalities: personalidades
connected/to connect: conectadas/conectar
known as: conhecidos como
least: menos
most tolerant: mais tolerantes
change: mudança
honest: honestos
straightforward: diretos
values: valores
has been defined/to define: foi definida/definir
probably: provavelmente
distinctive: característicos
relaxed attitudes: atitudes tranquilas
neighbors: vizinhos
hospitality: hospitalidade
museums: museus
regarded: apreciado, estimado
highly rated: altamente avaliadas
respected: respeitadas
mix: mistura
ethnic groups: grupos étnicos
every time: toda vez
say/to say: dizemos/dizer
volumes: muito
neutral tones: tons neutros
rapid speech: fala rápida
long drawl: o sotaque de fala lenta
characterizes/to characterize: caracteriza/caracterizar
certain: certa
word: palavra
phrase: frase
most likely: provavelmente
guess: adivinhar

central character: personagem central
colorful: colorido
ranching: rancheira
has played/to play: representou/representar
is embedded/to embed: está incorporada/incorporar
stories: histórias, contos
songs: músicas
legends: lendas
although: embora
generally: geralmente
considered/to consider: considerado/considerar
icon: ícone
comes from/to come from: origina-se de/originar-se de
Civil War: Guerra Civil
soldiers: soldados
drifting/to drift: a migrar/migrar
means/to mean: significa/significar
guns: armas
cattle: gado
gunfights: tiroteios
rugged country: uma terra rústica
amenities: conforto
danger: perigo
appealing: atrativos
open and untamed: abertos e indomados
owned/to own: possuíam/possuir
carry/to carry: carregar/carregar
horseback: em seus cavalos
ranchers: rancheiros
hired/to hire: contratavam/contratar
hard-working: trabalhadores
ranch hands: vaqueiros
tended to/to tend to: cuidavam/cuidar
the herd: rebanho
when the time came: quando chegava o momento
round up/to round up: reuniam/reunir
open prairie: pradaria aberta
drive/to drive: conduziam/conduzir
market: mercado
depicted/to depict: descreviam/descrever
rustlers: ladrões de gado
while: ainda que
in some cases: em alguns casos
often: muitas vezes
lonely: solitário
harsh conditions: condições difíceis
exposed: exposto
despite this: apesar disto
joked/to joke: brincavam/brincar
simple way of life: estilo de vida simples

The American Cowboy

The **central character** of America's **colorful ranching** heritage is the cowboy. The American cowboy **has played** an important part in American culture and history. The cowboy influence **is embedded** in **stories**, **songs**, **legends**, movies, art and fashion.

Although the cowboy is **generally considered** an American **icon,** the traditional cowboy actually **comes from** a Hispanic tradition, which originated in Central Mexico, known as "charro."

At the end of the **Civil War**, many **soldiers** had no home, and no place to go. They started **drifting** to the West. To many, this term **means guns**, **cattle,** horses and **gunfights**. It was a **rugged country** with few **amenities** and a lot of **danger**. The Western territories were **appealing** to the adventurous, and they were **open and untamed**. Many of these men only **owned** what they could **carry** on **horseback**. **Ranchers hired** these **hard-working** men as **ranch hands**. The ranch hands **tended to the herd** and did work around the ranch. **When the time came** to sell the beef, the ranch hands would **round up** the herd from the **open prairie** and **drive** the cattle to **market**.

Popular stories about the cowboys **depicted** them as **rustlers** or professional gunfighters. **While** this is true **in some cases**, the average American cowboy was **often lonely**, lived in **harsh conditions**, and was frequently **exposed** to danger. **Despite this**, the cowboys always kept their sense of humor and **joked** about everything. They did not make much money and enjoyed the **simple way of life**.

Tough as nails, but **generous** and **hospitable**, these were the true *Wild West* American cowboys. The cowboy was the **embodiment** of **rugged independence**. Some names you might be familiar with are Butch Cassidy and The Sundance Kid, Buffalo Bill, Billy the Kid, Wyatt Earp and Doc Holiday.

Many of these cowboys became legends in **real life** and **later** legends of the **silver screen**. They rode horses. They **sang** songs. Their horses **did tricks** and their guns were **shiny**. They became American heroes.

MODERN **WORKING** COWBOYS

Being a cowboy is certainly not **a thing of the past**. Throughout the U.S., you will find cowboys working on ranches and **farms**. The **exact** number of working cowboys is **unknown**. Cowboys are **responsible** for **feeding** the **livestock**, **branding** cattle and horses, and **tending to injuries**. They also **move** the livestock to different **pasture locations**, or **herd** them into corrals. In addition, cowboys **repair fences**, **maintain** ranch equipment, and **perform** other **odd jobs** around the ranch.

And **last, but not least**: the **cowgirl**! The history of women in the west is **not as well documented** as that of men. However, in recent years **companies have dedicated** time and money to **researching** the cowgirl tradition. The **National Cowgirl Museum and Hall of Fame** has made great efforts **to document** the history of cowgirls.

tough as nails: duros que nem pedra *(expressão idiomática)*
generous: generosos
hospitable: hospitaleiros
embodiment: personificação
rugged independence: forte independência
real life: vida real
later: mais tarde
silver screen: cinema
sang/to sing: cantavam/cantar
did tricks: faziam truques
shiny: brilhantes
working: trabalhadores
being: ser
a thing of the past: uma coisa do passado
farms: fazendas
exact: exato
unknown: desconhecido
responsible: responsáveis
feeding: alimentar
livestock: criação
branding/to brand: marcar/marcar
tending to: cuidando de
injuries: ferimentos
move: mudam
pasture locations: localizações de pasto
herd/to herd: arrebanha/arrebanhar
repair/to repair: conserta/consertar
fences: cercas
maintain/to maintain: conservar/conservar
perform/to perform: realiza/realizar
odd jobs: trabalhos esporádicos
last, but not least: último, mas não menos importante
cowgirl: vaqueira
not as well documented: não é tão bem documentada
companies: empresas
have dedicated/to dedicate: tem dedicado/dedicar
researching/to research: pesquisa/pesquisar
National Cowgirl Museum and Hall of Fame: Museu Nacional e Galeria da Fama da Vaqueira
to document: para documentar

culture 7

American Jazz

Jazz **is considered** the most **significant**, influential and innovative music **to emerge** from the United States. New Orleans, Louisiana, is **widely known** as the **birthplace** of jazz.

Jazz can **make** the **listener feel happy** or **sad**, **mellow** or **energetic**. Jazz can **sound loud** or **soft**. **Performers** of jazz **improvise** and **create** music as they play.

Jazz **has its roots** in the nineteenth **century**. In the late 1880's, African-Americans began **to develop** new forms of music. They created blues music from the **gospel music** and **sad songs** of their years in **slavery**. From the blues came **the first true** jazz music. This **happened during** the early 1900's in Louisiana. Classic, traditional or Dixieland jazz **came out of** the music originating in New Orleans.

During the 1920's, jazz continued **to gain popularity**. Louis Armstrong **became** famous for his performances on the **trumpet** and for his **unusual** voice. Louis Armstrong became one of the most influential and loved U.S. jazz musicians. Historians **call** the 1920's the **Golden Age** of American Jazz.

As time passed, a jazz form called "swing" became very popular in America. People **danced** to swing music until after World War II. Benny Goodman **led** one of America's most successful **swing bands**. People called Goodman "The King of Swing." Goodman also **presented** black and white jazz musicians **playing together** for the **first time**.

---

is considered: é considerado
significant: importante
to emerge/to emerge: que surgiu/surgir
widely known: amplamente conhecido
birthplace: local de nascimento
make/to make: fazer/fazer
listener: ouvinte
feel/to feel: sentir-se/sentir
happy: feliz
sad: triste
mellow: tranquilo
energetic: energizado
sound/to sound: soar/soar
loud: alto
soft: suave
performers: músicos
improvise/to improvise: improvisam/improvisar
create/to create: criam/criar
has its roots: tem suas raízes
century: século
to develop: a desenvolver
gospel music: música gospel
sad songs: músicas tristes
slavery: escravidão
the first true: a primeira verdadeira
happened/to happen: aconteceu/acontecer
during: durante
came out of/to come out of: veio à tona/vir à tona
to gain popularity: ganhar popularidade
became/to become: tornou-se (famoso)/tornar-se (famoso)
trumpet: trompete
unusual: peculiar
call/to call: chamam/chamar
Golden Age: Era de Ouro
as time passed: com o passar do tempo
danced/to dance: dançaram/dançar
led/to lead: liderou/liderar
swing bands: bandas de swing
presented/to present: apresentou/apresentar
playing together: tocando juntos
first time: primeira vez

culture

After World War II, swing jazz became **less** popular. Americans **began to listen** to different **sounds**. One was bebop. **Young** musicians had created bepop in the 1940's and it **gained** popularity **slowly** over the years. The music seemed **harshly different** to the **ears** of the public. Bebop appeared to sound **racing**, **nervous**, and often **fragmented**. **Nevertheless**, bebop was an exciting and beautiful **revolution** in the art of jazz.

In the 1950's, cool jazz became popular. Cool jazz instruments **sound softer** than bebop and the rhythm is **more even.**

With cool jazz came many **new** listeners. People went to jazz **clubs** and **bought** jazz **recordings**. The introduction of the **long-playing record** also **helped** the music become more popular.

In the 1960's a new kind of music, rock and roll, grew very popular in the United States. People **throughout** the world **listened to** the rock music of Elvis Presley and the Beatles. This new music **cut into** the popularity of jazz.

In the 1980's, trumpet player Wynton Marsalis helped **lead a return** to more traditional jazz. This **mainstream** jazz **borrows** sounds from swing, bebop and cool jazz. Marsalis is one of the **most well known** and **praised** jazz musicians.

Today, jazz musicians play **all types** of music. Jazz can sound like swing or bebop. It can sound like rock and roll. It can sound like American Western music. It can sound like the music of several nations and ethnic groups. Or, it can sound traditional. With **so many options to choose from**, people of all **ages** and **all walks of life** can **find enjoyment** and an **appreciation** for American jazz.

less: menos
began to listen: começaram a escutar
sounds: sons
young: jovens
gained/to gain: ganhou/ganhar
slowly: lentamente
harshly different: bem diferente
ears: ouvidos
racing: rápido
nervous: agitado
fragmented: quebrado
nevertheless: contudo
revolution: revolução
sound/to sound: soam/soar
softer: mais suaves
more even: mais uniforme
new: novos
clubs: clubes
bought/to buy: compravam/comprar
recordings: gravações
long-playing record: LP (disco de vinil)
helped/to help: ajudou/ajudar
throughout: por todo
listened to/to listen to: ouviam/ouvir
cut into/to cut into: reduziu/reduzir
lead a return: liderou o retorno
mainstream: corrente dominante
borrows/to borrow: apropria-se/ apropriar-se
most well known: mais famosos
praised: elogiados
today: atualmente
all types: todos os tipos
so many options: tantas opções
to choose from/to choose: para serem escolhidas/escolher
ages: idades
all walks of life: todas as classes sociais
find/to find: encontrar/encontrar
enjoyment: diversão
appreciation: apreço

Singing the Blues

America's **beginnings** in music **can be traced back to** "the blues." **Bar room singers** in the south, **gospel choirs**, rock and roll, pop styles and **early** jazz all **have their roots** in blues music.

The blues **started** in Mississippi after the Civil War. **At first** blues **were recorded only** by memory, and **performed** only **live** and in person. The blues **passed down** from generation to generation through an **oral tradition** much like **storytelling**.

Mississippi **produced** many **leading** blues musicians, including Charley Patton, Robert Johnson, Howlin' Wolf, Muddy Waters and B.B. King. These musicians **came out** of the area **known as** the Mississippi Delta. Three blues **museums are located** in the Mississippi Delta—the Delta Blues Museum in Clarksdale, the Blues & Legends Hall of Fame Museum in Robinsonville and the Highway 61 Blues Museum located in Leland.

Because of the early African-American experience and slavery, "singing the blues" **served as** functional music offering African-Americans a **vehicle to convey** their **daily** experiences. **Early forms** of the blues include the "field holler," **which allowed laborers** in the **fields to keep in contact** with each other, while the "ring shout" was used for **dancing**.

The blues **combined** the styles of the past **with a new type** of song. The popularity of the blues **marked a new era** for music. The result was the creation of a style of music that **would eventually contribute** to the development of jazz.

You can experience the blues live at festivals all **around** the U.S. For a complete listing of **legendary** rhythm and blues festivals visit: www.bluesfestivals.com

---

beginnings: origens
can be traced back to: remontam a
bar room singers: cantores de bar
gospel choirs: coros de gospel
early: original
have their roots: têm suas raízes
started/to start: começou/começar
at first: a princípio
were recorded/to record: eram gravados/gravar
only: apenas
performed/to perform: interpretados/interpretar
live: ao vivo
passed down/to pass down: passou/passar
oral tradition: tradição oral
storytelling: narração de histórias
produced/to produce: produziu/produzir
leading: principais
came out/to come out: surgiram/surgir
known as: conhecida como
museums: museus
are located: estão localizados
because of: por causa da
served as/to serve as: servia como/servir como
vehicle: veículo
to convey: expressar
daily: cotidianas
early forms: primeiras formas
which allowed: que permitiam
laborers: trabalhadores
field: campo
to keep in contact: ficarem em contato
dancing: dançar
combined/to combine: combinava/combinar
with a new type: com um novo tipo
marked a new era: marcou uma nova era
eventually: finalmente
would contribute to/to contribute to: contribuiria para/contribuir para
you can/can: você pode/poder
around: por todo
legendary: lendário

Native American Culture

The America **discovered by** the **first** Europeans was not an **empty wilderness**. Approximately 2 – 18 million people **lived** in **what is now called** the United States. These people, Native American Indians, were the first people to live here. The name "Indian" was first **applied** by Christopher Columbus. Columbus **mistakenly thought** America was part of the Indies, in Asia.

Indian customs and culture were extremely diverse due to the **expanse** of the land and the many different **environments** they **had adapted to**. Most tribes **combined gathering**, **hunting**, and the **cultivation** of corn and other products for their food supplies. The women **cared for** the children, and were **in charge of farming** and the distribution of food. The men hunted and **participated in** war. Indian culture in North America was **tied closely** to the land. Nature was part of their religious **beliefs**.

Initially, the Europeans **were welcomed enthusiastically** by the Native Americans. Conflicts soon **arose**. The **value systems** were different for each group. The natives were **in tune** to the **rhythms** and **spirit** of **nature**. Nature to the Europeans was a **commodity**: a **beaver colony** was a number of **pelts**, a **forest** was **timber** for **building**. The Europeans **expected to** own land and **claimed** it. The Indians, **on the other hand**, were considered by the Europeans as **nomadic** with no interest in land **ownership**.

It was the Europeans' materialistic **view** of the land that the Indians **found repellent**. The conflicts and wars continued until the end of the 19th **century**. On June 2, 1924, Congress **granted citizenship** to all Native Americans born in the U.S. The right to vote **was governed** by state law. In some states, Native American Indians **were prohibited** from voting until 1948.

Many Native Americans are politically and socially active, **holding fast** to the **ancient** values of their ancestors. **Prayers** for peace, respect for the environment, and love for all things living is a **legacy** that **remains** today.

discovered by: descoberta pelos
first: primeiros
empty wilderness: vazia imensidão
lived/to live: viviam/viver
what is now called: que é agora chamado
applied: usado
mistakenly: erroneamente
thought/to think: pensou/pensar
expanse: extensão
environments: ambientes
had adapted to/to adapt to: adaptaram-se/ adaptar
combined/to combine: combinavam/ combinar
gathering: colheita
hunting: caça
cultivation: cultivo
cared for/to care for: cuidavam das/ cuidar de
in charge of: encarregados de
farming: agricultura
participated in: participavam da
tied closely: estreitamente ligada
beliefs: crenças
were welcomed: foram recebidos
enthusiastically: com entusiasmo
arose/to arise: apareceram/aparecer
value systems: sistemas de valores
in tune: em sintonia
rhythms: ritmos
spirit: espírito
nature: natureza
commodity: mercadoria
beaver colony: colônia de castores
pelts: peles
forest: floresta
timber: madeira
building: construção
expected to: esperavam
claimed/to claim: reivindicaram/ reivindicar
on the other hand: por outro lado
nomadic: nômades
ownership: posse, propriedade
view: visão
found/to find: achavam/achar
repellent: repulsiva
century: século
granted citizenship: concedeu cidadania
was governed/to govern: foi determinado/determinar
were prohibited/to prohibit: foram proibidos/proibir
holding fast: agarrando-se
ancient: antigos
prayers: orações
legacy: legado
remains/to remain: persiste/persistir

unlike: ao contrário de
many: muitos
came/to come: chegaram/chegar
against their will: contra sua vontade
were caught up: foram envolvidos
slave trade: tráfico de escravos
waged/to wage: travaram/travar
centuries-long: secular
freedom: liberdade
full involvement: plena participação
society: sociedade
transformed/to transform: transformou/transformar
shaped/to shape: moldou/moldar
the world we live in today: o mundo em que vivemos atualmente
remade: refeitos
workers: trabalhadores
activists: ativistas
organizers: organizadores
thinkers: pensadores
more than: mais de
claim/to claim: alegam/alegar
ancestry: descendência
increases/to increase: aumenta/aumentar
every year: a cada ano
explorers: exploradores
colonists: colonos
free will: livre arbítrio
century: século
Age of Exploration: Era do Descobrimento
open up/to open up: explorar/explorar
Southwestern: sudoeste
during: durante
were transported/to transport: foram transportados/transportar
British colonies: colônias britânicas
later: posteriormente
precise: preciso
current estimates: cálculos aproximados
report/to report: relatam/relatar
died/to die: morreram/morrer
journey: jornada
today: hoje
again: de novo
making their way: encontrando seu caminho
shores: costas
to start: para começar

African Heritage

Unlike other immigrants, **many** Africans **came** to North America **against their will**. They **were caught up** in a brutal system of human exploitation—the transatlantic **slave trade**.

African Americans **waged** a **centuries-long** battle for dignity, **freedom**, and for **full involvement** in American **society**. Their participation **transformed** the United States, and **shaped the world we live in today**. Our customs have been influenced or **remade** by the efforts of African American **workers**, artists, **activists**, **organizers**, and **thinkers**.

More than 35 million Americans **claim** African **ancestry**. The number of African immigrants to the U.S. **increases every year**.

Explorers and Colonists

When Africans first came to the Americas, they came of their own **free will**. They arrived at the same time in history as the first Europeans. During the sixteenth **century**, African adventurers participated in the **Age of Exploration**. In the early 1500s, Africans explored Ecuador, Mexico, and Peru. The African explorer Estevanico helped the Coronado expedition **open up** what is now the **Southwestern** United States.

During the 300 years of the transatlantic slave trade, approximately 20 million Africans **were transported** to the Americas as slaves. Of these, more than 400,000 were sent to the 13 **British colonies** and, **later**, the United States. We may never know a **precise** number, but **current estimates report** that more than 1 million Africans **died** on the **journey**.

Today, Africans are coming to America **again**.

From Togo, Ghana, Ethiopia, Mali, Nigeria—Africans are again **making their way** to American **shores to start** new lives.

12 culture

More than 500,000 Africans came to the United States in the 1990's **alone**. This is more African immigrants **than had come** in all the 150 years **before**.

Today, Africans are immigrating to a **country profoundly shaped** by the long African experience in the United States. America is a country where people of African ancestry now **hold positions** of power, prestige, and influence, even as the nation **continues** to **grapple** with the **aftermath** of segregation and **inequality**. The United States is a country that has seen three of its most prominent African American citizens awarded the Nobel Peace Prize; the diplomat Ralph Bunche, the **civil rights leader** Martin Luther King Jr., and the novelist Toni Morrison.

Perhaps most important, America is a country that continues to be **enriched** by and **to recognize** its African heritage.

alone: sozinhos
than had come: do que os que vieram
before: antes
country: país
profoundly: profundamente
shaped: moldado
hold positions: ocupam postos
continues/to continue: continua/continuar
grapple: lutar
aftermath: consequências
inequality: desigualdade
civil rights: direitos civis
leader: líder
perhaps: talvez
enriched: enriquecido
to recognize: a reconhecer

Martin Luther King Jr.,
was the **most famous leader** of the **American civil rights movement,** a political activist, a Baptist **minister**, and was one of America's greatest orators.

In 1964, King became the youngest man awarded the **Nobel Peace Prize** for his work as a **peacemaker,** promoting **nonviolence** and equal treatment for different races.

On April 4, 1968, King **was assassinated** in Memphis, Tennessee. In 1977, he **was posthumously awarded** the **Presidential Medal of Freedom** by Jimmy Carter.

In 1986, *Martin Luther King Day* was established as a United States **holiday.** Martin Luther King is **one of only** three persons to receive this **distinction** (including Abraham Lincoln and George Washington), and of these persons the only one not a U.S. president, **indicating** his extraordinary position in American history.

In 2004, King was posthumously awarded the **Congressional Gold Medal.** King **often called for** personal responsibility in **fostering world peace.** King's most influential and well-known public address is the "I Have A Dream" **speech, delivered** on the **steps** of the Lincoln Memorial in Washington, D.C. in 1963.

most famous: mais famoso
leader: líder
American civil rights movement: movimento norte-americano pelos direitos civis
minister: pastor
Nobel Peace Prize: Prêmio Nobel da Paz
peacemaker: pacificador
non violence: não violência
was assassinated/to assassinate: foi assassinado/assassinar
was posthumously awarded: foi premiado postumamente com
Presidential Medal of Freedom: Medalha Presidencial da Liberdade
holiday: feriado
one of only: um de apenas
distinction: título de honra
indicating: indicando
Congressional Gold Medal: Medalha de Ouro do Congresso
often: muitas vezes
called for/to call for: chamou para si/chamar para si
fostering: promover
world peace: paz mundial
speech: discurso
delivered/to deliver: pronunciado/pronunciar
steps: escadarias

culture 13

myths: mitos
legends: lendas
songs: músicas
written: escrita
perhaps: talvez
documented: documentada
journals: jornais
recounting: relatando
topics: temas
were prompted by: foram inspirados no
discussing: debatendo
religious foundations: fundações religiosas
increasing desire to produce: crescente desejo de produzir
emerged/to emerge: surgiu/surgir
key: principais
shocking: chocante
work: obra
he claimed/to claim: ele alegou/alegar
to do away with: acabar com
reach/to reach: alcança/alcançar
spiritual state: estado espiritual
studying/to study: estudando/estudar
responding to/to respond to: respondendo a/responder a
nonconformist: inconformista
wooded: arborizada
pond: lagoa
urges/to urge: encoraja/encorajar
organized society: sociedade organizada
first: primeiro
major: grande
away from: longe de
masterpieces: obras-primas
literary style: estilo literário
highly evocative: altamente evocativo
irreverently funny: irreverentemente divertido
changed the way: mudou a forma
set the scene: preparou o terreno
working-class people: classe operária
struggle: luta
to lead: levar
masterpiece: obra-prima
tells/to tell: conta/contar
entering/to enter: admitidos em / entrar
will find/to find: descobrirão/descobrir
will include/to include: incluirão/incluir
stunningly: surpreendentemente
will chronicle/to chronicle: registrarão/registrar

Early American Literature

Early American literature began with the **myths**, **legends**, and **songs** of Indian cultures. There was no **written** literature during this time. **Perhaps** the first **documented** written literature is historical literature in **journals recounting** the exploration of early settlers of the United States.

Topics of early American writings **were prompted by** discussions of religion. John Winthrop wrote a journal **discussing** the **religious foundations** of the Massachusetts Bay Colony. The War of 1812 prompted an **increasing desire to produce** unique American work. From this **emerged** a number of **key** literary figures, including Edgar Allan Poe, Washington Irving, and James Fennimore Cooper.

In 1836, Ralph Waldo Emerson published a **shocking** nonfiction **work** called *Nature*. In it, **he claimed** it was possible **to do away with** organized religion and **reach** a **spiritual state** by **studying** and **responding to** the natural world.

Emerson's friend was Henry David Thoreau. Thoreau was a **nonconformist**. After living alone for two years in a cabin by a **wooded pond**, Thoreau wrote *Walden*, a memoir that **urges** resistance to **organized society**.

Mark Twain was the **first major** American writer to be born **away from** the East Coast—in the state of Missouri. His **masterpieces** were the memoir *Life on the Mississippi* and the novel *Adventures of Huckleberry Finn*. Twain's **literary style** was direct, **highly evocative**, and **irreverently funny**. Mark Twain's literature **changed the way** Americans write.

John Steinbeck was born in Salinas, California, which **set the scene** for many of his stories. Steinbeck wrote about poor, **working-class people** and their **struggle to lead** a decent life. *The Grapes of Wrath*, considered his **masterpiece,** is a novel that **tells** the story of a family's journey to California.

At universities across the United States, students **entering** a class in American literature **will find** that their studies **will include** books that are **stunningly** diverse. Future American writers will write of a new experience. New American literature **will chronicle** the experiences of different ethnic groups and immigrants that make up the United States.

Artistic Expression

The **artistic expression** of Americans is **as diverse as** the people who live in America. Two **famous** American artists **who believed** that art **belonged to** the **people** are **featured** in this article; Norman Rockwell, whose work **represented** life in America; and Andy Warhol, who **sparked a revolution** in art during the 1960's.

NORMAN ROCKWELL *(February 3, 1894–November 8, 1978)* Rockwell is most famous for the **cover illustrations** he created for *The Saturday Evening Post* **magazine**.

In 1943, **during** the Second World War, Rockwell painted the *Four Freedoms* series. The work **was inspired by** a speech by Franklin D. Roosevelt, who **had declared** that there were four **principles** for **universal rights**: Freedom from Want, **Freedom of Speech**, Freedom to **Worship**, and Freedom from **Fear**. Rockwell considered "Freedom of Speech" to be **the best** of the four.

Norman Rockwell was very **prolific**, and **produced** over 4000 original **works**, most of which have been either **destroyed** by **fire** or are in permanent collections. Original magazines in **mint condition** that **contain** his work are **rare** and are **worth** thousands of dollars.

ANDY WARHOL *(August 6, 1928–February 22, 1987)* Warhol was an American artist **associated with** the definition of **Pop Art**. Warhol was a painter, a **commercial illustrator**, an **avant-garde filmmake**r, music industry **producer**, **writer** and celebrity.

Warhol studied commercial art at Carnegie Mellon University in Pittsburgh. He showed an early **artistic talent**. He moved to New York City in 1949 and **began** a **career** in advertising and magazine illustration.

During the 1960s Warhol began to make paintings of famous American products such as Campbell's Soup Cans and Coca-Cola, as well as paintings of **celebrities** like Marilyn Monroe. Warhol sparked a revolution in art—his work **quickly** became very controversial, and popular. Warhol became **one of the most famous** American artists of the day.

---

artistic expression: expressão artística
as diverse as: tão diversa quanto
famous: famosos
who believed: que acreditavam
belonged to/to belong to: pertencia a/pertencer a
people: pessoas
featured/to feature: retratados/retratar
represented/to represent: representava/representar
sparked a revolution: incitou uma revolução
cover illustrations: ilustrações de capa
magazine: revista
during: durante
was inspired by/to inspire: foi inspirado por/inspirar
had declared/to declare: tinha declarado/declarar
principles: princípios
universal rights: direitos universais
freedom of speech: liberdade de expressão
worship: adoração, culto
fear: medo
the best: o melhor
prolific: criativo
produced/to produce: produziu/produzir
works: obras
destroyed/to destroy: destruídas/destruir
fire: fogo
mint condition: em perfeito estado
contain/to contain: contém/conter
rare: raras
worth/to be worth: valem/valer
associated with: associado com
Pop Art: arte pop *(popular)*
commercial illustrator: ilustrador comercial
avant-garde filmmaker: cineasta vanguardista
producer: produtor
writer: escritor
artistic talent: talento artístico
began/to begin: começou/começar
career: carreira
celebrities: celebridades
quickly: rapidamente
one of the most famous: um dos mais famosos

culture

birthplace of: local de nascimento de
characterized by: caracterizado por
simplicity: simplicidade
charm: charme
cultural center: centro cultural
fascinated/to fascinate: encantou/encantar
middle-class people: pessoas da classe média
in search of: em busca de
best seats in the house: melhores lugares da casa
relationship: relação
audience: público
lively: ativo
high-spirited: animado
caught up in: envolvida com
hissing/to hiss: assobiando/assobiar
booing/to boo: vaiando/vaiar
clapping/to clap: aplaudindo/aplaudir
cheering/to cheer: ovacionando/ovacionar
to escape the reality: para escapar da realidade
getaway: fuga
however: no entanto
assisting/to assist: apoiando/apoiar
war: guerra
effort: esforço
raise money: levantar fundos
relief: assistência
after: após
was filled/to fill: estava recheado/rechear
crowds: pilhas
enthusiastic citizens: cidadãos entusiasmados
flags: bandeiras
since that day: desde aquele dia
gathering place: ponto de encontro
reached its prime: atingiu seu auge
fresh ideas: novas ideias
hope: esperança
organizer: organizador
dazzling: deslumbrante
influenced/to influence: influenciou/influenciar
stock-market crash: quebra da bolsa de valores
plunged/to plunge: afundou/afundar
declined/to decline: diminuiu/diminuir
put...out of work: desempregou/desempregar
to write/to write: escrevendo/escrever
plays: peças
state of affairs: situação
included/to include: incluíam/incluir
weapon: arma
playwrights: dramaturgos
social commentary: crítica social

16 culture

The Birthplace of Broadway

New York City is the **birthplace of** Broadway, which began in the early 1900s. **Characterized by simplicity** and **charm**, Broadway soon became the **cultural center** of New York. The theatre district **fascinated** large groups of **middle-class people in search of** music, excitement, and romance. The **best seats in the house** cost only $2.00.

The **relationship** between **audience** and actors was **lively** and **high-spirited**. Audiences became **caught up in** the plays, talking to the actors, **hissing** and **booing**, or **clapping** and **cheering**.

To escape the reality of World War II, many used Broadway plays as an entertaining **getaway**. **However**, the Broadway community became especially active in **assisting** the **war effort**. The play *Yip, Yip, Yaphank* at the Century Theatre helped **raise money** for war **relief**.

After World War II ended, Times Square **was filled** with **crowds** of **enthusiastic citizens** carrying **flags** and celebrating. **Since that day**, Times Square has continued as a **gathering place** for the people of New York City.

Broadway **reached its prime** during the 1920s. **Fresh ideas** and **hope** filled the theatre. Lawrence Langner, **organizer** of the Theatre Guild, helped Broadway become a **dazzling** performing arts center that **influenced** the theatre of the world.

After the **stock-market crash** of 1929 and the Great Depression, Broadway **plunged**. The number of productions **declined** and **put** many theatre people **out of work**. Ironically, this became a creative period. Established writers organized the Playwrights Company, and continued **to write** interesting **plays** that were concerned with the **state of affairs** in America.

Many off Broadway theatres now **included** dramas of social protest, using the slogan "Theatre as a **Weapon**." Many **playwrights** used the theatres to make **social commentary**.

Broadway began **to compete with** television and movies during the 1940s. Most theatres on Broadway **were being turned into** film houses. Movies **were beginning to take over** the **entertainment business**. Also **by this time**, television was becoming a **competitor**. Television was providing the public with **free** entertainment.

In the 1950's Broadway had become **less of** an industry **and more of a loose array of** individuals. This period in America was one of increasing intolerance and political persecution, but Broadway **was not afraid** to **express nonconformist opinions**. Broadway **did not fear** the government. Although Broadway theatre **had lost some of its range**, it still **retained** its liveliness and joyfulness. In a country that now required **conventionality**, Broadway held onto a sense of **freedom of speech** and action. These were the ideals on which the nation **was founded**.

Many memorable **musicals emerged** in 1950-1970. Some of these included *West Side Story, My Fair Lady, The Sound of Music, Fiddler on the Roof, Man of La Mancha,* and *Hair.*

Modern day Broadway is **alive and well** and Broadway theatre is considered the most prestigious form of professional theatre in the United States, as well as the most well known to the general public.

Seeing a Broadway **show** is a **popular tourist activity** in New York. Some **ticket booths sell same-day tickets** for many Broadway shows at **half price**. This service helps sell **seats** that would **otherwise go empty**, and makes seeing a show in New York more affordable. Many theatres also offer special student **rates, same-day "rush" tickets**, or **standing-room tickets** to help **ensure** that their theatres are **full**.

Theatres all across America **produce** Off-Broadway and original plays, musicals and dance productions. American Theatre offers a diverse **range** of entertainment. With many **themes to choose from** you are **certain to find** a show that **interests you**.

---

to compete with: a competir com
were being turned into: estavam se transformando em
were beginning to/to begin to: estavam começando a/ começar a
to take over: assumir/assumir
entertainment business: indústria do entretenimento
by this time: nesse meio tempo
competitor: concorrente
free: grátis
less of...and more of: menos de... e mais de
a loose array of: uma série solta de
was not afraid: não estava com medo
express nonconformist opinions: expressar opiniões inconformistas
did not fear/to fear: não temia/temer
had lost/to lose: tenha perdido/perder
some of its range: parte de seu alcance
retained/to retain: preservava/preservar
conventionality: convencionalismo
freedom of speech: liberdade de expressão
was founded/to found: foi fundada/fundar
musicals: musicais
emerged/to emerge: surgiram/surgir
modern day: atualmente
alive and well: sã e salva
seeing: assistir
show: espetáculo
popular tourist activity: atividade turística popular
ticket booths: bilheterias
sell/to sell: vendem/vender
same-day tickets: entradas para o mesmo dia
half price: metade do preço
seats: lugares
otherwise: caso contrário
go empty: teriam ficado vazios
rates: preço
same day "rush" tickets: entradas "urgentes" para o mesmo dia
standing-room tickets: entradas populares para assistir em pé
ensure: assegurar
full: lotado
produce/to produce: produzem/produzir
range: série
themes to choose from: temas para serem escolhidos
certain to find: certamente encontrará
interests you: do seu interesse

ask/to ask: perguntar/perguntar
cultural values: valores culturais
you might receive blank stares: talvez receba um olhar inexpressivo
no response: nenhuma resposta
society: sociedade
diverse: diversificada
likely: provável
answers: respostas
has been enriched/to enrich: tem sido enriquecida/enriquecer
belief systems: sistemas de crença
a few select: uns poucos escolhidos
core: centro
nearly: quase
would agree upon: poderiam concordar
individual freedom: liberdade individual
whether you call it: seja chamando isto de
cornerstone: alicerce
destiny: destino
influenced/to influence: influenciou/influenciar
government: governo
was established/to establish: foi estabelecido/estabelecer
guaranteed: garantidos
large corporations: grandes corporações
majority of: a maioria de
businesses: negócios
owned: de propriedade de
dream: sonho
own boss: próprio patrão
being: ser
most appealing ways to improve: formas mais atraentes para melhorar
is regarded/to regard: é considerado/considerar
key to opportunity: chave para a oportunidade
including: incluindo
approach: abordagem
classroom: sala de aula
internships: estágio
considered: consideradas
lifelong: vitalício
continuing education programs: programas de educação contínua
belief: crença
be all that you can be: ser tudo o que você puder ser
emanates/to emanate: emana/emanar
heritage: herança
early settlers: primeiros colonos
to improve themselves: melhorarem a si mesmos
to develop: para desenvolver
talents: talentos
neighbors: vizinhos

18 culture

Cultural Values

If you **ask** Americans what the **cultural values** in the U.S. are, **you might receive blank stares** and little or **no response**. In a **society** as **diverse** as the United States, there is **likely** to be a multitude of **answers**. American culture **has been enriched** by the values and **belief systems** of almost every part of the world. **A few select** values are at the **core** of the American value system.

INDIVIDUAL FREEDOM — One value that **nearly** every American **would agree upon** is **individual freedom**. **Whether you call it** individual freedom, or independence, it is the **cornerstone** of American values.

The concept of an individual having control over his/her own **destiny influenced** the type of **government** that **was established** here. Individual rights are **guaranteed** in the United States Constitution.

While our economic system may be dominated by **large corporations**, the **majority of** American **businesses** are small, and many are **owned** by an individual or a family. It is part of the "American **dream**" to "be your **own boss**." **Being** an entrepreneur is one of the **most appealing ways to improve** one's economic future.

CHOICE IN EDUCATION
Education **is regarded** as the **key to opportunity, including** financial security. Americans take a pragmatic **approach** to learning. What one learns outside the **classroom** through **internship** and extracurricular activities is often **considered** as important as what is learned in the classroom. **Lifelong** learning is valued which is why you will find many adult and **continuing education programs**.

The **belief** that Americans should "**be all that you can be**" **emanates** from our Protestant **heritage**. Since the majority of the **early settlers** were Protestant, they believed that they had a responsibility **to improve themselves**, to be the best they could be, **to develop** their **talents**, and to help their **neighbors**.

THE FAMILY — The **main purpose** of the American family is to bring about the **happiness** of each individual family member. The traditional family values **include love** and respect for **parents, as well as** for all members of the family.

The **emphasis** on the individual and his/her right to happiness can be **confusing**. It **allows** children **to disagree**, even **argue** with their parents. While in most other cultures such **action** would be a **sign** of **disrespect**, that is not the case in the United States. It is considered a part of **developing** one's independence.

PRIVACY — **Privacy** is important to Americans. The **notion** of individual privacy may make it **difficult** to make friends. Because Americans respect one's privacy, they **may not go beyond** a **friendly** "hello."

The **rugged** individualism valued by most Americans **stems from** our **frontier heritage**. Early settlers had to be **self-sufficient**, which **forced** them to be **inventive**. Their **success** gave them **optimism** about the future, a belief that problems could be **solved**. This positive spirit **enables** Americans **to take risks** in areas where others might only dream. This **results in** tremendous **advances** in technology, **health** and science.

In addition to such basic American values as individual freedom, self-reliance, equality of opportunity, **hard work**, **material wealth**, and **competition**, we see a **trend toward** conservation. There is an emphasis on **recycling** and **preserving** the **environment**. Also there is a greater sensitivity to cooperation on a **global scale**.

No matter what changes the next **century** brings or whether you **agree** with American values, the opportunity **to live** in the United States is a wonderful and new experience.

O artigo anterior foi escrito por Thomas E. Grouling, PhD, que é o Diretor Adjunto do Departamento de Programas e Serviços Internacionais da Universidade Drake. Trabalha como conselheiro dos estudantes e alunos de intercâmbio, e também é diretor do Programa de Inglês Intensivo. O professor Grouling trabalhou com alunos internacionais e minorias étnicas por aproximadamente 40 anos e realiza um seminário anual sobre os Estudos Americanos na Universidade Drake.

---

main purpose: objetivo principal
happiness: felicidade
include/to include: incluem/incluir
love: amor
parents: pais
as well as: assim como
emphasis: ênfase
confusing: confuso
allows/to allow: permite/permitir
to disagree: a discordarem
argue/to argue: discute/discutir
action: ação
sign: sinal
disrespect: desrespeito
developing: desenvolvimento
privacy: privacidade
notion: noção
difficult: difícil
may not go beyond: talvez não vão além de
friendly: amigável
rugged: determinado
stems from/to stem from: origina-se de/originar-se de
frontier heritage: herança de fronteira
self-sufficient: autossuficientes
forced/to force: forçou/forçar
inventive: criativos
success: sucesso
optimism: otimismo
solved/to solve: resolvidos/resolver
enables/to enable: permite/permitir
to take risks: se arrisquem
results in: resulta em
advances: avanços
health: saúde
in addition to: além disso
hard work: trabalho duro
material wealth: riqueza material
competition: competição
trend toward: inclinação para
recycling: reciclar
preserving: preservar
environment: meio ambiente
global scale: escala global
no matter what: não importam que
changes: mudanças
century: século
agree/to agree: concorde/concordar
to live: viver

culture 19

Test Your Comprehension

The American Dream, page 4

1. Com o que o sonho americano é geralmente associado?

2. De que forma o sonho americano determinou a revolução industrial?

3. Além de segurança econômica e comodidade material, o que mais o sonho americano significa?

A Melting Pot, page 5

1. O que é o caldeirão de raças e culturas?

2. Qual é a região dos EUA considerada a mais tolerante em relação às mudanças e diferenças?

3. Qual foi o grupo étnico que mais influenciou o sudoeste dos EUA?

The American Cowboy, page 6

1. Qual é a origem do *cowboy* norte-americano?

2. O que os *cowboys* modernos fazem atualmente nos EUA?

3. Onde você pode aprender sobre a tradição dos *cowboys*?

American Jazz, page 8

1. Onde o jazz nasceu?

2. Qual é o grupo étnico que é a raiz do jazz?

Teste sua Compreensão

Early American Literature, page 14

1. Qual foi o primeiro notório escritor norte-americano nascido longe da costa leste?

2. Qual escritor escreveu sobre as pessoas da classe operária e sua luta?

The Birthplace of Broadway, page 16

1. A Broadway teve início em qual cidade norte-americana?

2. As pessoas iam ao teatro para fugir da realidade da guerra, mas o que a Broadway apoiou?

Artistic Expression, page 15

1. Quais eram as Quatro Liberdades pintadas por Norman Rockwell?

2. Andy Warhol ficou famoso por qual tipo de arte?

Cultural Values, page 18

1. Qual valor faria com que a maioria dos norte-americanos concordasse?

2. Qual valor é considerado a chave da oportunidade, incluindo a segurança econômica?

Though we travel the world over to find the beautiful,
we must carry it with us or we find it not.

Ralph Waldo Emerson

Travel

several: várias
options: opções
camping: acampar
throughout: por todo
different types: tipos diferentes
to choose: para escolher
depends/to depend: depende/ depender
interests: interesses
level: nível
include/to include: incluem/incluir
car camping: acampar com carro
full-facility campgrounds: acampamentos com serviço completo
backcountry: campo
limited facilities: serviços limitados
wilderness: natureza selvagem
must carry out: deve levar
carry in: trouxer
accept/to accept: aceitam/aceitar
official site: site oficial
prefer/to prefer: prefere/preferir
things: coisas
to consider: a serem consideradas
questions: perguntas
to ask: a perguntar
making/to make: estiver fazendo/fazer
available: disponíveis
such as: como
water: água
power: eletricidade
hookups: transmissões
showers: duchas
picnic tables: mesas para piquenique
grills: churrasqueiras
maximum number: número máximo
vehicles: veículos
permitted: permitidos
consecutive: consecutivos
length: duração
stay: estadia
regarding pets: em relação aos animais de estimação
whatever: qualquer
help preserve: ajude a preservar
beauty: beleza
outdoors: ao ar livre
generations to come: próximas gerações
responsibly: com responsabilidade

Camping Trips

There are **several** opportunities and **options** for **camping throughout** the United States and several **different types** of camping **to choose** from. The type of camping you choose **depends** on your **interests** and your **level** of experience. The different options **include car camping** at **full-facility campgrounds**, **backcountry** camping with **limited facilities**, and **wilderness** camping with no facilities at all and you **must carry out** everything you **carry in**.

Many of the U.S. national parks with campgrounds that **accept** reservations are part of the National Park Reservation Service. The **official site** for the National Park Service where you can make reservations is: www.reservations.nps.gov

If you **prefer** backcountry camping, the website www.recreation.gov offers complete information and reservations.

If you are going camping at a campground, here are some **things to consider** and **questions to ask** when **making** reservations:

- What facilities are **available**, **such as water** and **power hookups**, bathrooms, **showers**, **picnic tables**, and **grills**.

- What is the **maximum number** of people and **vehicles permitted** per campsite?

- Is there a limit on the number of days or **consecutive** days you can camp at a park? Are there other restrictions on **length** of **stay**?

- What are the restrictions **regarding pets** in the campground?

Whatever type of camping you choose, please **help preserve** the **beauty** of the great **outdoors** for yourself and **generations to come** by camping **responsibly**.

Rafting the Grand Canyon

When most people **think** of the Grand Canyon they think of **peering over** the **rim** and **admiring** the **beauty** from **up above**.

But **what about** being in the canyon and **looking up**? The Grand Canyon is one of the seven **natural wonders** of the world and a **trip down** the Colorado **River allows** you to **experience** the beauty and **ruggedness** from the **heart** of the canyon. Over the **course** of 250 miles the river **runs through unruly rapids**, making for a **wilder ride** than you're **likely to find** on **dry land**.

A river trip down the Grand Canyon **ranges from navigating** through **world-class** rapids to **swimming** in the **side** canyons and **hiking** through **remote areas** not **seen** by most **travelers**. On this **once-in-a-lifetime** adventure you will experience astounding views of **hidden waterfalls** and you will **discover ancient Indian ruins**.

The **diversity** of Grand Canyon's **scenery** is **matched** by the **surprising** diversity of its **plant** and animal life. There are 287 species of **birds** in the Grand Canyon, 88 species of **mammals**, 26 species of **fish**, and 58 species of **reptiles** and **amphibians**.

A **guide** for your rafting trip is highly recommended and **required** in some parts of the river. There are several **tour companies** that **book weekend** or **weeklong** trips. Some tours **provide special interest** trips including history, **geology** and **photography** tours.

think/to think: pensa/pensar
peering over: observar sobre
rim: beirada
admiring/to admire: admirar/admirar
beauty: beleza
up above: de cima
what about: que tal
looking up: olhar para cima
natural wonders: maravilhas naturais
trip down...river: viagem rio abaixo
allows/to allow: permite-lhe/permitir
experience: experimentar
ruggedness: aspereza
heart: coração
course: curso
runs through: corre sobre
unruly: rebeldes
rapids: corredeiras
wilder ride: passeio mais turbulento
likely: provavelmente
to find: encontre
dry land: terra firme
ranges from: vai de
navigating: navegar
world-class: melhores do mundo
swimming: nadar
side: laterais
hiking: caminhar
remote areas: áreas remotas
seen/to see: vistas/ver
travelers: viajantes
once-in-a-lifetime: uma vez na vida
hidden waterfalls: cachoeiras escondidas
discover: descobrirá
ancient Indian ruins: antigas ruínas indígenas
diversity: diversidade
scenery: paisagem
matched/to match: igualada/igualar
surprising: surpreendente
plant: vegetal
birds: aves
mammals: mamíferos
fish: peixes
reptiles: répteis
amphibians: anfíbios
guide: guia
required: necessário
tour companies: agências de viagens
book/to book: reservam/reservar
weekend: fim de semana
weeklong: uma semana inteira
provide/to provide: fornecem/fornecer
special interest: interesse especial
geology: geologia
photography: fotografia

beaches: praias
were built/to build: foram construídos/construir
late: no final de
designed: projetados
walkways: caminhos, passarelas
beachgoers: banhistas
stroll: passear
along: ao longo
shore: costa
tracking: deixar rastro
sand: areia
hotel lobbies: saguões dos hotéis
have something: têm algo
arcades: galerias
carnival rides: atrações de parques de diversões
clothing boutiques: lojas de roupa
gourmet candy shops: lojas especializadas em doces
nightclubs: clubes noturnos
sunup: nascer do sol
sundown: pôr do sol
packed: lotadas
making the most of: aproveitando ao máximo
summertime: veraneio
fun: diversão
true: verdadeira
celebrate/to celebrate: celebramos/celebrar
to offer: a oferecer
largest: maior
started/to start: começou/começar
has become/to become: tornou-se/tornar
recent years: últimos anos
still: ainda
alike: igualmente
family-friendly: para a família
found/to find: encontrada/encontrar
promenade: passeio
runs/to run: corre/correr
beside: ao lado de
wide: vastas
feel: toque
reminiscent: que lembra
seaside resorts: estâncias balneárias
once: uma vez
populated/to populate: povoou/povoar
will find/to find: encontrará/encontrar
fresh: fresca
family-owned shops: lojas familiares
another: outra

Down by the Boardwalk

The boardwalks of American **beaches** are major tourist attractions. The first boardwalks **were built** in New Jersey in the **late** 1800's. They were originally **designed** as **walkways** so **beachgoers** could **stroll along** the **shore** without **tracking sand** into the **hotel lobbies**. Today's boardwalks **have something** for everyone; **arcades, carnival rides, clothing boutiques, gourmet candy shops**, restaurants and **nightclubs**. From **sunup** to **sundown**, boardwalks are **packed** with people of all ages, **making the most of** their **summertime fun**.

The boardwalk is a **true** American beach tradition. We **celebrate** the boardwalk with a list of the best America has **to offer**.

Atlantic City is the **largest** of New Jersey's boardwalks and it is where it all **started** in 1870. Atlantic City **has become** more famous for its casinos in **recent years**, but the boardwalk is **still** packed in the summer with locals and tourists **alike**. A **family-friendly** boardwalk can be **found** in Ocean City. This popular **promenade runs beside** beautiful **wide** sand beaches. The boardwalk has a Victorian **feel, reminiscent** of the **seaside resorts** that **once populated** the mid-Atlantic coast. At all of the New Jersey coast towns you **will find fresh** saltwater taffy being made at **family-owned shops**. Saltwater taffy is **another** beachside tradition that started in New Jersey.

The west coast is not **as well known** for its boardwalks but Santa Cruz, California has a seaside **amusement park** that is one of the best in the nation. It is California's **oldest** amusement park and the **only** major seaside amusement park on the Pacific Coast. Here you will find a **wonderful blend** of **old** and **new** carnival rides. The Looff Carousel and the Giant Dipper **roller coaster** are National Historic Landmarks.

Virginia Beach's famous **oceanfront** boardwalk has been **named** by many the most **beautiful** boardwalk in the **country**. Its popular **three-mile** walkway has **recently** been **updated**. There is also a **bike path** that runs **alongside** the boardwalk making it popular for bikes, skateboards and rollerblades. **Concerts** are a big **attraction** here at one of the three oceanfront **stages**.

Myrtle Beach, South Carolina was **nearly empty** of boardwalk attractions **twenty years ago**. **Since that time** an **enormous growth** of shops, amusement parks, **theaters** and restaurants has **transformed** the boardwalk at Myrtle Beach into a major tourist center. **In addition to** the usual boardwalk **fare**, Myrtle Beach also **boasts** an **aquarium** and an IMAX theater. A wonderful new **addition** to Myrtle Beach is a **glass butterfly pavilion**.

Ocean City Maryland is home to a famous boardwalk that **buzzes** with activity. You will find **activities** and **events** that **appeal** to all ages. Ten miles of white-sand beaches and three miles of world-famous Boardwalk make Ocean City **picture-perfect**. From the **tiny train** that **chugs** along the three-mile promenade to the **antique** carousel that **dates back to** 1902, Ocean City has **kept** its **sense** of a **bygone era** while **keeping** its attractions fresh.

---

as well known: tão famoso
amusement park: parque de diversões
oldest: mais antigo
only: único
wonderful blend: maravilhosa mistura
old: velho
new: novo
roller coaster: montanha russa
oceanfront: margens do mar
named: chamado
beautiful: bonito
country: país
three-mile: três milhas (4,828 quilômetros)
recently: recentemente
updated: modernizado
bike path: ciclovia
alongside: ao lado de
concerts: concertos
attraction: atração
stages: palcos
nearly: quase
empty: vazio
twenty years ago: há vinte anos
since that time: desde aquela época
enormous growth: grande crescimento
theaters: teatros
transformed/to transform: transformou/transformar
in addition to: além de
fare: comida
boasts/to boast: ostenta/ostentar
aquarium: aquário
addition: acréscimo
glass butterfly pavilion: pavilhão de vidro para borboletas
is home to: sedia
buzzes/to buzz: zune/zunir
activities: atividades
events: eventos
appeal/to appeal: atraem/atrair
picture-perfect: maravilhoso
tiny train: pequeno trem
chugs/to chug: ruge/rugir (trem)
antique: antigo
dates back to: remonta à
kept/to keep: mantido/manter
sense: sensação
bygone era: época passada
keeping/to keep: mantém/manter

travel 27

islands:	ilhas
have long been considered:	têm sido consideradas há tempos
treasure:	tesouro
gorgeous sandy beaches:	maravilhosas praias arenosas
spectacular sunsets:	pores do sol espetaculares
breathtaking beauty:	beleza de tirar o fôlego
surprise:	surpresa
spots:	pontos
packed full:	repleta
diversity:	diversidade
find/to find:	encontrará/encontrar
depending:	dependendo
also:	também
see:	ver
miles:	milhas
barren lava flow:	fluxo de lava estéril
museums:	museus
skiing:	esquiar
snow-peaked mountain:	montanha com o pico nevado
often:	geralmente
landing spot:	local de aterrissagem
largest city:	maior cidade
probably best known:	provavelmente mais conhecida
hums/to hum:	zune/zunir
activity:	atividade
outdoor activities:	atividades ao ar livre
well worth your time:	bom aproveitamento do seu tempo
to visit:	visitar
world-famous surf:	surfe mundialmente famoso
relaxed:	relaxada
friendly:	amigável
spread across:	espalhadas por
bicycling:	andar de bicicleta
volcano:	vulcão
shopping:	fazer compras
snorkeling:	mergulhar
lovely cove:	encantadora enseada
tropical rain forest:	floresta tropical pluvial

Treasure Islands

The **islands** of Hawaii **have long been considered** the **treasure** of the United States. **Gorgeous sandy beaches**, **spectacular sunsets** and **breathtaking beauty**, it is no **surprise** that Hawaii is one of the most popular vacation **spots** in the U.S.

Oahu, Maui, Kauai and The Big Island are the four most popular islands. Each island is **packed full** of beauty and **diversity**. You will **find** perfect beaches on each island, but **depending** on your destination, you may **also see miles** of **barren lava flow**, **museums** and even **skiing** on a **snow-peaked mountain**!

OAHU

Oahu is **often** the **landing spot** for most visitors and home to the **largest city** in the state, Honolulu. Oahu is **probably best known** for the city and beaches of Waikiki. Waikiki **hums** with **activity**. Here you can do more than just  experience the **outdoor activities** of the islands. It is **well worth your time to visit** Pearl Harbor and the Polynesian Cultural Center. And you must visit the North Shore of Oahu for **world-famous surf**.

MAUI

Relaxed and **friendly**, Maui is home to some of the most beautiful resorts and gorgeous sandy beaches in the world. Activities are **spread across** the entire island and you can easily find something different to do every day. **Bicycling** down a **volcano**, **shopping** in historic Lahaina Town, world-class golf, **snorkeling** in a **lovely cove** or camping in a **tropical rain forest**; the Island of Maui has a lot to offer for all ages.

KAUAI

Known also as the **garden isle**, Kauai is **considered by many** to be the most beautiful of the islands. Poipu Beach **is consistently voted** one of the prettiest beaches in the world. **Lush** tropical rain forests **compete** for your attention with **dramatic canyons** and **coastline**. You won't find a **great deal** of **night life** here, but your time will be best **spent hiking**, **exploring** and kayaking during the day. Kauai is one of the **wettest** spots on Earth, with an **annual average rainfall** of 460 inches. The high annual rainfall has **eroded deep valleys** in the central mountain, **carving out** canyons and **creating** the many **scenic waterfalls**.

THE BIG ISLAND

Larger than all the other islands **combined**, The Big Island of Hawaii is a **remarkable contrast** of geography and **climates**. Tropical forests with beautiful waterfalls on one side, **stark** lava beds on the other. The **landscape** is **dominated** by mountains, particularly the **twin peaks** of Mauna Kea and Mauna Loa. Mauna Kea is the only **place** in Hawaii where you can **strap on skis** and **hit the slopes**.

If you can't **make up your mind** about which Island to visit you can **take** an **island-hopping cruise**. Norwegian Cruise Line has seven-day **itineraries** visiting Oahu, Maui, Kauai and the Big Island.

By **land** or **sea**, Hawaii is a great place for your **next** vacation!

---

known also as: também conhecida como
garden isle: ilha jardim
considered by many: considerada por muitos
is consistently voted: é votada constantemente
lush: exuberantes
compete/to compete: competem/competir
dramatic canyons: desfiladeiros emocionantes
coastline: litoral, costa
great deal: muita
night life: vida noturna
spent: gasto/gastar (tempo)
hiking: caminhando
exploring: explorando
wettest: mais úmidos
annual average rainfall: precipitação média anual
eroded/to erode: erodiu/erodir
deep valleys: vales profundos
carving out/to carve out: escavando/escavar
creating/to create: criando/criar
scenic waterfalls: deslumbrantes cachoeiras
larger: maior
combined: juntas
remarkable contrast: extraordinário contraste
climates: climas
stark: inóspitas
landscape: paisagem
dominated/to dominate: dominada/dominar
twin peaks: picos gêmeos
place: lugar
strap on skis: colocar esquis
hit the slopes: descer ladeira abaixo
make up your mind: se decidir
take: fazer
island-hopping cruise: cruzeiro que passa em todas as ilhas
itineraries: itinerários
land: terra
sea: mar
next: próxima

The First National Park

offer/to offer: oferecem/oferecer
more than: mais que
outdoor recreation: passatempos ao ar livre
chance: oportunidade
to learn: para aprender
first: primeiro
inspired: inspirado
beauty: beleza
worried: preocupado
natural wonders: maravilhas naturais
appealed/to appeal: pediram/pedir
protect: proteger
signed/to sign: assinou/assinar
granting/to grant: concedendo/conceder
inalienable public trust: patrimônio público tombado
time: vez
set aside/to set aside: destinado/destinou
scenic lands: terras deslumbrantes
to allow: para permitir
enjoyment: divertimento
spark: faísca
known/to know: conhecido/conhecer
waterfalls: cachoeiras
square miles: milhas quadradas
find: encontrar
abundance: abundância
wildlife: vida silvestre
spectacular scenery: paisagem espetacular
vast wilderness: muita natureza selvagem
to explore: para explorar
to see: para ver
spring: primavera
snowmelt: degelo
occurs/to occur: ocorre/ocorrer
tallest: mais altas
separate: separadas
flows/to flow: flui/fluir
walk: caminhar
ancient: antigas
found/to find: encontradas/encontrar
grove: bosque
generally considered: geralmente considerada
located: localizada

The National Parks in the United States **offer more than** just **outdoor recreation**—they offer a **chance to learn** about our nation's diverse history, geography, and culture.

The **first** official national park of the United States was California's Yosemite National Park. **Inspired** by the **beauty** of Yosemite and **worried** about the possible exploitation of Yosemite's **natural wonders**, conservationists **appealed** to Senator John Conness to help **protect** the park. On June 30, 1864, President Abraham Lincoln **signed** a bill **granting** Yosemite Valley and the Mariposa Grove of Giant Sequoias to the State of California as an **inalienable public trust**. This was the first **time** in history that a federal government had **set aside scenic lands** to protect them and **to allow** for their **enjoyment** by all people. This idea was the **spark** that made Yosemite the first official national park in 1890.

Yosemite National Park is best **known** for its **waterfalls**, but within its nearly 1,200 **square miles** you will **find** an **abundance** of **wildlife, spectacular scenery** and **vast wilderness to explore**.

The best time **to see** waterfalls is during **spring**, when most of the **snowmelt occurs**. Yosemite Falls is one of the world's **tallest** and is made up of three **separate** falls: Upper Yosemite Fall (1,430 feet), the middle cascades (675 feet), and Lower Yosemite Fall (320 feet). Another popular waterfall, Bridal Veil, **flows** all year and you can **walk** to the base in just a few minutes.

Ancient giant sequoias can be **found** in the Mariposa **Grove**. The Mariposa Grove is the largest group of giant sequoias in Yosemite. The General Sherman, a Giant Sequoia, is **generally considered** to be the largest tree in the world. This tree is **located** in Sequoia National Park, just south of Yosemite.

30 travel

Two famous **rock formations** in Yellowstone are Half Dome and El Capitan. Half Dome is **perhaps** the most **recognized symbol** of Yosemite. **Rising** nearly 5,000 feet **above** the Valley floor, some people **attempt** the **treacherous hike** or **rock climb** to the **top**. Experienced rock climbers enjoy El Capitan. It rises more than 3,000 feet above the Valley floor and is the largest **monolith** of **granite** in the world.

Yosemite National Park is home to **hundreds** of American **black bears**. These bears are very **curious** and have an amazing **sense of smell**. Most bears that **rely** on natural **food sources** are **active** during the day. However, when **hungry**, they **quietly sneak around** and **grab unattended** food at night. **Precautions** and information on bear **safety** can be found at **nature centers** in the park.

You don't need reservations **to visit** Yosemite National Park, but reservations **to stay overnight** in the park are **mandatory**. **Lodging** options in Yosemite National Park **range from** simple **cabins** to **deluxe rooms** at The Ahwahnee Hotel. Camping is the most popular way **to spend the night** in Yosemite National Park. There are 13 campgrounds located throughout the park and reservations are **necessary** for **most** locations. Information and reservations for Yosemite, **as well as** every national park in the United States, can be **found** online at: www.nps.gov.

rock formations: formações rochosas
perhaps: talvez
recognized: reconhecido
symbol: símbolo
rising: com elevação de
above: acima
attempt/to attempt: tentam/tentar
treacherous hike: excursão traiçoeira
rock climb: escalada em rochas
top: topo
monolith: monólito
granite: granito
hundreds: centenas
black bears: ursos negros
curious: curiosos
sense of smell: olfato
rely/to rely: dependem/depender
food sources: fontes de alimento
active: ativos
hungry: famintos
quietly sneak around: aproximam-se sorrateiramente
grab/to grab: roubam/roubar
unattended: não vigiada
precautions: precauções
safety: segurança
nature centers: centros de informações sobre a natureza
you don't need: você não precisa
to visit: visitar
to stay overnight: passar a noite
mandatory: obrigatórias
lodging: alojamento
range from: vão desde
cabins: cabanas
deluxe rooms: quartos de luxo
to spend te night: para passar a noite
necessary: necessárias
most: a maioria de
as well as: assim como
found/to find: encontrados/encontrar

most: a maioria de
think/to think: pensa/pensar
visiting: visitar
lifetime: para toda a vida
hard to arrange: difícil de conseguir
arrangements: planos, organização
through: através de
requires/to require: requer/requerer
extensive: extenso
planning: planejamento
ahead of time: adiantado
of course: naturalmente
worth: digno
effort: esforço
successful: bem sucedido
besides: além de
packed full: repleta
places: lugares
to visit: para visitar
taking: fazer
self-guided tour: visita autoguiada
learning/to learn: aprende/aprender
government: governo
prominent landmark: ponto de referência mais importante
stands/to stand: eleva-se/elevar
tall: altura
landing: patamar
views: vistas
unique feature: característica única
carved memorial stones: lápides entalhadas
line/to line: enfileiram-se/enfileirar
pay tribute: prestam homenagem
achievements: realizações
honors/to honor: honra/honrar
symbolizes/to symbolize: simboliza/simbolizar
belief: crença
should be free: deveriam ser livres
contains/to contain: contém/conter
statue: estátua
houses/to house: aloja/alojar
stone tables: mesas de pedra
engraved: gravadas
building: edifício
based on: baseia-se em
classic style: estilo clássico
introduced/to introduce: introduziu/introduzir
walls: paredes
describe/to describe: descrevem/descrever
belief: crença
freedom: liberdade

A Walking Tour of D.C.

When **most** people **think** of a trip to Washington, D.C. they think of **visiting** the White House. A trip to the White House is an experience of a **lifetime**; however it can be **hard to arrange**. You must have a group of ten or more people and make your **arrangements through** your member of Congress. This **requires extensive planning** well **ahead of time**. It is, **of course**, **worth** the **effort** if you are **successful**.

Besides the White House, Washington, D.C. is **packed full** of interesting, historical and educational **places to visit**. **Taking** a **self-guided tour** of the national monuments is a great way to explore the city while **learning** about the history, **government** and people of the United States.

THE WASHINGTON MONUMENT

The most **prominent landmark** in Washington, D.C. is the Washington Monument. It **stands** 555 feet **tall**. An elevator takes visitors to the 500-foot **landing** for magnificent **views** of the city. A **unique feature** of the Washington Monument is the 193 **carved memorial stones** that **line** the interior of the monument. These stones **pay tribute** to the **achievements** of George Washington.

THE LINCOLN MEMORIAL

The Lincoln Memorial **honors** Abraham Lincoln, the 16th President of the United States. The memorial **symbolizes** Lincoln's **belief** that all people **should be free**. The chamber inside the memorial **contains** a **statue** of Lincoln. The chamber also **houses** two **stone tables**; one **engraved** with Lincoln's Second Inaugural Address, and the other with the Gettysburg Address.

THE JEFFERSON MEMORIAL

The Jefferson Memorial honors Thomas Jefferson, author of the Declaration of Independence, first Secretary of State, and third President. The structure of the **building** is **based on** the **classic style** of architecture Jefferson **introduced** into this country. In the center of the memorial is a statue of Jefferson. On the **walls** are four inscriptions. They **describe** his **belief** in **freedom** and education.

32 travel

VIETNAM VETERANS MEMORIAL

The Vietnam Veterans Memorial honors the men and women who **served** in the Vietnam War. The memorial **consists** of three parts: the Wall of **names**, the Three **Servicemen** Statue and **Flagpole**, and the Vietnam Women's Memorial. The Memorial Wall **contains** the names of the 58,220 men and women who were **killed** and **remain missing** from the war.

KOREAN WAR VETERANS MEMORIAL

The Korean War Veterans Memorial is a **reminder** of the Korean War and the sacrifices and **hardships** of those who **fought** in this war. This memorial consists of a **platoon** of **stainless steel** soldiers. Engraved on a **nearby** wall are the total **casualties** of **both** the United States and the United Nations' **troops** along with the words "FREEDOM IS NOT FREE".

NATIONAL WORLD WAR II MEMORIAL

The National World War II Memorial is a National memorial to Americans who served and **died** in World War II. The **design** of the National World War II Memorial **incorporates** many **symbolic elements** representing **unity**, **sacrifice**, **victory** and freedom.

UNITED STATES MARINE CORPS MEMORIAL

The Marine Corps War Memorial is a symbol of America's **gratitude** to the U.S. Marines who died in **combat**. The statue **portrays** one of the most famous **events** of World War II: the U.S. victory of Iwo Jima.

THE TOMB OF THE UNKNOWNS

The **Tomb** of the **Unknown Soldier** is **located** at Arlington National Cemetery. It was **constructed to mark** the **grave** of an **unidentified** American soldier from World War I. Three **Greek figures** are engraved into the **marble** and represent **Peace**, Victory, and Valor. **On the back** of the Tomb is the **following inscription**: **HERE RESTS** IN HONORED **GLORY** AN AMERICAN SOLDIER **KNOWN** BUT TO **GOD**.

served/to serve: serviram/servir
consists/to consist: consiste/consistir
names: nomes
servicemen: militares
flagpole: mastro de bandeira
contains/to contain: contém/ conter
killed/to kill: mortos/matar
remain missing: permanecem desaparecidos
reminder: lembrança
hardships: dificuldades
fought/fight: lutaram/lutar
platoon: pelotão
stainless steel: aço inoxidável
nearby: próxima
casualties: baixas
both: ambos
troops: tropas
died/to die: morreram/morrer
design: projeto
incorporates/to incorporate: inclui/ incluir
symbolic elements: elementos simbólicos
unity: unidade
sacrifice: sacrifício
victory: vitória
gratitude: gratidão
combat: combate
portrays/to portray: representa/ representar
events: acontecimentos
tomb: tumba, túmulo
unknown: desconhecido
soldier: soldado
located: localizada
constructed/to construct: construída/ construir
to mark: para sinalizar
grave: sepultura
unidentified: não identificado
Greek figures: figuras gregas
marble: mármore
peace: paz
on the back: na parte de trás
following: seguinte
inscription: inscrição
here rests: aqui jaz
glory: glória
known: conhecido/conhecer
God: Deus

travel 33

ready:	preparado/a
something:	algo
next:	próximas
skip/to skip:	pule/pular
spend/to spend:	passe/passar
lighthouse:	farol
romantic towers:	torres românticas
provide/to provide:	fornecem/fornecer
unique:	únicas
accommodations:	acomodações
country:	país
allow/to allow:	permitem/permitir
guests:	hóspedes
to perform:	realizar
keeper's duties:	obrigações do guardião
raising/to raise:	içar/içar
flag:	bandeira
recording/to record:	registrando/registrar
odd jobs:	trabalhos avulsos
maintain:	conservar
scenery:	paisagem
surroundings:	arredores
range from:	vão de
upscale:	elegante
gourmet meals:	refeições gastronômicas
rugged:	rústico
bunk beds:	camas beliche
tiny:	minúscula
entire:	todo
yourself:	só para você
restored:	restaurado
open:	abertos
daily:	diariamente
departs/to depart:	parte/partir
own:	particular, só sua
rent:	alugar
second-floor:	segundo andar
agree to do:	aceitarem fazer
hour's worth:	o equivalente a uma hora
record-keeping:	manutenção de registros
chores:	tarefas
landmark:	ponto de referência
red-brick:	tijolo vermelho
built/to build:	construído/construir
overnight:	passar a noite
public tours:	excursões públicas
operational:	em funcionamento
enjoy:	aproveitar
swimming:	natação
picnicking:	fazer um piquenique
bird watching:	observar as aves
reached/to reach:	alcançado/alcançar
boat:	barco
nature trail:	trilha ecológica
village:	povoado

Unique Accommodations

Ready for **something** different? On your **next** vacation **skip** the hotel and **spend** the night in a **lighthouse**! These **romantic towers provide** some of the most **unique accommodations** in the **country**. Some lighthouses **allow guests to perform** various **keeper's duties** such as **raising** the **flag**, **recording** the weather, and other **odd jobs** to help **maintain** the property. All lighthouses provide spectacular **scenery**, historic **surroundings**, and an extraordinary opportunity. The lighthouses **range from upscale** bed and breakfasts with **gourmet meals** to more **rugged** accommodations with **bunk beds** and no electricity.

The lighthouse on **tiny** Rose Island, in Rhode Island's Narragansett Bay, is one of the few authentic lighthouses in America that allows you to have the **entire** lighthouse to **yourself** and become keeper for a week. The island and **restored** lighthouse are **open** from 10 a.m. to 4 p.m. **daily**. But when the last ferry **departs**, the island becomes your **own**. Up to four adults can **rent** the **second-floor** apartment if they **agree to do** an **hour's worth** of daily **record-keeping** and **chores**.

A **landmark** on the Hudson River, the Saugerties Lighthouse, is a **red-brick** lighthouse **built** in 1869. The lighthouse offers **overnight** bed and breakfast accommodations, **public tours** and special events. The **operational** light-tower offers a panoramic view of the Hudson River. On this small island you can **enjoy swimming**, **picnicking** and **bird-watching**. The Lighthouse can be **reached** by **boat** or the half-mile **nature trail** at the end of Lighthouse Drive in the **village** of Saugerties, New York.

34 travel

The East Brother Light Station is located **less** than an hour from San Francisco but **once** you **arrive**, **city life feels** a **world away**. The Light Station operates as a four-room bed and breakfast and is **accessible only** by boat. **Gourmet dinners** are **served** with **wine** and breakfasts **have been made popular** by the Lighthouse French Toast Soufflé. The day can be **spent hiking** the island, bird and **whale** watching or **learning** about the history of the lighthouse.

Travel **back in time** with a stay at the Isle Au Haut Lighthouse in Maine. This authentic Keeper's House is **without telephones** and electricity. Guests **use kerosene lanterns** for **light** and **woodstoves** for **heat**. To reach this 1907 lighthouse, take a 40-minute boat ride to the **remote** island of Isle au Haut. **Bikes** are **provided** to guests for **transportation around** the island. There are six **bedrooms furnished** with **antiques**, island **crafts** and **coastal memorabilia**.

Charity Island Lighthouse in Au Gres, Michigan, offers overnight lodging in the **spring** and **fall**. It is operational as a bed and breakfast with four bedrooms. **Upon arrival** guests **receive** a 30-minute **presentation** on the history of the island and the lighthouse. The island **consists** of **almost three hundred acres** of **forest** and is home to a **multitude** of **wildlife** including **songbirds**, **bald eagles**, **raccoons**, and **foxes**. The island is **preserved** as a wildlife **sanctuary** and is considered a bird-watcher's **paradise**.

less: menos
once: uma vez
arrive/to arrive: chega/chegar
city life: vida urbana
feels/to feel: sente/sentir
world away: um mundo de distância
accessible only: acessível apenas
gourmet dinners: jantares gastronômicos
served/to serve: servidos/servir
wine: vinho
have been made popular: tornaram-se populares
spent/to spend: gasto/gastar
hiking/to hike: caminhando/caminhar
whale: baleia
learning/to learn: aprendendo/aprender
back in time: de volta no tempo
without telephones: sem telefones
use/to use: usam/usar
kerosene lanterns: lanternas de querosene
light: luz
woodstoves: fogões a lenha
heat: calor
remote: remota
bikes: bicicletas
provided/to provide: fornecidas/fornecer
transportation: transporte
around: ao redor
bedrooms: quartos
furnished: mobiliados
antiques: antiguidades
crafts: artesanatos
coastal memorabilia: lembranças litorâneas
spring: primavera
fall: outono
upon arrival: recém-chegados
receive/to receive: recebem/receber
presentation: apresentação
consists/to consist: consiste/consistir
almost: quase
three hundred acres: trezentos acres
forest: floresta
multitude: grande quantidade
wildlife: vida selvagem
songbirds: pássaros cantantes
bald eagles: águia-de-cabeça-branca
raccoons: guaxinim
foxes: raposas
preserved: preservada
sanctuary: santuário
paradise: paraíso

travel 35

all over: por toda parte
cities: cidades
big and small: grandes e pequenas
will find/to find: encontrará/encontrar
factories: fábricas
give/to give: oferecem/oferecer
tours: excursões
visit: visitar
educational: educativas
entertaining: divertidas
behind-the-scenes: os bastidores
everyday things: coisas do cotidiano
made/to make: feitas/fazer
both: ambos
taking/to take: fazendo/fazer
road trip: longa viagem de carro
stopping: parar
break: descanso
provide: fornecer
valuable insight: valiosa perspectiva nova
end: final
guide: guia
hand out/to hand out: distribui/distribuir
free samples: amostras grátis
in addition: além disso
resulting in: resultando em
affordable activity: atividade acessível
list: listar
great place: excelente lugar
to plan: para planejar
put on/to put on: coloque/colocar
white paper hat: chapéu branco de papel
follow/to follow: siga/seguir
friendly: amigáveis/amistosos
sweet-smelling: cheirosa
watch/to watch: observe/observar
flavors: sabores
range from: vão de
buttered popcorn: pipoca manteigada
unique: única
candy: doce
made/to make: feito/fazer
bills: notas
large reams: grandes resmas
blank paper: papel em branco
intricately inked currency: papel moeda detalhadamente pintado
locations: localizações
favorite ice cream brand: marca de sorvete favorita
tasted/to taste: provados/provar
to eat: para comer
breakfast: café da manhã
guitar-making process: processo de fabricação de guitarras
assembling/to assemble: acumulando/acumular
quality: qualidade
by hand: feito à mão

36   travel

Made in the USA

All over the United States, in **cities big and small**, you **will find factories** that **give tours** to the public. Why **visit** a factory? Factory tours are **educational** and **entertaining**. The **behind-the-scenes** view of how **everyday things** are **made** can be interesting to **both** kids and adults. If you are **taking** a **road trip**, **stopping** to visit a factory can make a nice **break**. If you are visiting a new city it can **provide valuable insight** into what makes that city special. At the **end** of the tour, the tour **guide** will often **hand out free samples** of their products. **In addition**, factory tours are generally free to the public, **resulting in** an **affordable activity** for you and your family.

There are more tours than we could **list** in one article. A **great place to plan** your factory tour is at Factory Tours: www.factorytoursusa.com

Jelly Belly Factory (www.jellybelly.com) **Put on** a **white paper hat**, **follow friendly** tour guides through the **sweet-smelling** factory and **watch** how Jelly Bellies are made. With the interesting **flavors** that **range from buttered popcorn** to jalapeño, the Jelly Belly tour is a **unique candy** experience.

U.S. Department of the Treasury (www.moneyfactory.com) Do you want to see how money is **made**? Here you can watch **bills** go from **large reams** of **blank paper** into **intricately inked currency**. There are two **locations**—one in Washington, D.C., and the other in Fort Worth, Texas.

Ben and Jerry's (www.benjerry.com) This **favorite ice cream brand** is one of the most popular tours in the United States. Samples are **tasted** in their FlavoRoom and tours starting at 9am give you the perfect excuse **to eat** ice cream for **breakfast**.

Gibson Guitar Factory (www.gibsonmemphis.com) At this factory in Memphis, Tennessee, you will watch the **guitar-making process**. For over 100 years, the company has been **assembling quality** American guitars **by hand**.

Home on the Range

Have you **ever wanted to live** like a **cowboy**? **Well**, you can **spend** a **weekend** as a cowboy at one of the many "dude ranches" **located across** the United States.

The dude ranch, **also known as** a **guest ranch**, is a ranch that is **open** for **visitors**. They **allow** visitors **to experience** ranch activities **first-hand** on weekend or weeklong vacations. **Daily** activities usually **include horseback riding lessons**, **trail rides**, picnics, **hiking**, **cook-outs**, and rodeos. They **often host nightly** entertainment around a **campfire**.

Working ranches are another option for a more authentic experience. As the name **implies**, they are real working ranches that are in the **business** of **raising cattle** or horses and/or **farming**. They usually offer more rustic **accommodations** for **a smaller** number of guests and **less organized** activities. Daily activities include horseback riding and **sightseeing**, but you also have the opportunity to work with real cowboys in their daily ranch work.

Most dude ranches are **located out west** in the "**big sky country**" **states** such as Montana, Idaho, Colorado and Wyoming. Part of the **joy** of visiting a Dude Ranch is the spectacular **scenery** that you get to experience. The majestic mountains, green **rolling hills**, beautiful **rivers and lakes** are a **delight to view** and an **adventure to explore**. Exploring the **countryside** on horseback **allows** you to see things at a **slower pace** and the chance to see more wildlife such as **eagles**, buffalo, **deer** and even **wild bears**.

Before you **pick** a dude ranch to visit, go to websites such as www.ranchweb.com and www.duderanches.com to **read reviews** from other travelers. And, before you go, **make sure** you are prepared to **dress the part—don't forget to pack** your cowboy hat!

---

ever wanted: alguma vez já quis
to live: viver
cowboy: caubói, vaqueiro
well: bom
spend: passar
weekend: fim de semana
located: localizados
across: através de
also known as: também conhecido como
guest ranch: hotel fazenda
open: aberto
visitors: visitantes
allow/to allow: permitem/permitir
to experience: experimentar
first-hand: primeira mão
daily: diárias
include/to include: incluem/incluir
horseback riding lessons: aulas de equitação
trail rides: passeios em trilhas
hiking: caminhadas
cook-outs: churrasco
often: geralmente
host/to host: apresentam/apresentar
nightly: todas as noites
campfire: fogueira
working: em funcionamento
implies/to imply: indica/indicar
business: negócio
raising cattle: criação de gado
farming: agricultura
accommodations: acomodações
a smaller: um menor
less organized: menos organizadas
sightseeing: turismo
located out west: localizados no oeste
"big sky country" states: estados "com grandes áreas de céu aberto"
joy: diversão
scenery: paisagem
rolling hills: colinas ondulantes
rivers and lakes: rios e lagos
delight to view: vistas prazerosas
adventure: aventura
to explore: a explorar
countryside: campo
allows/to allow: permite/permitir
slower pace: ritmo mais lento
eagles: águias
deer: cervo
wild bears: ursos selvagens
before: antes
pick: escolher
read: leia
reviews: opiniões
make sure/to make sure: certifique-se/certificar-se
dress the part: vestir-se a caráter
don't forget/to forget: não se esqueça de/esquecer-se
to pack: colocar na mala

travel 37

best: melhor
whale watching: mirante de baleias
is found: encontra-se
is home to: abriga
protected waters: águas protegidas
coastline: costa
camping: acampar
kayaking: navegar em caiaque
wildlife: vida silvestre
called: chamadas
largest: maiores
dolphin family: família dos golfinhos
striking: impressionantes
markings: marcas
feed/to feed: alimentam-se/alimentar-se
fish: peixes
meal: comida
during certain times: durante certas épocas
guaranteed: tem a garantia
predictably: previsivelmente
seen: vistas
spring: primavera
autumn: outono
follow/to follow: seguem/seguir
migrating: migrantes
shore: litorâneas
warmest: mais quente
driest: mais seco
tours: excursões
will take/to take: levarão/levar
aboard: a bordo
vessels: barcos, navios
swimming: nadando
breaching: rompendo
chasing/to chase: perseguindo/perseguir
all of the above: todo o anterior
communicate/to communicate: se comunicam/comunicar-se
regular basis: regularmente
underwater: embaixo d'água
listen: escutar
adds/to add: agrega/agregar
magical dimension: dimensão mágica
even closer view: vista ainda mais próxima
multi-day: de vários dias
paddle: remar
stopping/to stop: parando/parar
hike: caminhar
around: ao redor
explore/to explore: explora/explorar
guides: guias
point out: indicar
explain: explicar
land: terra
while: enquanto
miss/to miss: perca/perder
museum: museu

38 travel

San Juan Orcas

Some of the **best whale watching** on the continent **is found** in the San Juan Islands off the coast of Washington.

The Puget Sound **is home to** 400 islands and home to 90 orcas. The **protected waters** and miles of **coastline** are ideal for **camping** and **kayaking**, and seeing pods of orcas and other **wildlife**.

Orcas, also **called** "killer whales," are the **largest** members of the **dolphin family**. Orcas are beautiful whales with **striking** black and white **markings**. Orcas **feed** almost exclusively on **fish**, with chinook salmon being their favorite **meal**. **During certain times** of the year you are **guaranteed** a whale sighting in this area.

The whales are **predictably seen** from **spring** until **autumn**, when they **follow** the **migrating** salmon through **shore** waters. July, August and September are the **warmest** and **driest** months and the best time to see orcas, porpoises and also gray whales.

There are many whale watching **tours** that **will take** you **aboard** one of their "whale-friendly" **vessels**. You may see the whales **swimming, breaching, chasing** fish—or **all of the above**! Orcas **communicate** with each other on a **regular basis**. Some boats have an **underwater** microphone so you can **listen** to their "conversations." This **adds** another **magical dimension** to the experience.

For an **even closer view** you can kayak with orcas in the San Juan Islands. On **multi-day** trips, you will **paddle** four to five hours a day, **stopping** to watch wildlife or **hike around** the islands. As you **explore**, the **guides** will **point out** wildlife and **explain** the ecology of the area.

The best place to see orcas from **land** is Lime Kiln Point State Park in Friday Harbor. This park is also called "Whale Watch Park." **While** you are there, don't **miss** the Whale Watch **Museum**.

Go to Jail!

Alcatraz, which is **also known** as 'the Rock', is the famous American **prison located** on Alcatraz Island, in San Francisco Bay. A **trip** to the island **offers** a **close-up look** at a **historic** and **notorious** federal prison. More than a million visitors a year **climb** the **steep hill** from the **ferry dock to view crumbling cell blocks**, and the **former living quarters** of prisoners and **guards**.

Before **being used as** a prison it was home to the **first** and **oldest operating lighthouse** (1854) and the first US **Fort** on the West Coast (1859).

This **military fortress** that had **protected** San Francisco Bay since California's Gold Rush days was a federal prison between 1934 and 1963. The bay's **icy water** and **strong currents** made "The Rock" **escape-proof**. **However,** it is **reported** that five prisoners tried to escape and are **officially listed** as **missing** and **presumed drowned**.

Between 1969 and 1971 the island was **taken over** by Native Americans. **Today**, the **entire** island is **preserved** as part of the National Park **System** and is a **venue** for tourists rather than criminals. A few former prisoners and guards can be **heard** on the prison's **audio tour** of the famous *Cell House*.

The **refreshing ferryboat ride**, with **stunning views** of San Francisco Bay, **adds** a special **beginning** and **end** to this popular **tour**.

also known as: também conhecida como
prison: prisão
located: localizada
trip: viagem
offers/to offer: oferece/oferecer
close-up look: olhada de perto
historic: histórica
notorious: notória
climb/to climb: escalam/escalar
steep hill: colina íngreme
ferry dock: cais de balsa
to view: para ver
crumbling cell blocks: blocos de celas desmoronando
former living quarters: antigos alojamentos
guards: guardas
being used as: ser usado como
first: primeiro
oldest: mais antigo
operating lighthouse: farol em funcionamento
fort: forte
military fortress: fortaleza militar
protected/to protect: protegido/proteger
icy water: água gélida
strong currents: correntes fortes
escape-proof: à prova de fuga
however: contudo
reported/to report: informado/informar
officially: oficialmente
listed/to list: listados/listar
missing: desaparecidos
presumed: dados por
drowned: afogados
taken over/to take over: tomada/tomar
today: hoje
entire: inteira
preserved/to preserve: preservada/preservar
system: sistema
venue: ponto de encontro
heard/to hear: ouvidos/ouvir
audio tour: excursão em áudio
refreshing: refrescante
ferryboat ride: passeio de balsa
stunning views: maravilhosas paisagens
adds/to add: adiciona/adicionar
beginning: começo
end: final
tour: excursão

travel 39

Test Your Comprehension

Camping Trips, page 24

1. Quais são os três tipos de acampamento disponíveis nos parques nacionais?

2. O que você deveria fazer primeiro se estivesse planejando uma viagem de acampamento?

3. Quando se deixa um acampamento norte-americano, o que não se deve esquecer de fazer para as gerações futuras?

Rafting the Grand Canyon, page 25

1. Que rio corre pelo Grand Canyon?

2. Quais são algumas das viagens de interesse especial oferecidas no Grand Canyon?

Down by the Boardwalk, page 26

1. Quando e onde foram construídos os primeiros calçadões pavimentados?

2. Qual é o maior calçadão?

3. Qual é a novidade do Passeio Marítimo da Praia Myrtle, na Carolina do Sul?

Treasure Islands, page 28

1. Qual é a ilha havaiana que tem a maior praia?

2. Qual a ilha, também conhecida como a Ilha Jardim, considerada por muitos a mais bonita?

3. A grande ilha do Havaí tem várias paisagens. Com o que se parece?

Teste sua Compreensão

America's First National Park, page 30

1. Qual foi o primeiro parque nacional dos Estados Unidos?

2. Quem assinou o projeto de lei que colocou este parque nacional como patrimônio tombado?

3. Quais são as famosas formações rochosas que estão neste parque nacional?

Walking Tour of D.C, page 32

1. Qual é a altura do Monumento de Washington?

2. O que está gravado nas duas pedras de mesa do monumento comemorativo de Lincoln?

3. O que representam os 4 elementos simbólicos incorporados no projeto do monumento comemorativo da Segunda Guerra Mundial?

Made in the USA, page 36

1. Quais são alguns dos sabores dos doces encontrados numa excursão à fábrica Jelly Belly?

2. Aonde você iria para ver como o dinheiro é feito?

San Juan Orcas, page 38

1. As ilhas San Juan estão de frente para o litoral de qual estado?

2. Quando as baleias migram e podem ser vistas?

3. Qual é a melhor maneira de ver as orcas de perto?

A love for tradition has never weakened a nation, indeed it has strengthened nations in their hour of peril.

Sir Winston Churchill

Tradition

choice: escolha
free: grátis
tax-funded: pagas através de imposto
public schools: escolas públicas
tuition-based: *(com mensalidades)* com base em matrícula
private schools: escolas particulares
required/to require: requeridos/requerer
to provide: fornecer
free of charge: gratuita
monitored/to monitor: controladas/controlar
standarized testing: testes padrões
made/to make: tomadas/tomar (decisões)
to attend: a frequentar
trouble: conflito
with the law: com a lei
divided: dividida
levels: níveis
elementary: ensino fundamental do 1º segmento
junior high: ensino fundamental do 2º segmento
senior high: ensino médio
grade: séries
vary/to vary: variam/variar
grade school: escola primária
first: primeiros
basic subjects: matérias básicas
science: ciências
taught/to teach: ensinadas/ensinar
depending upon: de acordo com
expanded on/to expand on: ampliados/ampliar
foreign language: língua estrangeira
added/to add: adicionada/adicionar
runs/to run: vai de/percorrer
required: devem
to complete: completar
to receive: receber
become/to become: tornam-se/tornar-se
official transcript: histórico escolar
to apply: para se candidatarem
post-secondary: ensino superior
consists of: consiste em
criteria: critérios
earned/to earn: tiradas/tirar (notas)
GPA (Grade Point Average): CRA (Coeficiente de Rendimento Acadêmico)
scores: pontuação
finishing: terminar
master's degree: mestrado
as a whole: como um todo
becoming: tornando
valued: valorizada
highly: em alto grau
status: posição social

44 tradition

Choices in Education

People in the United States have a **choice** between **free tax-funded public schools** or **tuition-based private schools**.

All public school systems are **required to provide** an education **free of charge** to everyone of school age. All schools, public and private, are **monitored** by the Department of Education. Educational standards and **standardized testing** decisions are **made** by state governments.

People are required **to attend** school until the age of 16–18. If a child is not attending school the parents could be in **trouble with the law**.

Education is **divided** into three **levels**: **elementary**, **junior high**, and **senior high**. **Grade** levels **vary** from area to area.

Elementary school, also known as **grade school**, is a school of the **first** six grades. The **basic subjects** of math, English and **science** are **taught**.

Junior high school is grades 5–8 **depending upon** the school structure. The basic subjects are **expanded on**. A **foreign language** is often **added**.

High school **runs** from grades 9–12. Each grade number also has a name: freshman, sophomore, junior and senior. There are a minimum number of courses students are **required to complete to receive** a high school diploma. Starting in ninth grade, grades **become** very important because they are part of a student's **official transcript**. In the last two years of high school students take standardized tests **to apply** for college. The SAT and ACT are the most common standardized tests.

Post-secondary education in the United States is known as college or university. It **consists of** four years, or more, of study. Students apply to receive admission into college. Admissions **criteria** involve the grades **earned** in high school, **GPA**, and standardized test **scores**. After **finishing** a four-year degree students may continue to a more advanced degree such as a **master's degree**.

As a whole, the population of the United States is **becoming** more educated. Post-secondary education is **valued** very **highly** by American society and is one of the main determinants of class and **status**.

Prom and Homecoming

"Prom" is the **name** for a **special dance held** at the **end** of the **high school academic year**.

Traditionally the prom is a **special night** for the **junior and senior classes**. **Younger guests** may go to the prom only if their **date** is a junior or a senior. Prom is a memorable and important night for most high school students. **Some feel** that it is the most romantic **night** of their lives and the **highlight** of their senior year!

Shopping for the prom **dress** can be an event of its own. **Formal wear** is **worn** by both girls and boys. Sometimes there is a prom **theme** and the **couples** dress **according** to the theme.

The prom **festivities** generally **include dinner** and a dance. The prom is often held at the school; however, some schools **rent ballrooms** or hotels or more **unusual venues** such as a **cruise boat** to **host** prom night. A prom **king** and **queen** are **announced** and **crowned** during the night. Traditionally the prom queen and king are **chosen** by their **fellow students**. **Campaigns** are held in the **weeks before** the prom and students **cast votes** for who they want to be king and queen. The king and queen are crowned and dance together **to celebrate** their election.

Homecoming is another annual academic tradition that happens in high school and colleges. Homecoming is **largely associated** with football. People, **towns**, high schools and colleges **come together**, usually in late September or October, **to welcome** back **alumni**. The activities consist of a football game played on the school's football field, activities for students and alumni, a **parade** featuring the school's **marching band**, and the coronation of a homecoming queen and king, similar to the prom queen and king.

---

name: nome
special dance: festa especial
held/to hold: celebrada/celebrar
end: final
high school: ensino médio
academic year: ano acadêmico
special night: noite especial
junior and senior classes: turmas dos dois últimos anos do ensino médio
younger guests: convidados mais novos
date: encontro, parceiro
some: alguns
feel/to feel: sentem/sentir
night: noite
highlight: destaque
shopping: fazer compras
dress: vestido
formal wear: traje a rigor
worn/to wear: usado/usar
theme: tema
couples: casais
according: de acordo
festivities: festividades
include/to include: incluem/incluir
dinner: jantar
rent/to rent: alugam/alugar
ballrooms: salões de festa
unusual venues: locais de evento diferentes, incomuns
cruise boat: cruzeiro
host: hospedar
king: rei
queen: rainha
announced: anunciados
crowned: coroados
chosen/to choose: escolhidos/escolher
fellow students: colegas de escola
campaigns: campanhas
weeks: semanas
before: antes
cast votes: votam
to celebrate: celebrar
largely associated: muito associado com
towns: cidades
come together: reúnem-se
to welcome: dar as boas-vindas a
alumni: ex-alunos
parade: desfile
marching band: banda marcial

tradition

begin/to begin: começam/começar
parties: festas
sizes: tamanhos
held/to hold: celebradas/celebrar
across: através de
gather/to gather: se reúnem/reunir
watch/to watch: assistem/assistir
part of: parte de
midnight hour: meia-noite
approaches/to approach: se aproxima/aproximar-se
time zone: fuso horário
able to watch: pode ver
televised: televisionada
nationally: nacionalmente
before: antes de
brightly lit ball: bola muito iluminada
begins to drop: começa a descer
slowly: lentamente
pole: mastro
perched: colocado
count down: fazer contagem regressiva
seconds: segundos
reaches/to reach: chega/chegar
bottom: fim
hug/to hug: se abraçam/abraçar
kiss/to kiss: se beijam/beijar
cheers: saudações
heard/to hear: ouvidos/ouvir
another: outra
to sing: cantar
song: música
stroke: bater
played/to play: tocada/tocar
to welcome in: dar as boas-vindas a
literally: literalmente
means/to mean: significa/significar
households: lares
to spend: passar
afternoon: tarde
watching/to watch: assistindo/assistir
parade: parada, desfile
game: jogo

Traditions for the New Year

New Year's celebrations **begin** on December 31, New Year's Eve. New Year's **parties** of all **sizes** are **held across** the United States. Friends and family **gather** at home and **watch** television as **part of** the festivities. As the **midnight hour approaches** your own **time zone** you are **able to watch** New Year's celebrated all across the world.

Times Square in the heart of New York City hosts a very popular New Year's celebration and is **televised nationally**. At one minute **before** midnight, a **brightly lit ball begins to drop slowly** from a **pole perched** on one of the buildings. People begin to **count down** the **seconds** as the ball drops. When it **reaches** the **bottom**, it is the New Year. People **hug** and **kiss**, confetti falls, and **cheers** of "Happy New Year!" are **heard** everywhere.

Another New Year's tradition is **to sing** the **song** "Auld Lang Syne" at the **stroke** of midnight. This song is **played** in English-speaking countries **to welcome in** the new year. "Auld Lang Syne" **literally means** "old long ago," or "the good old days."

New Year's Day

On January 1, it is a tradition in many **households** for families and friends **to spend** the **afternoon watching** the Rose Bowl. The Tournament of Roses **parade** and the Rose Bowl football **game** are on many television sets across America.

The parade first **started** in 1890 and is held in Pasadena, California. In 1902, the parade committee **decided to add** a football game to the day's celebrations. By 1920 the **crowds outgrew** the football stands. The tournament's president **envisioned** a grand stadium and **put** his vision into action. He **built** a **new stadium** and **named** it the Rose Bowl.

Today the Tournament of Roses Parade is **more than** five miles **long** with **thousands** of people **participating, marching** in bands or **dance troops** and on **floats**. **City officials ride** in the cars **pulling** the floats and **waving** at the crowd. A celebrity is **chosen** to be the official **master** of ceremonies. The **queen** of the tournament rides on a special float **made from more than** 250,000 **flowers**.

New Year's resolutions are made on New Year's Day. Americans **write down** their resolutions and **promise to keep** them for the year **to come**. New Year's resolutions usually **include** things like **getting healthy** or **losing weight** and generally **encompass** something that **involves bettering** your **life**.

Regardless of the way the New Year is celebrated, the sentiments are the **same**. With a new year, people **hope for** a **fresh start**. They **wish** each other **good luck** and **best wishes** for the upcoming year.

started/to start: começou/começar
decided/to decide: decidiu/decidir
to add: adicionar
crowds: multidões
outgrew/to outgrow: lotavam/lotar
envisioned/to envision: previam/prever
put/to put: colocaram/colocar
built/to build: construiu/construir
new: novo
stadium: estádio
named/to name: denominou/denominar
more than: mais de
long: distância
thousands: milhares
participating/to participate: participando/participar
marching/to march: marchando/marchar
dance troops: grupos de dança
floats: carros alegóricos
city officials: funcionários municipais
ride/to ride: vão em/ir
pulling/to pull: puxando/puxar
waving/to wave: acenando/acenar
chosen/to choose: escolhida/escolher
master: mestre
queen: rainha
made from more than: feito com mais de
flowers: flores
write down/to write down: escreve/escrever
promise/to promise: prometem/prometer
to keep: mantê-las
to come: vindouro
include/to include: incluem/incluir
getting healthy: ficar saudável
losing weight: perder peso
encompass/to encompass: abrange/abranger
involves/to involve: envolve/envolver
bettering: melhorar
life: vida
regardless: independentemente
same: mesmos
hope for/to hope for: esperam/esperar
fresh start: novo começo
wish/to wish: desejam/desejar
good luck: boa sorte
best wishes: felicidades

wedding: casamento
some of: algumas das
most flexible: mais flexíveis
world: mundo
due to: devido a
ethnic backgrounds: formações étnicas
vary widely: variam muito
bride's: da noiva
first: primeiro
wears/to wear: veste/vestir
dress: vestido
veil: véu
considered: considerado
bad luck: má sorte
groom: noivo
to see: ver
before: antes
receive: receberá
gifts: presentes
to be used: para serem usados
honeymoon: lua de mel
weeks: semanas
intended: planejada
single man: homem solteiro
include: incluir
vows: votos
written: escritos
speak of: falam de
love: amor
newlyweds: recém-casados
kiss: beijam-se
seal/to seal: selam/selar
their union: sua união
after: após
celebrated/to celebrate: celebrado/celebrar
dance: dança
husband: marido
wife: mulher
toasts: brindes
given/to give: dados/dar
wishing/to wish: desejando/desejar
couple: casal
happiness: felicidade
cut: corte
cake: bolo
shared future: futuro compartilhado
it is thought: acredita-se
to throw: jogar
backwards over her shoulder: para trás, acima do ombro
single female guests: convidadas solteiras
catches it/to catch: o pega/pegar
supposed to be: supostamente será
do not wish: não querem
choose: escolhem
to elope: fugir para casar
involves/to involve: envolve/envolver
much less: muito menos
second: segundo
quickly: rápidamente
justice of the peace: juiz de paz
may or may not invite: podem convidar ou não
a small number: um pequeno número de

Going to The Chapel

Wedding traditions in the United States are **some of** the **most flexible** in the **world**. **Due to** the many religions and **ethnic backgrounds**, the wedding ceremonies and traditions can **vary widely**.

Weddings in the United States can be very elaborate, especially when it is the **bride's first** wedding. Traditionally the bride **wears** a white wedding **dress** and **veil**. It is **considered bad luck** for the **groom to see** the bride in her wedding gown **before** the wedding.

It is traditional for the bride to have a bridal shower and the groom to have a bachelor party before the wedding. During the bridal shower the bride-to-be will **receive gifts**, usually gifts **to be used** on her **honeymoon**. A bachelor party is held for the groom in the **weeks** before the wedding and is **intended** as a "final celebration" as a **single man**!

Wedding ceremonies may be religious or civil. The ceremony may **include vows written** by the bride and the groom. The vows **speak of** their **love** and promises to each other. The **newlyweds kiss** at the end of the ceremony to **seal their union**.

After the ceremony the wedding is **celebrated** at a reception. The newlyweds have their first **dance** together as **husband** and **wife**. **Toasts** are **given** by family and friends, **wishing** the **couple happiness**. The bride and the groom make the first **cut** in the **cake** together, symbolizing their **shared future**. **It is thought** of as good luck for the bride **to throw** her wedding bouquet **backwards over her shoulder** towards the **single female guests**. The one who **catches it** is **supposed to be** the next one married.

Couples who **do not wish** to have an elaborate wedding ceremony may **choose to elope**. An elopement **involves much less** preparation and is becoming more common, especially for **second** weddings. The couple is **quickly** married at the **justice of the peace**. They **may or may not invite a small number** of friends and/or family.

April Fools!

April Fool's Day is a **lighthearted holiday** that **takes place** on April 1st. It is a **time** for **playful pranks** and **practical jokes**. The history of April Fool's Day is not well **documented** or **clearly known**. There does not **seem** to be a first April Fool's Day that can be **declared** on the calendar. The **closest date** that can be **identified** as the start of this tradition was in the **late** 1500s, in France.

Today, on April 1, Americans **play tricks** on friends and **strangers alike**. Pranks **performed** on April Fool's Day **range from** simple jokes, **such as** saying, "Your **shoe's untied!**," **to** more elaborate pranks, such as **setting** a **roommate's alarm clock back an hour**, making them late. **School children** might **tell** a **classmate** that school has been **canceled**. Whatever the prank, the trickster **ends** the joke by **yelling**, "April Fool!"

April Fool's Day is not a **serious** holiday. Schools are not **closed**, **gifts** are not given and no one gets the day **off from work**. It's **considered** a **fun** holiday. It is also a holiday in which you must **remain** alert; you **never know** when you might be the **next** April Fool!

KNOCK-KNOCK! Knock-Knock jokes are **well-known jokes** in the United States and a favorite "**call and answer**" **game** among **children**. They are the **best-known format** of the **pun**. **In addition** to being **silly** and fun, they are also **helpful** in children **advancing** their **language skills**. The **standard** format has five **lines**. The person **telling** the joke says "Knock, knock." The other person **answers accordingly**, and hopefully, **laughs**!

Knock, knock!   Who's there?
Cow go.   Cow go who?
Cow go moo!

Knock, knock!   Who's there?
Olive   Olive who?
Olive you!   (I love you!)

lighthearted: alegre
holiday: feriado
takes place: ocorre
time: momento
playful: divertidas
pranks: brincadeiras
practical jokes: trotes
documented: documentada
clearly: clareza
known: conhecida
seem/to seem: parece/parecer
declared: declarado
closest date: data mais próxima
identified/to identify: identificada/identificar
late: final de
today: hoje
play tricks: fazem brincadeiras
strangers: estranhos
alike: também com
performed/to perform: realizadas/realizar
range from...to: vão de... até
such as: como
shoe's untied: sapato está desamarrado
setting...back an hour: atrasando uma hora
roommate's: colega de quarto
alarm clock: despertador
school children: colegiais
tell/to tell: dizem/dizer
classmate: colega
canceled/to cancel: cancelada/cancelar
ends/to end: acabar/acabar
yelling/to yell: gritando/gritar
serious: sério
closed/to close: fechadas/fechar
gifts: presentes
off from work: dia de folga
considered/to consider: considerado/considerar
fun: divertido
remain: permanecer
never: nunca
know/to know: sabe/saber
next: próxima
well-known jokes: piadas bem conhecidas
call and answer game: jogo de chamar e responder
children: crianças
best-known format: formato mais conhecido
pun: trocadilhos
in addition: além de
silly: bobos
helpful: úteis
advancing: melhorarem
language skills: vocabulário
standard: padrão
lines: linhas
telling/to tell: contando/contar
answers/to answer: responde/responder
accordingly: consequentemene
laughs/to laugh: riem/rir

consistently: constantemente
referred: referidos
blended together: misturadas juntas
another indication: outro indício
sing/to sing: cantam/cantar
England: Inglaterra
decorate trees: decoram árvores
Germany: Alemanha
red suit: traje vermelho
arrival: chegada
chimney: chaminé
to fill: encher
stockings: meias
Netherlands: Holanda
sleigh: trenó
pulled/to pull: puxado/puxar
reindeer: renas
range/to range: variam/variar
legend: lenda
set aside/to set aside: reservam/reservar
own: próprias
star: estrela
placed/to place: colocada/colocar
symbolizing: simbolizando
presses/to press: aperta/apertar
magically: magicamente
lights up/to light up: ilumina/iluminar
enormous: enorme
outdoor: ao ar livre
festivities: festividades
they follow: seguem
gather together: se reúnem
meal: refeição
consists/to consist: consiste/consistir
stuffed turkey: peru recheado
mashed potatoes: purê de batatas
gravy: caldo ou molho de carne
pumpkin pie: torta de abóbora
exchanging gifts: trocando presentes
believe/to believe: acreditam/acreditar
until: até
naughty: malcriados
nice: bonzinhos
checks/to check: checa/checar
presents: presentes
filled/to fill: cheio/encher
coal: carvão

An American Christmas

The United States is **consistently referred** to as a "melting pot"—a nation of cultures and traditions **blended together**. Christmas celebrations in the U.S. are **another indication** of this melting pot. Americans **sing** Christmas carols from **England** and **decorate trees**, a tradition that came from **Germany**. Santa Claus, in a **red suit**, originated in Scandinavia. His **arrival** through the **chimney to fill stockings** is a tradition that started in the **Netherlands**. His **sleigh pulled** by **reindeer** began in Switzerland. American Christmas traditions and customs **range** from religious symbols to the **legend** of Santa Claus. The origins and history are Christian and pagan.

Regions of the United States **set aside** their **own** Christmas traditions.

- In Colorado, a **star** is **placed** on a mountain **symbolizing** the star of Bethlehem.
- In Washington, D.C., the president **presses** a button and **magically lights up** an **enormous outdoor** tree.
- In Boston, carol singing **festivities** are more famous than anywhere else in the United States.
- In Arizona, **they follow** the Mexican tradition, *Las Posadas*.

American families **gather together** for a special Christmas **meal** that **consists** of **stuffed turkey, mashed potatoes** and **gravy**, and **pumpkin pie**. The majority of Americans celebrate Christmas by **exchanging gifts** with family and friends. Children generally **believe** in Santa **until** the age of 10. They are told that Santa has a **naughty** and a **nice** list. He **checks** the list before Christmas and if you are on the naughty list you might not get any **presents** and your stocking might be **filled** with **coal**!

Every family has different traditions during the holiday season. Some traditions are **passed on** from generation to generation. The **following** list **highlights** some traditions that are representative of American families **celebrating** Christmas.

- A Christmas Carol is a **song** or **hymn sung** during the Christmas season. Christmas Carolers can be **heard** at parties, **malls** and Christmas festivals.

- Americans **send** Christmas **cards** to their friends and family during the holiday season. Some families **include letters reviewing** the **past year** and a family photo.

- The Christmas **shopping** season officially **begins** the day **after** Thanksgiving. A Christmas shopping trip is made extra special by the Christmas decorations in all of the **stores**.

- Eggnog is a very popular holiday **drink**. It is **made** with **milk**, cream, **sugar**, **beaten eggs** and generally **flavored** with **rum** or brandy.

- **For children and grownups alike**, Christmas **cookies** may be the best Christmas tradition of all.

- Each Christmas season, stockings can be **found** throughout American homes. Children **awake** on Christmas **morning** to find their stockings full of **treats**.

- The brilliant colors and **cheer** of Christmas **lights** are a **sight to behold**. In some **neighborhoods** all of the houses **participate** in decorating their homes and **allow** people to take a **driving tour to enjoy** the lights.

Whatever your region or tradition, Christmas is one of the most celebrated and enjoyed holidays in the nation. The most important thing **to remember** during the holiday season is to make **cherished memories** with your **loved ones**. Celebrate **deep-rooted** traditions and **continue to create** new holiday traditions **to share** with your family and friends.

every: cada
passed on/to pass on: transmitidas/transmitir
following: seguinte
highlights/to highlight: destaca/destacar
celebrating: celebração
song: música
hymn: hino
sung/to sing: cantado/cantar
heard/to hear: ouvidos/ouvir
malls: centros comerciais
send/to send: enviam/enviar
cards: cartões
include/to include: incluem/incluir
letters: cartas
reviewing/to review: reconsiderando/reconsiderar
past year: ano passado
shopping: compras
begins/to begin: começam/começar
after: após
stores: lojas
drink: bebida
made: feita
milk: leite
sugar: açúcar
beaten eggs: ovos batidos
flavored: misturado
rum: rum
for... and... alike: tanto para... quanto para
children: crianças
grownups: adultos
cookies: biscoitos
found/to find: encontradas/encontrar
awake/to awake: acordam/acordar
morning: manhã
treats: presentes
cheer: vibração
lights: luzes
sight to behold: espetáculo a ser contemplado
neighborhoods: bairros
participate/to participate: participam/participar
allow/to allow: permitem/permitir
driving tour: excursão
to enjoy: para disfrutar
whatever: qualquer
to remember: para se lembrar de
cherished memories: estimadas lembranças
loved ones: entes queridos
deep-rooted: fortemente enraizadas
continue/to continue: continue/continuar
to create: criando
to share: para compartilhar

a time: uma época
giving thanks: agradecer
sharing: compartilhar
family members: membros da família
gather together: reúnem-se
to enjoy: para curtir
give thanks: agradecer
good things: boas coisas
spirit: espírito
homeless shelters: abrigos
offer/to offer: oferecem/oferecer
free meals: refeições grátis
falls on/to fall on: cai em/cair em
date: data
every year: cada ano
has held/to hold: tem organizado/organizar
abundant harvest: colheita abundante
began/to begin: começou/começar
ago: atrás
started/to start: iniciou/iniciar
early days: princípio
boat: barco
sailed/to sail: navegou/navegar
across: através de
to settle in: para estabelecer-se
called/to call: chamados/chamar
winter: inverno
too late: muito atrasados
season: estação
to grow: para plantar
crops: cultivos, culturas
limited food: comida limitada
half: metade
died/to die: morreu/morrer
disease: doenças
spring: primavera
arrived/to arrive: chegou/chegar
taught them: os ensinaram
corn: milho
showed them: os mostraram
unfamiliar soil: solo desconhecido
to hunt: caçar
fish: pescar
fall: outono
beans: feijões
pumpkins: abóboras
thankful for: agradecidos por
help: ajuda
planned/to plan: planejaram/planejar
invited/to invite: convidaram/convidar
chief: chefe
brought/to bring: trouxeram/trazer
deer: cervo
to roast: para assar
turkeys: perus
prepared/to prepare: preparados/preparar
learned/to learn: aprendido/aprender
to cook: cozinhar
squash: abóbora
dishes: pratos
served/to serve: servidos/servir

52 tradition

Giving Thanks

Thanksgiving is **a time** for **giving thanks** and **sharing**. **Family members** and friends **gather together** on this day **to enjoy** a feast and **give thanks** for the many **good things** they have. In the **spirit** of sharing, **homeless shelters offer free meals** to homeless people in their communities. Thanksgiving **falls on** the fourth Thursday of November, a different **date every year**.

Almost every culture in the world **has held** celebrations of thanks for an **abundant harvest**. The American Thanksgiving holiday **began** almost 400 years **ago**. It **started** in the **early days** of the American colonies.

In 1620, a **boat sailed across** the Atlantic Ocean **to settle in** the New World. These people were **called** Pilgrims. The Pilgrims settled in what is now the state of Massachusetts. Their first **winter** was difficult. They arrived **too late** in the **season to grow** new **crops**. They had **limited food** and almost **half** of their people **died** from **disease**. When **spring arrived** the Indians **taught them** how to grow **corn**. Corn was a new food for the colonists. The Indians **showed them** other crops to grow and taught them about the **unfamiliar soil**. They showed them how and where **to hunt** and **fish**.

In the **fall** of 1621, crops of corn, **beans** and **pumpkins** were harvested. The colonists were **thankful for** the **help** from the Indians and the abundance of food. They **planned** a feast and **invited** the local Indian **chief** and several Indians. The Indians **brought deer to roast** with the **turkeys** that had been **prepared** by the colonists. The pilgrims had **learned** how **to cook** cranberries and different kinds of **squash** from the Indians and these **dishes** were also **served**.

For **years to come**, the pilgrims **continued** to celebrate the fall harvest with a feast. After the United States became an independent country, Congress **recommended** that the whole nation **set aside** one day a year for thanksgiving. George Washington **suggested** the date November 26 as Thanksgiving Day. In 1863, at the **end** of a **long civil war**, Abraham Lincoln **asked** all Americans to set aside the last Thursday in November as a day of thanksgiving.

On **dinner tables** throughout the United States, the same foods eaten at the first thanksgiving are the traditional foods **still** served today. Turkey, corn and pumpkins are symbols that represent Thanksgiving. You will **find** many of these symbols on holiday decorations and **greeting cards**. Cranberry **sauce**, or cranberry **jelly**, was on the first Thanksgiving table and is still served today.

For millions of Americans, Thanksgiving Day traditions are **closely connected to** football. From football games in the **backyard** to **watching** the **yearly** games of the Detroit Lions and Dallas Cowboys, football is **linked with** the **holiday season**.

America's Thanksgiving Day **Parade** is also an important tradition. It was **first held** in 1924 in Detroit, Michigan. The parade **began** as a small event. Its popularity **grew** with each **passing year** and so did its **size**. In 1952 the parade **received national coverage** on TV and is to this day a very popular televised event.

The most popular parade is the Macy's Thanksgiving Day Parade. The three-hour event is held in New York City starting at 9:00 A.M. on Thanksgiving Day and is televised nationwide. Important **features** of Thanksgiving parades are **enormous floats**, **scenes** from Broadway **plays** or TV **shows**, **gigantic balloons** of **cartoon characters**, and **marching bands**. The parade **ends** with Santa Claus's **image passing by** the **crowds**. The Thanksgiving Day parade tradition is **meant** to celebrate Thanksgiving and American traditions and **call forth** the next holiday, Christmas.

---

years to come: anos vindouros
continued/to continue: continuaram/ continuar
recommended/to recommend: recomendou/recomendar
set aside: reservasse
suggested/to suggest: sugeriu/sugerir
end: final
long civil war: longa guerra civil
asked/to ask: pediu/pedir
dinner: jantar
tables: mesas
still: ainda
find: encontrará
greeting cards: cartões de cumprimentos
sauce: molho
jelly: geleia
closely connected to: conectado intimamente a
backyard: quintal
watching: assistir
yearly: anuais
linked with: ligado com
holiday season: temporada de férias
parade: desfile
first held: realizado pela primeira vez
began/to begin: começou/começar
grew/to grow: cresceu/crescer
passing years: passar dos anos
size: tamanho
received/to receive: recebeu/receber
national coverage: cobertura nacional
features: características
enormous floats: carros alegóricos enormes
scenes: cenários
plays: peças
shows: espetáculos
gigantic balloons: balões gigantes
cartoon characters: personagens de desenho animado
marching bands: bandas marciais
ends/to end: termina/terminar
image: imagem
passing by/to pass by: passando/passar
crowds: multidão
meant: tem o objetivo de
call forth: inspira

tradição **53**

American's Favorite Sport

became/to become: se tornou/tornar
annual event: evento anual
has developed/to develop: tem contraído/contrair
following: séquito
dedicated: dedicados
fans: fãs
visitors: visitantes
watch: assistir
see for themselves: ver por si mesmos
spirit: espírito
feel/to feel: sentem/sentir
sport: esporte
spectator: assistido
reported/to report: relatou/relatar
towns: cidades
founded: fundada
league: liga
consists/to consist: consiste/consistir
biggest event: maior evento
gather/to gather: se reúnem/reunir
noticeable: perceptível
lack of traffic: trânsito vazio
roads: ruas
watching: assistindo
food: comida
beer: cerveja
chips and dip: batatinhas fritas e molho
second-largest: segundo maior
consumption: consumo
following: seguindo
associated: associadas com
some: alguns
consider/to consider: consideram/considerar
as much or more fun: tão ou mais divertidos
pre-game: pré-jogo
takes place/to take place: ocorre/ocorrer
parking lot: estacionamento
served/to serve: servida/servir
open: aberta
participate/to participate: participam/participar
even if: mesmo se
range from ... to: vão de... até
kitchens: cozinhas
motor homes: trailers
pick-up trucks: caminhonetes
hibachi grills: grelhas portáteis
lawn chairs: cadeiras de jardim
cooler: geladeira portátil

Football is an important part of American life. Since 1916, when the Rose Bowl game **became** a famous **annual event**, football **has developed** a national **following** of **dedicated fans**. **Visitors** to the United States can **watch** a game to **see for themselves** the **spirit** and enthusiasm Americans **feel** for this **sport**. Football is the most popular **spectator** sport in the United States. The Gallup Poll has **reported** football to be America's favorite sport every year since 1972.

Professional football developed in small **towns** of Pennsylvania and the Midwest. The National Football League (NFl), **founded** in Canton, Ohio, is the largest professional American football **league** and **consists** of thirty-two American teams.

The Super Bowl is the **biggest event** in the football season. On Super Bowl Sunday people of all ages **gather** for large parties in celebration of the big game. There is a **noticeable lack of traffic** on the **roads** as almost everyone is at home **watching** the game on TV. Traditional **food** at Super Bowl parties consists of **beer**, pizza, barbecue, and **chips and dip**. Super Bowl Sunday is the **second-largest** U.S. food **consumption** day, **following** Thanksgiving.

Tailgate parties are another tradition **associated** with football. **Some consider** the tailgate party **as much or more fun** than the actual game. Tailgating is a **pre-game** party that **takes place** in the **parking lot** or stadium where the game is held. The food is **served** and the party is held on and around the **open** tailgate of a vehicle. People still **participate even if** their vehicles do not have tailgates. Tailgate parties **range from** full **kitchens** set up in **motor homes to pick-up trucks** with **hibachi grills** to **lawn chairs** set around a **cooler** full of beer.

54 tradition

The **halftime show** is a very popular and important **element** of an American football game. During the **interval between** the second and third **quarters**, 20 minutes of **entertainment** is **presented** on the football field. A halftime show can consist of performances by **cheerleaders**, **dance teams**, **marching bands**, or an assortment of other performances. At high school and most college games, the bands of the two **competing** teams perform at halftime. For the Super Bowl game, an elaborate show involving famous musicians, dancers, **fireworks** and **special effects** is customary. The halftime show for the Super Bowl is a **highlight** of the event and can **cost** millions to create.

Football and cheerleading **go hand in hand**. Cheerleading **first started** at Princeton University in the 1880s. **Surprisingly**, cheerleading started as an **all-male** activity as a way **to encourage school spirit** at football games. Females started **to participate** in cheerleading in the 1920s. Today 97% of cheerleaders are female. In the 1960s, NFL teams began **to organize** professional cheerleading teams. The Dallas Cowboys Cheerleaders **gained** the **spotlight** with their **revealing outfits** and **sophisticated** dance **moves** first **seen** at the 1976 Super Bowl. This **caused** the **image** of cheerleaders to permanently **change**, as many other teams began **to copy** them. The Dallas Cowboys Cheerleaders are one of the most famous cheerleading teams in the world.

Marching bands are part of every football game. At college football games they play the college **fight songs**. College fight songs are songs **written** specifically for that college team. In professional and **amateur** sports, fight songs are a popular way for fans **to cheer** for their team. Fight songs are a **time-honored** tradition. In **singing** a fight song, fans **feel** like they are **part of** the team.

The **true spirit** of a football game **can only be felt** by **attending** a **live** game. **Whether** it's a high school, college or professional game, you will feel part of this American tradition and part of America's favorite sport —football!

---

halftime show: show do intervalo
element: componente
interval: intervalo
between: entre
quarters: quartos
entertainment: entretenimento
presented/to present: apresentado/apresentar
cheerleaders: líderes de torcida
dance teams: grupos de dança
marching bands: bandas marciais
competing: adversários
fireworks: fogos de artifício
special effects: efeitos especiais
highlight: destaque
cost: custar
go hand in hand: caminham de mãos dadas
first started: se originou
surprisingly: surpreendentemente
all-male: só de homens
to encourage: para fomentar
school spirit: espírito escolar
to participate: participar
to organize: a organizar
gained/to gain: ganhou/ganhar
spotlight: holofote
revealing: reveladores
outfits: trajes
sophisticated: sofisticados
moves: movimentos
seen: vistos
caused/to cause: causou/causar
image: imagem
change: mudar
to copy: copiar
fight songs: músicas de torcida
written: escritas
amateur: amador
to cheer: torcerem
time-honored: consagrada
singing: cantando
feel/to feel: se sentem/sentir
part of: parte de
true spirit: verdadeiro espírito
can only be felt: pode ser sentido apenas
attending/to attend: assistindo/assistir
live: ao vivo
whether: seja

beloved: adoradas
since: desde
called/to call: chamado/chamar
national pastime: passatempo nacional
appeals/to appeal: atrai/atrair
wide age range: para todas as idades
learning: aprendendo
to catch: pegar
ball: bola
lifelong fans: fãs vitalícios
strong: fortes
ties: laços
unite/to unite: unem/unir
developed/to develop: desenvolvidos/desenvolver
eating: comer
peanuts: amendoins
Cracker Jacks: *pipoca caramelada com amendoim*
chants: gritos de torcida
cheers: aclamações
stadium: estádio
bring/to bring: trazem/trazer
gloves: luvas
hope/to hope: esperam/esperar
catch: pegar
foul balls: bolas fora de campo
wear/to wear: vestem/vestir
team jerseys: camisas do time
pride: orgulho
player: jogadores
away from: longe de
continue/to continue: continuam/continuar
trading: trocando
baseball cards: cartões de beisebol
collecting: colecionando
autographs: autógrafos
joining: unindo-se a
fan clubs: fã-clubes
broken up/to break up: dividida/dividir
leagues: ligas
season: temporada
played: jogados
advance/to advance: avançam/avançar
begins/to begin: começa/começar
first: primeira
next round: rodada seguinte
playoffs: eliminatórias
declared/to declare: declarado/declarar
chance: oportunidade
to become: tornar-se
grand finale: grande final
common social ground: tema social de interesse comum
strangers: estranhos
love: amor
turns/to turn: transforma/transformar
friends: amigos
rich: rica
legends: lendas

56 tradition

The National Pastime

Baseball is one of America's most **beloved** traditions. **Since** 1856, The United States has **called** baseball its "**national pastime**."

Baseball **appeals** to a **wide age range** — from children just **learning** how **to catch** a **ball** to **lifelong fans** of the game. **Strong ties unite** Americans and baseball. Rituals and customs have **developed** from America's personal connection to the game, from **eating** hot dogs, **peanuts**, and **Cracker Jacks** to **chants** and **cheers** in the **stadium**.

At the ballpark, many **bring** their own **gloves** and **hope** to **catch foul balls**. Some fans **wear team jerseys** with **pride** for their favorite **player**. **Away from** the stadium, the traditions **continue** by **trading baseball cards**, **collecting autographs**, and **joining fan clubs**.

American major league baseball is **broken up** into two **leagues**, the American League and the National League. The baseball **season** is 162 games, **played** from April through September. The best teams in these 162 games **advance** to the post-season. The post-season **begins** the **first** week in October with the division championship series. The first team to win three games advances to the **next round** of the **playoffs**. The first team in each league to win four games is **declared** league champion, and advances to the World Series for the **chance to become** world champion. Called the Fall Classic, the World Series is the **grand finale** of the sport's postseason and takes place in October. The first World Series was held between Boston of the American League and Pittsburgh of the National League in 1903.

Baseball is more than just a game. It is part of American culture and a **common social ground** between **strangers**. At baseball games all across the nation the **love** for this sport **turns** strangers into **friends**. Baseball is an American tradition **rich** in **legends** and history.

Famous Names in Baseball

Babe Ruth is **regarded** by many historians and fans as the greatest baseball player of **all time**. He was the first player **to hit** 60 **home runs** in a season and the only player to hit 3 home runs **twice** in a World Series game.

Hank Aaron played from 1954 to 1976. He is **best known** for **breaking** Babe Ruth's **long-standing** record of 714 home runs in a **career** with his own record of 755. He is regarded by many as the greatest **hitter** of all time. He is the first player **to reach** 3,000 hits and 500 home runs and the **only** player to hit at least 30 home runs in 15 seasons.

In 1998 Mark McGuire and Sammy Sosa **battled it out** for **most** home runs in a season with McGuire **winning** with 69 to Sosa's 66.

In 2001 Barry Bonds hit the most home runs in one season with 73 home runs. On August 7, 2007, Bonds hit his 756th home run, breaking the record held for 33 years by Hank Aaron.

Baseball **Lingo**

Another tradition **associated** with baseball is the **language** of baseball. Paul Dickson **says** in his introduction to *The New Dickson Baseball Dictionary*, "The influence of baseball on American English is **stunning** and **strong**. **No other sport has contributed** so richly to American English as baseball."

Listed below are some American idioms that **derived** from baseball lingo. They have **dual meanings**, phrases **used** in and out of the game.

1. curveball — A **surprise**. "She really **threw** me a curveball." *The curveball is a* **pitch** *in baseball* **designed to fool** *the* **batter**.

2. **drop** the **ball** — To **fail** in one's responsibilities, make an error, or **miss** an opportunity.

3. **play** ball — To **get going**, or **to start**. *Before every baseball game, the* **umpire shouts** *"play ball" to start the game.*

4. **cover** one's bases; cover all the bases — **Ensure safety** *In baseball, a player covers a base by* **standing close** *to it.*

---

regarded/to regard: considerado/ considerar
all time: todos os tempos
to hit: bater
home runs: correr todas as bases e marcar ponto
twice: duas vezes
best known: mais conhecido
breaking/to break: quebrando/quebrar
long standing: duradouro
career: carreira
hitter: batedor
to reach: alcançar
only: único
battled it out: disputaram
most: mais
winning: ganhando
high: alto
lingo: jargão
another: outra
associated: associada
language: linguagem
says/to say: diz/dizer
stunning: surpreendente
strong: forte
no other sport: nenhum outro esporte
has contributed/to contribute: contribuiu/contribuir
listed below: listadas abaixo
derived: derivaram
dual meanings: significados duplos
used: usadas
surprise: surpresa
threw/to throw: lançou/lançar
pitch: lançamento
designed to fool: destinado a enganar
batter: batedor
drop: deixar cair
ball: bola
fail: falhar
miss: perder
play: jogar
get going: começar
to start: iniciar
umpire: árbitro
shouts/to shout: grita/gritar
cover: cobrir
to ensure: assegurar
safety: segurança
standing close: ficando parado perto

The American Flag

For **many** Americans the American flag **symbolizes freedom** and **pride** in their **country**. The American **public** and the American **government take** the flag very **seriously**.

National flag **laws** and **regulations** were **amended** and **documented** in 1976. **Rules**, **customs** and **etiquette** were **set forth pertaining to** the **display** and use of the flag. **Included** in the regulations are such rules as the national flag cannot **cover** a monument or any **ceilings**. It must not be **folded** while being displayed. No one should **write** on an American flag. **Ships** can **lower** their flags **slightly** in **greeting each other**, but **otherwise** should not be lowered for any other object or person.

It is **customary** to **fly** the flag on national holidays, and many people fly the flag **daily** from their homes. Flying the flag is **meant** to **demonstrate** patriotism and **loyalty** to the United States. The flag flown on Memorial Day and Veterans Day **honors** the men and women who **served** in **wars** and in honor of those who **died** during war.

Also called "Stars and Stripes," or "Old Glory," the American flag is one of the most complicated flags in the world. Sixty four **pieces** of **fabric** are **needed to complete** its construction. The flag has 13 red and white **alternating stripes** and 50 **stars** on a blue **background**. The stripes **represent** the original 13 **states of the Union**. The 50 stars represent each of the 50 states. Betsy Ross, who was a **seamstress**, is **credited** as the American woman who **sewed** the first American flag.

---

many: muitos
symbolizes/to symbolize: simboliza/simbolizar
freedom: liberdade
pride: orgulho
country: país
public: público
government: governo
take/to take: leva/levar
seriously: muito a sério
laws: leis
regulations: regulamentos
amended/to amend: emendadas/emendar
documented/to document: documentadas/documentar
rules: regras
customs: hábitos
etiquette: etiqueta
set forth/to set forth: estabelecidos/estabelecer
pertaining to: relativos a
display: exposição
included: incluídas
cover: cobrir
ceilings: tetos
folded: dobrada
write: escrever
ships: navios
lower: abaixar
slightly: levemente
greeting/to greet: saudando/saudar
each other: um ao outro
otherwise: caso contrário
customary: habitual
fly: hastear
daily: diariamente
meant/to mean: significa/significar
demonstrate: demostrar
loyalty: lealdade
honors/to honor: honra/honrar
served/to serve: serviram/servir
wars: guerras
died/to die: morreram/morrer
also called: também chamada
pieces: peças
fabric: tecido
needed/to need: são necessárias/ser necessário
to complete: para completar
alternating: alternadas
stripes: listras
stars: estrelas
background: fundo
represent/to represent: representam/representar
states of the Union: estados da União
seamstress: costureira
credited/to credit: atribuída/atribuir
sewed/to sew: costurou/costurado

58 tradition

In 1949, President Harry S. Truman **proclaimed** June 14 as Flag Day. Flag Day celebrates the adoption of the flag of the United States. The President **announces** the commemoration **each year**, and **encourages** all Americans to display the flag. Individual states **determine** how they will observe the day. Pennsylvania is the **only** state that declares Flag Day a **public holiday**.

The Pledge of Allegiance is an **oath of allegiance** to the United States as **represented** by its national flag. It is regularly **recited** at public events, and public school children across the nation recite The Pledge of Allegiance **in front of** the flag every **morning**.

The Pledge of Allegiance was **written** by author and **Baptist minister** Francis Bellamy. It **appeared** in the popular children's **magazine** *Youth's Companion* in 1892. The **owners** of *Youth's Companion* were **selling** flags to schools, and asked Bellamy to write something for their **advertising campaign**. The Pledge was **published** in the September 8th issue. A few **changes** were made to the pledge **over** the years. The current Pledge of Allegiance reads: I pledge allegiance to the flag of the United States of America, and to the republic for which it stands, one nation under God, indivisible, with liberty and justice for all.

During the War of 1812 lawyer Francis Scott Key was **transporting** a prisoner **abroad** a **ship** when he **saw** an American flag flying in Baltimore **Harbor**. The flag **inspired** him to write a **poem**. This poem is "The Star-Spangled Banner," the national **anthem** of the United States. The **actual** flag that inspired the song now **hangs** in the Museum of American History in Washington, D.C. "The Star-Spangled Banner" was **officially made** the national anthem by Congress in 1931.

The "Star-Spangled Banner" is sung at large public **gatherings** and at **sporting events**. When the song is **performed** in public, it is customary for American citizens **to stand** and **face** the flag while **placing** their **right hand over** their **heart**. This **formality** also **applies** to the Pledge of Allegiance. Men are encouraged **to remove** their **hats** during the performance.

proclaimed/to proclaim: proclamou/proclamar
announces/to announce: anuncia/anunciar
each year: cada ano
encourages/to encourage: incentiva/incentivar
determine/to determine: determinam/determinar
only: único
public holiday: feriado público
oath of allegiance: juramento de fidelidade
represented: representado
recited/to recite: recitado/recitar
in front of: em frente de
morning: manhãs
written/to write: escrito/escrever
Baptist: batista
minister: pastor
appeared/to appear: apareceu/aparecer
magazine: revista
owners: donos
selling/to sell: vendendo/vender
advertising campaign: campanha publicitária
published/to publish: publicado/publicar
changes: mudanças
over: decorrer dos anos
during: durante
transporting/to transport: transportando/transportar
aboard: a bordo
ship: navio
saw/to see: viu/ver
harbor: porto
inspired/to inspire: inspirou/inspirar
poem: poema
anthem: hino
actual: real
hangs/to hang: pendurada/pendurar
officially: oficialmente
made/to make: feito/fazer
gatherings: reuniões
sporting events: eventos esportivos
performed/to perform: interpretada/interpretar
to stand/stand: parar/para
face/to face: olha/olhar
placing/to place: colocam/colocar
right hands: mãos direitas
over: sobre
heart: corações
formality: formalidade
applies/to apply: aplica-se/aplicar
to remove: tirar
hats: chapéus

Trick or Treat

evening: começo da noite
take a walk down: passear
neighborhood: bairro
street: rua
you might see: você talvez veja
pirates: piratas
ghosts: fantasmas
princesses: princesas
witches: bruxas
don't be alarmed: não fique alarmado
costumed children: crianças fantasiadas
knocking/to knock: batendo/bater
opens/to open: abre/abrir
hold out/to hold out: estendem/estender
a bag: um saco
yell/to yell: gritam/gritar
hoping/to hope: esperando/esperar
bags: sacos
candy: doces
end: fim
popular holiday: feriado popular
young and old alike: tanto para os jovens quanto para os adultos
masquerade: de máscaras
games: jogos
played/to play: jogados/jogar
at a time: de cada vez
tub of water: bacia de água
without using hands: sem usar as mãos
sinking/to sink: afundando/afundar
face: rosto
attempting/to attempt: tentam/tentar
to bite: morder
typical: típicas
homemade: caseiras
treats: delícias
include/to include: incluem/incluir
dried pumpkin seeds: sementes secas de abóboras
popcorn balls: bolas de pipoca
started/to start: começou/começar
evil spirits: espíritos malignos
flying on broomsticks: voando em vassouras
black cats: gatos pretos
since: desde então
evolved/to evolve: evoluído/evoluir
decorate/to decorate: decoram/decorar
windows: janelas
silhouettes: silhuetas
carving: esculpir
let...know/to let know: informam/informar
goodies: coisas boas, doces
waiting/to wait: esperando/esperar

In the **evening** of October 31, if you **take a walk down** a **neighborhood street you might see pirates**, **ghosts**, **princesses** and **witches**! But **don't be alarmed**, these "ghosts" are **costumed children knocking** on their neighbors' doors. When the door **opens** the children **hold out a bag** and **yell**, "Trick or Treat." They are **hoping** their **bags** will be full of **candy** by the **end** of the night. Halloween is a **popular holiday** in the United States for **young and old alike**.

Halloween parties or **masquerade** parties for adults are common. At children's parties traditional **games** are **played**. One of the most popular games is "bobbing for apples." One child **at a time** has to get apples from a **tub of water without using hands**. They do this by **sinking** their **face** into the water and **attempting to bite** the apple. **Typical homemade** Halloween **treats include dried pumpkin seeds**, caramel apples and **popcorn balls**.

Halloween **started** as a celebration connected with ghosts and **evil spirits**. Witches **flying on broomsticks**, **black cats**, ghosts, goblins and skeletons have **since evolved** as symbols of Halloween. Black and orange are the traditional Halloween colors. In the weeks before October 31, Americans **decorate windows** of houses and schools with **silhouettes** of the various Halloween symbols. Pumpkins are another main symbol of Halloween. **Carving** pumpkins into "jack-o-lanterns" is a Halloween custom that came from Ireland. Today jack-o'-lanterns in the windows of a house on Halloween night **let** children **know** that there are **goodies waiting** if they knock and say "Trick or Treat!"

60 tradition

Remembrance and Honor

Memorial Day, **originally** called Decoration Day, is **observed** on the **last** Monday in May. Memorial Day is a day of **remembrance** for those who were **killed** in **war defending** the United States.

Waterloo, N.Y. was **officially declared** the **birthplace** of Memorial Day. However it's **difficult to confirm** the exact origins of the day. Most people **agree** that it is not important where or when it **first started**. What is important is that Memorial Day was **established**. Memorial Day is about **coming together** to honor those who **gave** their lives for their country. The day is **celebrated** with **parades**, memorial **speeches** and ceremonies, and the decoration of **graves** with **flowers** and **flags**. On Memorial Day, the President or Vice President gives a speech and **lays** a **wreath** on the Tomb of the Unknown Soldier at Arlington Cemetery in Washington, D.C.

Veterans Day was originally called Armistice Day. It is observed **either** on November 11th **or** on the fourth Monday of October. Veterans Day **honors** the men and women who **served** during wars with the U.S. **armed forces**. On November 11, 1918, a **treaty** was **signed bringing** World War I **to an end**. November 11, 1919 was **set aside** as Armistice Day in the United States, to remember the sacrifices that men and women made during World War I. In 1954 the holiday was **changed** to Veterans Day and **declared** a National holiday.

Americans still **give thanks** for **peace** on Veterans Day. There are ceremonies and speeches and, in some towns, parades. Throughout the day, many Americans **observe** a moment of silence, remembering those who **fought** for peace.

American Veterans have established **support groups** such as the American Legion and Veterans of Foreign Wars. These groups **sell paper poppies** made by **disabled** veterans to **raise funds** for their **charitable activities**. The **poppy** is a **bright** red flower that became a symbol of World War I after a **bloody battle took place** in a **field** of poppies in Belgium.

originally: originalmente
observed: observado
last: último
remembrance: recordação
killed/to kill: mortos/matar
war: guerra
defending/to defend: defendendo/defender
officially: oficialmente
declared/to declare: declarado/declarar
birthplace: lugar de nascimento
difficult to confirm: difícil de confirmar
agree/to agree: concorda/concordar
first started: se originou
established/to establish: estabelecido/estabelecer
coming together: reunir-se
gave/to give: deram/dar
celebrated/to celebrate: celebrado/celebrar
parades: desfiles
speeches: discursos
graves: túmulos
flowers: flores
flags: bandeiras
lays/to lay: coloca/colocar
wreath: coroa de flores
either ... or ...: tanto em... quanto
honors/to honor: honra/honrar
served/to serve: serviram/servir
armed forces: forças armadas
treaty: tratado
signed/to sign: assinado/assinar
bringing...to an end: dando fim a
set aside/to set aside: reservado/reservar
changed/to change: mudado/mudar
declared/to declare: declarado/declarar
give thanks: agradecem
peace: paz
observe/to observe: reservam/reservar
fought/to fight: lutaram/lutar
support groups: grupos de apoio
sell/to sell: vendem/vender
paper poppies: papoulas de papel
disabled: portadores de necessidades especiais
raise funds: levantar fundos
charitable activities: atividades beneficentes
poppy: papoula
bright: brilhante
bloody: sangrenta
battle: batalha
took place/to take place: ocorreu/ocorrer
field: campo

Test Your Comprehension

Choices in Education, page 44

1. Até qual idade os alunos devem frequentar a escola nos Estados Unidos?

2. Os Estados Unidos fornecem educação gratuita nos três primeiros níveis escolares. Quais são eles?

3. O ensino superior é conhecido como "college" ou universidade. Qual é a sua duração?

April Fools!, page 49

1. Qual é o dia do mês de abril conhecido como o "Dia dos Bobos"?

2. Segundo o que sabemos, esta tradição começou em que país?

3. O que acontece neste dia?

Traditions for the New Year, page 46

1. Quando começam as celebrações do Ano Novo?

2. Qual cidade recebe o Ano Novo com uma bola iluminada descendo, enquanto a multidão faz a contagem regressiva?

3. Que partida de futebol americano é assistida no dia do Ano Novo nos Estados Unidos?

An American Christmas, page 50

1. Cite alguns dos países europeus que levaram a celebração natalina aos Estados Unidos.

2. Qual é a bebida festiva popular?

Teste sua Compreensão

Giving Thanks, page 52

1. Quando se celebra o Dia de Ação de Graças nos Estados Unidos?

2. Quem foram os convidados para o primeiro Dia de Ação de Graças em 1621?

The National Pastime, page 56

1. Quais foram os rituais e costumes desenvolvidos a partir da ligação entre os EUA e o beisebol?

2. Qual foi o grande jogador de beisebol a conseguir bater 60 *home runs* numa única temporada?

America's Favorite Sport, page 54

1. O futebol americano se tornou uma parte importante da vida norte-americana em 1916, quando ocorreu um famoso evento anual. Que evento foi este?

2. Onde foi fundada a Liga Nacional de Futebol Americano?

3. Quais são as líderes de torcida mais famosas?

The American Flag, page 58

1. O que simboliza a bandeira norte-americana?

2. Quem escreveu o "Juramento de Lealdade"?

Remembrance and Honor, page 61

1. Como se chamava, originalmente, o "Dia da Lembrança"?

2. Por que o "Dia da Lembrança" é festejado?

The more you praise and celebrate your life,
the more there is in life to celebrate.

Oprah Winfrey

Celebration

Luck of the Irish

Irish immigrants **brought** the tradition of **celebrating** Saint Patrick's Day to the United States. The **first** U.S. celebration of Saint Patrick's Day **took place** in 1737 in Boston, Massachusetts. **During** this first celebration The Irish Society of Boston **organized** the **first** Saint Patrick's Day **Parade** on March 17.

Today, Americans of all **ethnicities** celebrate Saint Patrick's Day on March 17. Many people **wear green-colored clothing** or **pin** a **shamrock** to their **shirt**. Traditionally, those who are **caught** not wearing green on Saint Patrick's Day are **pinched**. The most common traditions on Saint Patrick's Day **include enjoying** Irish **folk music** and **food,** and **consuming** large **quantities** of Irish **beer**, often **dyed green**.

Parades are a big part of the Saint Patrick's Day celebration. The New York parade **has become** the **largest** Saint Patrick's Day parade in the **world**.

The city of Chicago has a very **unique** Saint Patrick's Day tradition of **coloring** the **river** water green. This tradition **started** in 1962 when 100 **pounds** of green vegetable dye were **added** to the river, and the river water **stayed** green for a **week**. The tradition **still continues** today!

Irish-American **heritage** has become an important part of American culture. Saint Patrick's Day celebrations in the United States are a **wonderful way** for people **to honor** Irish heritage and celebrate its **rich** culture and traditions.

Irish: Irlandeses
brought/to bring: trouxeram/trazer
celebrating: celebrar
first: primeira
took place/to take place: ocorreu/ocorrer
during: durante
organized/to organize: organizou/organizar
first: primeiro
parade: desfile, parada
today: hoje
ethnicities: etnias
wear/to wear: vestem/vestir
green-colored clothing: roupas verdes
pin/to pin: fixam/fixar (prender com alfinete)
shamrock: trevo de quatro folhas
shirt: blusa
caught/to catch: pegos/pegar
pinched/to pinch: beliscados/beliscar
include/to incluye: incluem/incluir
enjoying: desfrutar
folk music: música popular, folclórica
food: comida
consuming: consumir
quantities: quantidades
beer: cerveja
dyed green: tingidas de verde
has become/to become: tornou-se/tornar-se
largest: maior
world: mundo
unique: exclusiva
coloring: pintar
river: rio
started/to start: começou/começar
pounds: libras (1 libra = 0,45 kg)
added/to add: adicionados/adicionar
stayed/to stay: ficou/ficar
week: semana
still: ainda
continues/to continue: continua/continuar
heritage: herança
wonderful way: maravilhosa forma
to honor: de honrar
rich: rica

66 celebration

Groundhog Day

Groundhog Day, February 2nd, is a **whimsical holiday** in the United States. It is the day that the groundhog **comes out** of his **hole** after a **long winter sleep to look for** his **shadow**.

If he **sees** his shadow, he **regards it** as an **omen** of six more **weeks** of **bad weather** and **returns** to his hole.

If the day is **cloudy** and he doesn't see his shadow, he takes it as a **sign** of **spring** and **stays above ground**.

The **first** official Groundhog Day was **announced** on February 2, 1886 in Punxsutawney, Pennsylvania, with a **proclamation** by the **newspaper's editor**, Clymer Freas: "Today is Groundhog Day and **up to the time** of **going to press** the **beast has not seen** its shadow."

The **legendary** first Groundhog Day celebration was made

the **following year** by a group of **spirited** groundhog **hunters** who **called themselves** "The Punxsutawney Groundhog Club." Clymer, a member of the club, used his editorial **clout to name the one and only** official **weather predicting** groundhog, Phil, the Punxsutawney groundhog.

Today a trip to the Punxutawney Groundhog Day celebration is a **weekend** of **action-packed** events **including trivia contests**, **dances**, Groundhog Day **weddings**, music, **food**, **fun** and **games**. **If you happen** to be celebrating a **birthday** on February 2nd, then you are **invited to join** others who **share** the special day with Phil the groundhog and **receive** a **free souvenir**.

---

groundhog: marmota
whimsical holiday: feriado estranho
comes out/to come out: sai/sair
hole: toca, buraco
long winter sleep: longa hibernação
to look for: para procurar
shadow: sombra
sees/to see: vê/ver
regards it: considera isto
omen: presságio
weeks: semanas
bad weather: mau tempo
returns/to return: volta/voltar
cloudy: nublado
sign: sinal
spring: primavera
stays/to stay: fica/ficar
above: sobre
ground: solo
first: primeiro
announced/to announce: declarado/declarar
proclamation: proclamação
newspaper's editor: editor do jornal
up to the time: até o momento
going to press: do fechamento da edição
beast: animal
has not seen: ainda não viu
legendary: lendário
following year: ano seguinte
spirited: espirituosos
hunters: caçadores
called themselves: que se autodenominavam
clout: influência
to name: para nomear
the one and only: a única
weather predicting: que prevê o tempo
weekend: fim de semana
action-packed: com muita ação
including: incluindo
trivia contests: competição de perguntas e respostas
dances: festas
weddings: casamentos
food: comida
fun: diversão
games: jogos
if you happen: se por acaso você
birthday: aniversário
invited/to invite: convidado/convidar
to join: se unir
share/to share compartilham/compartilhar
receive: receber
free souvenir: brinde

celebration 67

Powwows

A powwow is a **gathering** of North America's **indigenous people**. The word powwow is **derived from** a **term** which **referred to** a gathering of **medicine men** and **spiritual leaders**. The powwow is North America's **oldest** public festival. Native Americans have celebrated with seasonal ceremonies of **feasting, dancing, singing** and **drumming**. Originally powwows were **planned** around **seasonal changes**, but as non-Native people **interacted** with the Native, customs were **altered**.

Typically, a powwow consists of people **meeting** to dance, sing and socialize. Native American and non-Native American **alike** are **invited to attend**. A powwow always **begins** with the **grand entry** of the **eagle feather standard**. All **spectators remove** their **hats** and **stand** as a **sign of respect**. The standard is **followed by** the tribal **chiefs** and the **esteemed village elders**, then by a procession of all of the dancers until the entire arena is **filled with** Indian dancers **adorned** in **colorful** and elaborate **costumes**.

The annual Denver Powwow in March begins the season of pow-wows. In 1990, it **attracted** thirty-thousand people, **half of whom** were not Native Americans. In the Denver Coliseum different tribes sing songs that have been **passed down** for **thousands of years**. They are **accompanied by** the **beat** of a large drum, played by five to ten drummers. Dancers of different tribes **show** their **skills**. Dancers with **fancy shawls look like** delicate **flying birds** as they **raise** their **cloth-covered arms to the beat of** the drums. **Grass dancers** wear costumes of **brightly-colored yarn**.

---

gathering: reunião
indigenous people: povo indígena
derived from: deriva-se
term: termo
referred to: lembra a
medicine men: curandeiros
spiritual leaders: líderes espirituais
oldest: mais antigo
feasting: banquete
dancing: dança
singing: canto
drumming: tamboreio
planned/to plan: planejados/planejar
seasonal changes: mudanças de estação
interacted/to interact: interagiam/interagir
altered/to alter: alterados/alterar
typically: tipicamente
meeting/to meet: reunindo-se/reunir
alike: da mesma forma
invited/to invite: convidados/convidar
to attend: assistir
begins/to begin: começa/começar
grand entry: grande entrada
eagle feather standard: estandarte de penas de águia
spectators: espectadores
remove/to remove: tiram/tirar
hats: chapéus
stand/to stand: levantam-se/levantar-se
sign of resepct: sinal de respeito
followed by: seguido por
chiefs: chefes
esteemed village elders: estimados anciões da vila
filled with: ocupada com
adorned: ornamentados
colorful: coloridos
costumes: trajes
attracted/to attract: atraiu/atrair
half of whom: metade das quais
passed down: transmitidas
thousands of years: milhares de anos
accompanied by: acompanhadas por
beat: batida
show/to show: mostram/mostrar
skills: habilidades
fancy shawls: xales de fantasia
look like: se parecem com
flying birds: pássaros voando
raise/to raise: erguem/erguer
cloth-covered: cobertos com tecido
arms: braços
to the beat of: ao ritmo do
grass dancers: dançarinos que dançam na grama
brightly-colored yarn: fios de cores vivas

Native American culture **comes alive** at the Gathering of Nations powwow in Albuquerque, New Mexico. Over 3,000 Native American dancers and singers representing more than 500 tribes from Canada and the United States **gather together** in April at North America's **biggest** powwow. The Indian Traders **Market** is also part of the celebration and **offers** a very special **shopping** experience and exhibition of Native American **artifacts**. Over 800 artists, **crafters**, and **traders** place their **wares** on **display** and **for sale**.

One of the **longest-running contest** powwows in the country is held each year in North Dakota. The United Tribes International Powwow typically **attracts** 800 dancers, more than two dozen drum groups, and over 15,000 spectators. Held annually since 1969, the **four-day** event is a large **outdoor** powwow that takes place at the **end** of the **summer season**.

Powwows **mean** different **things** to different people. They are **still religious** or **war** celebrations, but **themes** and **goals** have **changed with the times**. Now **instead of giving thanks** to their **gods** for a war victory, Indians **honor** those of their tribes who have **served in** the American **armed forces**. **Young people return** from the bigger cities **to learn** traditional dances and songs **in order to keep** their heritage **alive**. People who are not Native Americans are **encouraged to participate** in the activities. **One thing** is **obvious** at every powwow: they are **true** community events. The tribal elders are always **held in high esteem** and the children are **cherished**. Family, tribe and **friendship** are **extolled**. Everyone is welcomed in a **spirit** of **peace** and friendship.

comes alive/to come alive: ganha vida/ganhar vida
gather together: reúnem-se
biggest: maior
market: mercado
offers/to offer: oferece/oferecer
shopping: compras
artifacts: artefatos
crafters: artesãos
traders: comerciantes
wares: mercadorias
display: exposição
for sale: para venda
longest-running: de maior duração
contest: competição
attracts/to attract: atrai/atrair
four-day: de quatro dias
outdoor: ao ar livre
end: final
summer season: temporada de verão
mean/to mean: significam/significar
things: coisas
still: ainda
religious: religiosas
war: guerra
themes: temas
goals: objetivos
changed with the times: mudaram com o tempo
instead of giving thanks: ao invés de agradecerem
gods: deuses
honor/to honor: honram/honrar
served in/to serve in: serviram em/servir em
armed forces: forças armadas
young people: jovens
return/to return: voltam/voltar
to learn: para aprender
in order to keep… alive: para manter… viva
encouraged to participate: encorajadas a participar
one thing: uma coisa
obvious: óbvia
true: verdadeiros
held in high esteem: estar em alta estima
cherished/to cherish: amadas/amar
friendship: amizade
extolled/to extol: exaltadas/exaltar
spirit: espírito
peace: paz

celebration 69

in addition to: além de
regional holidays: feriados regionais
originated from: originaram-se de
seasons: estações
climate: clima
country: país
northeastern states: estados do nordeste
main: principais
festivals: festivais
welcome: dão as boas-vindas
arrival: chegada
autumn: outono
leaves: folhas
changing colors: mudança de cores
trees: árvores
to turn: ficar
come from all over: vêm de todas as partes
spectacular: espetacular
foliage: folhagem
holds/to hold: organiza/organizar
offers/to offer: oferece/oferecer
wood-chopping contest: competição de corte de madeira
auction: leilão
drive/to drive: dirigem/dirigir
scenic mountain roads: pitorescas estradas da montanha
to view: para ver
later: depois, mais tarde
townspeople: cidadãos
demonstrating ways: demostrando formas
cooking: cozinhar
handed down: transmitidas, passadas
winters: invernos
long: longos
cold: frios
midwestern: meio-oeste
to get out of: para saírem de
house: casa
socialize: socializar
hosts/to host: apresenta/apresentar
ice skating shows: espetáculos de patinação no gelo
fishing: pesca
snowmobile races: corrida de motos de neve
best sculpture: melhor escultura
carved in ice: esculpida em gelo

Seasonal Celebrations

In addition to the traditional holidays celebrated in the United States, **regional holidays** have **originated from** the **seasons**, geography and **climate** of the different parts of the **country**.

In the **northeastern states**, the **main** attractions are **festivals** that **welcome** the **arrival** of **autumn** and the **leaves changing colors**. As the leaves on the **trees** begin **to turn** red, orange and yellow people **come from all over** the U.S. to see the **spectacular** and colorful **foliage**. Warner, New Hampshire **holds** a Fall Foliage Festival which **offers** a **wood-chopping contest** and an **auction**. Vermont welcomes tourists who **drive** along the **scenic mountain roads to view** the impressive colors of the leaves.

The leaves turn color **later** in Bedford, Pennsylvania. In October the **townspeople** celebrate the fall foliage by **demonstrating ways** of **cooking** that have been **handed down** to them by their ancestors.

Winters are **long** and **cold** in many **midwestern** states, so winter festivals have become events for people **to get out of** the **house** and **socialize**. In St. Paul, Minnesota, the Winter Carnival **hosts ice skating shows**, ice **fishing** competitions and **snowmobile races**. In Houghton Lake, Michigan, a winter festival called Tip-Up-Town USA offers a contest for the **best sculpture carved in ice**.

70 celebration

In Washington, **spring** is **welcomed in** with a **Daffodil** Festival. A **parade** of **floats rides through town** made from these brilliant yellow flowers. Oregon **boasts** a **rose** festival in Portland, where bands play music in a parade of **flowers** and floats. Aspen, Colorado holds an annual summer Music Festival where musicians of classical and contemporary music **perform** and **teach classes**. Santa Barbara, California **pays tribute to** the **early settlers** who **came from** Spain by performing **historical plays during** the Old Spanish Days in August.

Spring in the southwest **finds** the townspeople of Okeene, Oklahoma **catching snakes** in the Rattlesnake Roundup. In Houston, Texans come to the Astrodome to see **cowboys ride horses** and **rope cattle** during the Livestock Show and Rodeo. Visitors **watch** the Hopi Indians **carry on** their strong tradition of **rain dancing**, a combination of dancing and **prayer to invoke rain** in a **hot**, **dry** August.

Alaska and Hawaii have climates different **from each other** and the rest of the country. Nome, Alaska has **daylight** almost **twenty-four hours a day** in June, so **midnight baseball games** and raft races are the main events in the Midnight Sun Festival. In Kodiak, a King Crab Festival is held in May during **crab harvesting season**. Hawaii is **warm year round,** and flower and **sun** festivals were held there **even before** it became a state.

These are a **small** representation of the **hundreds** of holidays and celebrations observed throughout the United States. Each state **has its own** individual history and people, and the **right** to celebrate its own tradition. **But one thing is certain**—all Americans **welcome you** to celebrate **with them**!

spring: primavera
welcomed in: recebida
daffodil: narciso
parade: desfile, parada
floats: carros alegóricos
rides through town: atravessam a cidade
boasts/to boast: ostenta/ostentar
rose: rosa
flowers: flores
perform/to perform: se apresentam/se apresentar
teach/to teach: ensinam/ensinar
classes: aulas
pays tribute to: presta homenagem a
early settlers: primeiros colonos
came from: vieram de
historical plays: peças históricas
during: durante
finds/to find: encontra/encontrar
catching snakes: capturando cobras
cowboys: caubói
ride horses: cavalgando
rope cattle: laçando o gado
watch/to watch: assistem/assistir
carry on: continuando
rain dancing: dança da chuva
prayer: oração
to invoke rain: para evocar a chuva
hot: quente
dry: seco
from each other: um do outro
daylight: luz do dia
twenty-four hours a day: vinte e quatro horas por dia
midnight baseball games: jogos de beisebol à meia-noite
raft races: corrida de balsas
crab harvesting season: temporada de pegar caranguejo
warm: quente
year round: durante o ano todo
sun: sol
even before: ainda antes
small: pequena
hundreds: centenas
has its own: tem sua própria
right: direito
but one thing is certain: mas uma coisa é certa
welcome you: dão-lhe as boas-vindas
with them: com eles

celebration **71**

Flavor of America

lobsters: lagostas
potatoes: batatas
regional food specialities: especialidades gastronômicas regionais
worth/to be worth: merecem/merecer
big and small: grandes e pequenas
towns: cidades
hold/to hold: organizam/organizar
cooking competitions: competições de culinária
all types: todo os tipos
one thing in common: uma coisa em comum
enjoy/to enjoy desfruta/desfrutar
flavor: sabor
read about: lê sobre
craziest: mais loucas
tastiest: mais saborosas
avocados: abacates
used to create: usados para criar
phenomenon: fenômeno
feeds/to feed: alimenta/alimentar
hungry: famintas
started: começou
third-largest: terceiro maior
producer: produtor
free...to enter: entrada grátis
competition: competição
best: melhor
recipes: receitas
ice cream: sorvete
photography contest: concurso de fotografia
anything made with: qualquer coisa feita com abacate
goes: é válida
heritage: herança
local: local:
chef: chefe de cozinha
cooks/to cook: cozinha/cozinhar
help of: ajuda de
largest: maior
measures/to measure: mede/medir
feet: pés
diameter: diâmetro
stone-ground corn: milho moído na pedra
gallons: galões
vegetable oil: óleo vegetal
red chili sauce: molho de pimenta malagueta vermelha
chopped onions: cebolas picadas
grated cheese: queijo ralado
since: desde
polished off: acabaram com
cold beer: cerveja gelada
make ... complete: tornam ... completo

From Maine **lobsters** to the **potatoes** of Idaho, America's **regional food specialties** are always **worth** celebrating. **Big and small towns** across America **hold cooking competitions** and celebrations of **all types** with **one thing in common**—food! **Enjoy** the **flavor** of America as you **read about** a few of the **craziest** and **tastiest** food celebrations throughout the United States.

AVOCADO FESTIVAL

Over 2000 **avocados** are **used to create** this **phenomenon** that **feeds** a crowd of 12,000 **hungry** people. **Started** in 1987 because Santa Barbara County is the **third-largest** avocado **producer** in the country, the Avocado Festival is **free** for all **to enter.** There is a competition for the **best** guacamole and various other **recipes**, including avocado **ice cream!** There's also a **photography contest** and pop art show, where **anything made with** an avocado **goes.**

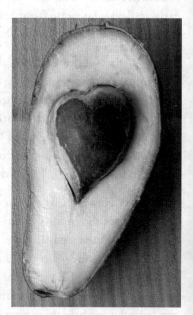

WHOLE ENCHILADA FIESTA

The city of Las Cruces, New Mexico celebrates its **heritage** every year when **local chef** Roberto Estrada **cooks** (with the **help of** eleven sous chefs) the world's **largest** enchilada. The enchilada **measures** over 30 **feet** in **diameter.** The ingredients are: 750 pounds of **stone-ground corn,** 175 **gallons** of **vegetable oil,** 75 gallons of **red chili sauce,** 50 pounds of **chopped onions,** and 175 pounds of **grated cheese.** Every year **since** 1980, over 70,000 hungry people have **polished off** the whole enchilada over the 3-day event. **Cold beer** and mariachi music **make** the event **complete.**

THE CRAWFISH CAPITAL OF THE WORLD

Celebrate **crawfish** in the crawfish capitol of the world: Bayou Teche, Louisana. Since 1959, the **first weekend** in May **brings** people, **crazy about** crawfish, **together to join** in the festivities. Enjoy crawfish **served any way** you can **imagine**: **boiled**, **fried**, etouffee, hot dogs, jambalaya, **pies**, bisque, gumbo, and the **list goes on**. **Make sure** you **stick around** for the crawfish **races** and the crawfish **eating contest**. The **winning crustacean** of the race is always **mounted** and **framed** for posterity. Other popular activities during this event include cooking contests, **fiddle** and **accordion** music, a dance contest, and the **crowning** of the Crawfish **Queen** and **King**.

NAPA VALLEY MUSTARD FESTIVAL

Napa Valley is a **wonderful place to visit** and **wine tasting feels like** a celebration any time of year! The months of February and March are an **especially lovely time** to visit **to partake in** the celebrations **surrounding** the Napa Valley **Mustard** Festival. **Fields**, **vineyards**, and **hillsides** vibrant with **wild** mustard **in bloom provide** a **breathtaking backdrop** during this event. **If** you have **never experienced** the Mustard Festival **you are in for a visual and culinary treat.**

SAY CHEESE!

Each year the town of Little Chute, Wisconsin celebrates the great Wisconsin Cheese Festival **to honor** one of their **largest exports**—cheese. The town **may be little** but its cheese production is **huge**, **producing two billion** pounds, or 25% of the **nation's** cheese per year.

The Great Wisconsin Cheese Festival is a three-day event the first weekend in June. The festival is a **family event** that **features** music, the Big Cheese parade, cheese tasting, a cheese **carving** demonstration, a cheese eating contest, **games** and entertainment.

---

crawfish: lagostim
first weekend: primeiro fim de semana
brings ... together: reúne
crazy about: loucos por
to join: para participar
served/to serve: servido/servir
any way: de todas as maneiras
imagine: imaginar
boiled/to boil: fervido/ferver
fried/to fry: frito/fritar
pies: tortas
list goes on: e a lista continua
make sure/to make sure: certifique-se/certificar-se
stick around: fique por aí
races: corridas
eating contest: competição de comer
winning crustacean: crustáceo vencedor
mounted/to mount: montado/montar
framed/to frame: emoldurado/emoldurar
fiddle: violino
accordion: acordeão
crowning: coroação
queen: rainha
king: rei
wonderful place: maravilhoso lugar
to visit: para visitar
wine tasting: prova de vinho
feels like: parece
especially lovely time: época especialmente encantadora
to partake in: para participar em
surrounding: ao redor
mustard: mostarda
fields: campos
vineyards: vinhedos
hillsides: encostas
wild: silvestre
in bloom: florescendo
provide/to provide: fornece/fornecer
breathtaking backdrop: pano de fundo de tirar o fôlego
if: se
never: nunca
experienced: teve a experiência
you are in for a: espera-lhe um
visual and culinary treat: prazer visual e gastronômico
say/to say: diga/dizer
cheese: queijo
to honor: para honrar
largest exports: maiores exportações
may be little: pode ser pequena
huge: enorme
producing: produzindo
two billion: dois bilhões
nation's: da nação
family event: evento familiar
features: características
carving: escultura
games: jogos

celebration 73

senator: senador
concerned about: preocupado com
state: estado
environment: meio ambiente
turned/to turn: transformou/transformar
solution: solução
called for/to call for: exigiu/exigir
teach-in: conferências ou seminários sobre temas polêmicos
held/to hold: realizado/realizar
wrote letters: escreveu cartas
colleges: universidades
newspapers: jornais
urging/to urge: encorajando/encorajar
to join together: a unirem-se
to teach: para ensinar
things: coisas
needed changing: precisavam mudar
participants/to participate: participaram/participar
observed/to observe: celebrado/celebrar
later: depois, mais tarde
around: ao redor
particpants: participantes
celebrants: celebrantes
thousand: mil
schools: escolas
hundreds: centenas
focus: foco
bring together: reunir
out into: em
spring sunshine: sol da primavera
peaceful demonstrations: manifestações pacíficas
in favor of: a favor de
reform: reforma
fairs: feiras
festivals: festivais
promote/to promote: promovem/promover
awareness: consciência
gather/to gather: reúnem-se/reunir-se
plant trees: plantar árvores
beach: praias
river: rios
cleanups: limpeza
laws: leis
were passed/to pass: foram aprovadas/aprovar
thanks to: graças a
continued efforts: contínuos esforços
to protect: para proteger
drinking water: água potável
creation: criação
reports/to report: informa/informar
largest secular holiday: maior feriado secular
half billion: meio bilhão

Earth Day

In 1962 Gaylord Nelson, a United States **senator** from Wisconsin, became **concerned about** the **state** of the **environment**. Over the next eight years he **turned** his concerns into a **solution** and **called for** an environmental **teach-in**, or Earth Day, to be **held** on April 22, 1970. He **wrote letters** to all of the **colleges** and **newspapers urging** people **to join together** on this special day **to teach** everyone about the **things** that **needed changing** in our environment. Over 20 million people **participated** that year, and Earth Day is now **observed** each year on April 22.

Earth Day became very popular in the United States and **later around** the world. The first Earth Day had **participants** and **celebrants** in two **thousand** colleges and universities, ten thousand primary and secondary **schools**, and **hundreds** of communities across the United States. The **focus** of the first Earth Day was to *"**bring together** Americans **out into** the **spring sunshine** for **peaceful demonstrations** in favor of environmental **reform**."*

Earth Day is now celebrated in communities worldwide. Celebrations include educational **fairs** and **festivals** that **promote** environmental **awareness**. People **gather** together to **plant trees** and participate in **beach** and **river cleanups**.

Many important **laws were passed** by the Congress **thanks to continued efforts** of the 1970 Earth Day. These significant laws include the Clean Air Act, laws **to protect drinking water** and the ocean, and the **creation** of the United States Environmental Protection Agency.

The Earth Day Network **reports** that Earth Day is now the **largest secular holiday** in the world, celebrated by more than a **half billion** people every year.

Parents Apreciation Day

On the **second Sunday** in May, Americans of **all ages treat** their **mothers** to **something** special. It is the one day out of the year when children, **young and old**, **express how much** they **appreciate** their mothers.

Celebrating Mother's Day is a tradition that **came from England** and **became** an official **holiday** in the United States in 1915.

On Mother's Day **morning** some American children **follow** the tradition of **serving** their mothers **breakfast in bed**. Other children **will give** their mothers **gifts** which they **have made themselves** or **bought** in **stores**. Adults give their mothers **red carnations,** the official Mother's Day **flower**. If their mothers are **deceased** they may bring **white** carnations to their **grave sites**. This is the **busiest** day of the year for American restaurants. On her special day, family members **do not want** Mom **to cook dinner**.

The United States is one of the **few countries** in the world that has an official day on which **fathers** are **honored** by their children. On the third Sunday in June, fathers all across the United States are given presents, **treated** to dinner or **otherwise made to feel** special.

The origin of Father's Day is **not clear**. **Some say** that it began with a **church service** in West Virginia in 1908. Others say the first Father's Day ceremony was **held** in Vancouver, Washington.

In 1916, President Woodrow Wilson **approved** of this idea, but it was not until 1924 when President Calvin Coolidge made it a national event to "**establish** more **intimate** relations **between** fathers and their children and **to impress upon** fathers the **full measure** of their **obligations**." **Since then,** fathers have been honored and recognized by their families **throughout** the country on the **third** Sunday in June.

second Sunday: segundo domingo
all ages: todas as idades
treat/to treat: convidam/convidar
mothers: mães
something: algo
young and old: pequenas e mais velhas
express/to express: expressam/expressar
how much: o quanto
appreciate/to appreciate: valorizam/valorizar
came from England: veio da Inglaterra
became/to become: tornou-se/tornar
holiday: feriado
morning: manhã
follow/to follow: seguem/seguir
serving: servir
breakfast in bed: café da manhã na cama
will give/to give: darão/dar
gifts: presentes
have made themselves: eles próprios fizeram
bought/to buy: compraram/comprar
stores: lojas
red carnations: cravos vermelhos
flower: flor
deceased: falecidas
white: brancos
grave sites: sepulturas
busiest: mais ocupado
do not want: não querem
to cook dinner: faça o jantar
few countries: poucos países
fathers: pais
honored: homenageados
treated/to treat: convidados/convidar
otherwise: de outra forma
made to feel: que os façam sentir-se especiais
not clear: não é clara
some say: alguns dizem
church service: serviço religioso
held/to hold: realizado/realizar
approved/to approve: aprovou/aprovar
establish: estabelecer
intimate: íntimas
between: entre
to impress upon: para inculcar, incluir
full measure: medida completa
obligations: obrigações
since then: desde então
throughout: por todo
third: terceiro

celebration

Season of Merriment

The **French expression** 'Mardi Gras' **literally translates to** 'Fat Tuesday'. It was called this **because of** the **feasting** that **took place** on this day. It is a celebration that is held **just before** the **beginning** of **Lent**.

By far the largest, most **lavish** Mardi Gras celebration in the U.S. is in New Orleans, Louisiana. Mardi Gras has been celebrated in New Orleans **since as early as** the 1700s. Festivities included **masked balls** and **bawdy street processions**, which by 1806 **had become so rowdy** that they were **forbidden**. In 1817 it became illegal **to wear** masks. These **laws** were **more or less ignored**. Both the festivities and masks became legal again by 1827, when New Orleans came under American control.

French **royals**, **feather-covered showgirls**, **painted clowns**, masked **lions—you can find** them all in the **streets** of New Orleans at Mardi Gras. By **dawn** on that most famous Tuesday, people have **claimed** the **best spots** on the streets **to watch** fabulous **floats**, outrageous **performers**, and **visiting celebrities** go by. Many **travel hundreds of miles to be a part of** the excitement.

Marching bands, some of them **founded** more than a **century** ago, also **take to the streets** with music and festive **dress**. They **open** the day by **spreading** jazz music through the city before more than 350 floats and 15,000 **costumed** people **take over** the **scene**. Crazy costumes and **wild make-up** are the **order of the day**.

French expression: expressão francesa
literally: literalmente
translates to/to translate to: traduz-se como/traduzir
because of: por causa de
feasting: banquete
took place/to take place: ocorreu/ocorrer
just before: logo antes
beginning: começo
Lent: quaresma
by far: de longe
lavish: luxuosa
since: desde
as early as: já em
masked balls: bailes de máscaras
bawdy street processions: obscenas procissões de rua
had become so: tornou-se tão
rowdy: ruidosas
forbidden: proibidas
to wear: usar
laws: leis
more or less: mais ou menos
ignored/to ignore: ignoradas/ignorar
royals: realeza
feather-covered showgirls: coristas cobertas de plumas
painted clowns: palhaços pintados
lions: leões
you can find: podem ser encontrados
streets: ruas
dawn: amanhecer
claimed/to claim: assegurado/assegurar
best spots: melhores lugares
to watch: para ver
floats: carros alegóricos
performers: intérpretes
visiting: visitantes
celebrities: celebridades
travel/to travel: viajaram/viajar
hundreds of miles: centenas de milhas
to be a part of: para fazerem parte de
marching bands: bandas marciais
founded/to found: fundadas/fundar
century: século
take to the streets: saem às ruas
dress: vestimenta
open/to open: abrem/abrir
spreading/to spread: difundindo/difundir
costumed: fantasiadas
take over: assumem/assumir
scene: cena
wild make-up: maquiagens estravagantes
order of the day: ordem do dia

KREWES: NEW ORLEANS ROYALTY

Mardi Gras **has long combined** wild street activities **open** to everyone with events **organized by private clubs known as** krewes. Today, thousands of people **belong to** about 60 krewes that **plan** the parades and balls of New Orleans' Mardi Gras. The **oldest** krewe, the Krewe of Comus, was founded in 1857 by men who **feared** the **outrageous antics** of Mardi Gras **would lead to** the holiday being **outlawed**. They **hoped** that **secret societies** could **keep** the celebrations **alive**.

In 1872 the **Russian grand duke** Alexis Romanoff **visited** New Orleans at Mardi Gras. A group of **businessmen** organized the Krewe of Rex **to host** a parade for the occasion, and **appointed** a "**king for the day**" so that the grand duke could have a royal reception. **Naming** kings and queens at Mardi Gras balls **has been** a tradition of the krewes **ever since**. Today, the Rex parade is the **main event** on Mardi Gras. The King of Rex is the King of Carnival.

CATCHING BEADS

The millions of **colorful beaded necklaces thrown** from floats are the **most visible symbols** and **souvenirs** of Mardi Gras. **In addition,** millions of **cups** and **toy coins** known as "doubloons" are **decorated** with krewe **logos** and thrown to **parade-watchers**. Some "throws" are **especially prized** and people do outrageous **things to catch** the most **goodies**. Some **dress** their children in **eye-catching** costumes and **seat them** on **ladders** that **tower over** the **crowds**. Others **give up** on the costume **altogether**, finding that the tradition of **taking clothes off** can be the **quickest attention-getter**!

---

has long combined: combina há muito tempo
open: abertas
organized by: organizados por
private clubs: clubes privados
known as: conhecidos como
belong to: pertencem a
plan/to plan: planejam/planejar
oldest: mais antigo
feared/to fear: temiam/temer
ourtrageous: escandalosas
antics: travessuras
would lead to: levariam a
outlawed: proibido
hoped/to hope: tinham esperança/ter esperança
secret societies: sociedades secretas
keep: manter
alive: vivas
Russian grand duke: Grão-duque russo
visited/to visit: visitou/visitar
businessmen: empresários
to host: para apresentar
appointed/to appoint: nomeou/nomear
king for the day: rei para o dia
naming: nomear
has been/to be: tornou-se/tornar-se
ever since: desde então
main event: evento principal
colorful beaded necklaces: colares de contas coloridas
thrown/to throw: jogados/jogar
most visible symbols: símbolos mais visíveis
souvenirs: lembranças
in addition: além de
cups: copos
toy coins: moedas de brinquedo
decorated: decorados
logos: logotipos
parade-watchers: espectadores do desfile
especially prized: particularmente apreciados
things: coisas
to catch: para pegar
goodies: presentes
dress/to dress: vestem/vestir
eye-catching: chamativas
seat them: os sentam
ladders: escadas
tower over: sobressaem-se
crowds: multidões
give up: deixam de lado
altogether: por completo
taking clothes off: tirar as roupas
quickest attention-getter: a maneira mais rápida de atrair a atenção

celebration 77

A Salute to Spring

People in the United States celebrate Easter **according to** their personal and **religious beliefs**. Christians **commemorate** Good Friday as the day that Jesus Christ **died** and Easter Sunday as the day that he was **resurrected**. Protestant **settlers brought** the custom of a **sunrise service**, a religious **gathering at dawn**, to the United States. All, **in some way or another,** are a **salute to spring**, **marking re-birth**.

On Easter Sunday **children wake up to find** that the **Easter Bunny** has **left them baskets** of **candy**. Children **hunt** for **eggs around** the **house** that they **decorated earlier** that **week**. **Neighborhoods** hold Easter egg hunts. The child who **finds** the most eggs **wins** a **prize**.

Traditionally, many celebrants **bought** new **clothes** for Easter which they **wore** to **church**. After church services, everyone went for a **walk** around the town. This **led to** the American custom of Easter **parades** all over the country.

In the **early** nineteenth **century**, Dolly Madison, the **wife** of the fourth American President, **organized** an **Easter egg roll** in Washington, D.C. She had been **told** that Egyptian children **used to roll** eggs **against** the **pyramids**, so she **invited** the children of Washington to roll **hard-boiled** eggs down the **lawn** of the new **Capitol building**! The event has **grown**, and today Easter Monday is the **only** day of the year when tourists **are allowed** on the White House **lawn**. The egg-rolling event is **open to** children **twelve years old** and **under**. Adults are allowed **only when accompanied** by children.

---

according to: de acordo com
religious beliefs: crenças religiosas
commemorate/to commemorate: comemoram/comemorar
died/to die: morreu/morrer
resurrected: ressuscitou
settlers: colonos
brought/to bring: trouxeram/trazer
sunrise service: cerimônia religiosa ao nascer do sol
gathering at dawn: reunião ao amanhecer
in some way or another: de uma forma ou de outra
salute to spring: saudação à primavera
marking re-birth: marcando o renascimento
children: crianças
wake up: acordam
to find: para descobrir
Easter Bunny: Coelhinho da Páscoa
left them: deixou-lhes
baskets: cestas
candy: doces
hunt/to hunt: caçam/caçar
eggs: ovos
around: ao redor
house: casa
decorated/to decorate: decoraram/decorar
earlier: previamente
week: semana
neighborhoods: vizinhanças, bairros
finds/to find: encontra/encontrar
wins/to win: ganha/ganhar
prize: prêmio
bought/to buy: compravam/comprar
clothes: roupas
wore/to wear: vestiam/vestir
church: igreja
walk: caminhada
led to/to lead to: levou a/levar a
parades: desfiles, paradas
early: começo
century: século
wife: esposa
organized/to organize: organizou/organizar
Easter egg roll: gincana de ovos de Páscoa
told/to tell: disseram-lhe/dizer
used to: costumavam
roll: rolar
against: contra
pyramids: pirâmides
invited/to invite: convidava/convidar
hard-boiled: cozidos
lawn: gramado
Capitol building: Capitólio
grown/to grow: cresceu/crescer
only: único
are allowed: são permitidos
lawn: gramado
open to: aberto para
twelve years old: doze anos
under: menores
only when accompanied: apenas quando acompanhados

Celebrating Workers

Every year, on the **first Monday** in September, **Labor Day commemorates workers** in America. The **timing** of the **holiday** makes it an ideal **bridge between summer vacations** and the **autumn season** and **new school year**. It is a federal holiday and all banks, schools, **post offices** and **government** offices are **closed** on Labor Day **throughout the country**.

First **celebrated** in New York City in 1882 with a **parade** of 10,000 workers, Labor Day **was made** a legal holiday in all states in 1894 **under** President Grover Cleveland. **Although** the U.S. government was **encouraged to change** the **date** and **adopt** May 1st **along with** the majority of the world, the September date **stuck**, and **remains to this day**.

It is now celebrated **mainly** as a **day of rest** and **even more so** as the unofficial **end** of the summer season. Popular resort areas are **packed with** people **enjoying** one **last three-day weekend** of summer vacation.

Forms of celebration include picnics, barbecues, **fireworks**, and **camping**. Families with **school-age children** take it as the last weekend **to travel before** the **school year begins**.

Leaders of the American Federation of Labor **called** the day a national tribute to the **huge contributions** workers have made to the **strength**, **prosperity** and **well-being** of the United States. The **principles behind** this holiday are as important **today** as they were 112 years **ago**, as **we continue to honor** the workers of America's **past**, present and **future**.

---

every year: todos os anos
first Monday: primeira segunda-feira
Labor Day: Dia do trabalho
commemorates/to commemorate: homenageia/homenagear
workers: trabalhadores
timing: momento
holiday: feriado
bridge: ponte
between: entre
summer vacations: férias de verão
autumn season: estação de outono
new school year: novo ano escolar
post offices: correio
government: governamentais
closed: fechados
throughout the country: por todo o país
celebrated: celebrado
parade: desfile, parada
was made: foi feito
under: sob (*a presidência de*)
although: embora
encouraged to change: encorajado a mudar
date: data
adopt: adotar
along with: junto a
stuck: ficou, pegou
remains to this day: permanece até hoje
mainly: principalmente
day of rest: dia de descanso
even more so: mais até
end: final
packed with: repletos de
enjoying/to enjoy: desfrutando/desfrutar
last: últimos
three-day weekend: fim de semana de três dias
fireworks: fogos de artifício
camping: acampamento
school-age children: crianças em idade escolar
to travel: para viajar
before: antes
school year: ano escolar
begins/to begin: comece/começar
leaders: líderes
called/to call: chamaram/chamar
huge contributions: enormes contribuições
strength: força
prosperity: prosperidade
well-being: bem-estar
principles: princípios
behind: por trás
today: hoje
ago: atrás
we continue: nós continuamos
to honor: a honrar
past: passado
future: futuro

celebration 79

poet: poeta
playwright: dramaturgo
widely regarded: amplamente considerado
greatest writer: maior escritor
language: idioma
preeminent dramatist: extraordinário dramaturgo
wrote/to write: escreveu/escrever
approximately: aproximadamente
sonnets: sonetos
as well as: bem como
works: obras
non-profit groups: grupos sem fins lucrativos
strive to/to strive to: esforçam-se para/esforçar-se para
provide: fornecer
stimulating: estimulante
atmosphere: atmosfera
watch: ver
participate in: participar
become immersed: ficar imersos
entertain/to entertain: entretém/entreter
enrich/to enrich: enriquece/enriquecer
educate/to educate: educa/educar
brings/to bring: traz/trazer
summer: verão
free: grátis
park: parque
welcomed tradition: tradição bem recebida
bringing: trazendo
audiences: públicos
in addition: além disso
reaches/to reach: alcança/alcançar
over: mais de
arts education programs: programas de educação artística
rely on/to rely on: dependem de/depender de
supporters: patrocinadores
share/to share: compartilham/compartilhar
belief: crença
power: poder
beauty: beleza
should be accessible: deveriam ser acessíveis
everyone: todos

Shakespeare Festivals

William Shakespeare was an English **poet** and **playwright**. He is **widely regarded** as the **greatest writer** of the English **language** and as the world's **preeminent dramatist**. He **wrote approximately** 38 plays and 154 **sonnets, as well as** a variety of other poems.

In the United States, small and large communities celebrate the **works** of Shakespeare through festivals. Both profit and **non-profit groups strive to provide** playgoers a **stimulating** festival **atmosphere** where they can **watch, participate in,** and **become immersed** in experiences that **entertain, enrich,** and **educate.**

The San Francisco Shakespeare Festival **brings** Shakespeare's greatest works to over 30,000 people in the Bay Area each **summer** with **Free** Shakespeare in the **Park.**

Free Shakespeare in the Park has become a **welcome tradition** in the Bay Area, **bringing** professional, free performances of Shakespeare's greatest works to diverse **audiences** for over 20 years.

In addition, each year The San Francisco Shakespeare Festival **reaches** a new audience of **over** 120,000 kids throughout the state with unique **arts education programs**—Shakespeare on Tour, Midnight Shakespeare, and Bay Area Shakespeare Camps.

Non-profit groups **rely on** donations from friends and **supporters** who **share** a **belief** that the **power** and **beauty** of William Shakespeare's work **should be accessible** to **everyone.**

Martin Luther King Day

All through the 1980s, **controversy surrounded** the idea of a Martin Luther King Day. Members of Congress and **citizens** had **petitioned** the President **to make** January 15, Dr. Martin Luther King, Jr.'s birthday, a **federal holiday**. Others wanted to make the holiday on the day he **died,** while **some** people **did not want** to have a holiday **at all**.

On Monday, January 20, 1986, in **cities** and **towns** across the country people celebrated the **first** official Martin Luther King Day. A **ceremony** which **took place** at an **old railroad depot** in Atlanta, Georgia was especially **emotional. Hundreds** had **gathered to sing** and **to march**. Many were the **same** people who, in 1965, had marched for **fifty miles between** two cities in the state of Alabama **to protest** segregation and discrimination of black Americans.

Today, Martin Luther King Day is **observed** on the **third** Monday of January each year, **around the time** of King's birthday, January 15. Schools, offices and federal agencies are **closed** for the holiday. On this Monday there are **quiet** memorial services **as well as elaborate** ceremonies and **parades** in honor of Dr. King. **Speeches** are given **reminding** everyone of Dr. King's **lifelong work** for **peace**.

Martin Luther King Day is **not only** for celebration and remembrance, education and tribute, **but also** a day of **service**. All across America people **perform** service in hospitals and **shelters** and **prisons** and **wherever** people **need** some **help**. It is a day of **volunteering to feed** the **hungry, rehabilitate housing,** tutor those who can't **read**, and a **thousand** other **projects** for **building** the **beloved** community of Martin Luther King's **dream**.

---

all through: durante todo
controversy: controvérsia
surrounded/to surround: rodeou/rodear
citizens: cidadãos
petitioned/to petition: pediram/pedir
to make: para tornar
federal holiday: feriado nacional
died/to die: morreu/morrer
some: algumas
did not want: não querem
at all: em absoluto
cities: cidades
towns: povoados
first: primeiro
ceremony: cerimônia
took place/to take place: ocorreu/ocorrer
old railroad depot: antiga estação ferroviária
emotional: emotiva
hundreds: centenas
gathered/to gather: reuniram-se/reunir
to sing: para cantar
to march: para marchar
same: mesmas
fifty miles: cinquenta milhas
between: entre
to protest: para protestar
observed: realizado
third: terceiro
around the time: próximo à data
closed: fechados
quiet: silenciosos
as well as: bem como
elaborate: elaboradas
parades: desfiles, paradas
speeches: discursos
reminding: lembrando
lifelong: de toda a vida
work: obra, trabalho
peace: paz
not only...but also: não apenas... mas também
service: serviço
perform/to perform: realizam/realizar
shelters: abrigos
prisons: prisões
wherever: em qualquer lugar que
need/to need: precisarem/precisar
help: ajuda
volunteering: voluntariado
to feed: para alimentar
hungry: famintos
rehabilitate: restaurar
housing: moradias
read: ler
thousand: milhares
projects: projetos
building: construir
beloved: amada
dream: sonho

ethnic groups: grupos étnicos
carry special meaning: têm um significado especial
Jews: judeus
for example: por exemplo
observe/to observe: celebram/celebrar
high holy days: dias santos
employers: patrões
allowing them to take these days off: permitindo-lhes tirar folga nestes dias
patron saint: padroeiro
townspeople: cidadãos
Dutch ancestry: ascendência holandesa
yearly tulip festival: festival anual de tulipas
folk fairs: feiras folclóricas
foods: comidas
have settled: estabeleceram-se
take place: tem lugar
crowds: multidões
gather/to gather: reúnem-se/reunir
narrow streets: ruas estreitas
settled/to settle: estabeleceram/estabelecer
Chinese New Year: Ano Novo Chinês
cloth dragon: fantasia de dragão
sways back and forth: balança de um lado para o outro
through: através
following: seguindo
playing drums: tocando tambores
dancers: dançarinos
carrying/to carry: carregando/carregar
paper lion heads: cabeças de leão em papel
sticks: varas
store: lojas
business: negócios
owners: donos
come outside: saem
money: dinheiro
holiday: feriado
all over the world: por todo o mundo
observe it/to observe: o comemoram/comemorar
over: mais de
Feast of the Holy Spirit: Festa do Divino Espírito Santo
oldest: mais antiga
ethnic: étnica
dating back to: remontando a
hosted by: comemorada por
includes/to include: inclui/incluir
games: jogos
held/to hold: realizado/realizar
Pentecost Sunday: Domingo de Pentecostes
honors/to honor: honra/honrar
known for serving: conhecida por servir
poor: pobres
feeding: alimentar
hungry: famintos
bread: pão
own table: própria mesa

Ethnic Celebrations

Various **ethnic groups** in America celebrate days that **carry special meaning** for them. **Jews**, **for example**, **observe** their **high holy days** in autumn, and most **employers** show consideration by **allowing them to take these days off**. Irish Americans celebrate the **patron saint**, Saint Patrick, on March 17. In May, the **townspeople** of Holland, Michigan celebrate their **Dutch ancestry** through a **yearly Tulip Festival**. **Folk fairs** in the American Midwest offer **foods** of ethnic diversity, because people of so many different nationalities **have settled** there. Many different ethnic celebrations **take place**, at different times, all across the United States.

In January and February large **crowds gather** in the **narrow streets** of Chinatown in New York, San Francisco, and other cities where Chinese have **settled,** to celebrate **Chinese New Year**. A huge **cloth dragon sways back and forth** through the streets. **Following** the dragon are people **playing drums** and **dancers carrying paper lion heads** on **sticks**. As they dance, **store** and **business owners come outside** to give them **money**. New Year is the most important **holiday** in China, and Chinese people **all over the world** actively **observe it**.

For **over** 700 years Portuguese people have celebrated the **Feast of the Holy Spirit**. In San Diego, California, this is the **oldest ethnic** religious celebration, **dating back to** the time when the first families settled here in 1884. This 3-day event is San Diego's oldest festival and is **hosted by** the Portuguese community. The celebration **includes** traditional music and dancing, and food and **games** for adults and children. The festival is **held** each year on **Pentecost Sunday**, seven weeks after Easter. It **honors** Queen Isabel, the Portuguese royal who was **known for serving** the **poor** and **feeding** the **hungry** with **bread** from her **own table**.

The festival begins with an **elaborate parade**. Girls **wear crowns** and Renaissance-style **gowns to symbolize** Queen Isabel, while the boys **escorting them** wear **tuxedos**. The **finely dressed** kings and queens **march** to St. Agnes Roman Catholic Church, where the new queen is **crowned**. The crown is the **same one used** since the first festival in 1910.

On May 5, Los Angeles, California is **alive** with color, **laughter** and dancing. More than 500,000 Mexicans and Americans of Mexican **origin** are celebrating Cinco de Mayo.

The celebration takes place in the streets **outside City Hall** where Mexican orchestras and **local bands play** Mexican patriotic **songs**. The streets are **colored** in **red, white** and **green** — the colors of the Mexican **flag**. Young boys are **proud** to be **seen** in Mexican **clothing** and girls wear red and green **ruffled dresses** with **wide skirts**. Famous musicians play popular **tunes** on their guitars while dancers **spin around** and **click** their **castanets**.

A temporary **stage** at the **steps** of City Hall is **decorated** with a **picture** of General Zaragoza, **flanked by** Mexican and American flags. Mexican **dignitaries** are **guests of honor**, **pleased to hear** the **mayor** of Los Angeles **making a speech** in Spanish. **Later**, celebrants **stroll** through the streets to the old section of the city. Others go to **city parks** where **sports events**, dances and **picnics featuring** Mexican food are taking place.

It is an occasion which Mexicans and Americans **share to emphasize** the **friendship between** their two **countries**.

elaborate parade: desfile elaborado
wear crowns: usam coroas
gowns: vestidos
to symbolize: para simbolizar
escorting them: que as acompanham
tuxedos: traje de gala
finely dressed: vestidos elegantemente
march/to march: marcham/marchar
crowned/to crown: coroada/coroar
same one used: mesma usada
alive: viva
laughter: risada
origin: origem
outside: fora de
City Hall: prefeitura
local bands: bandas locais
play/to play: tocam/tocar
songs: músicas
colored: coloridas
red: vermelho
white: branco
green: verde
flag: bandeira
proud: orgulhosos
seen/to see: vistos/ver
clothing: roupas
ruffled dresses: vestidos bufantes
wide skirts: saias largas
tunes: melodias
spin around: dão voltas
click: estalam
castanets: castanholas
stage: palco
steps: degraus
decorated: decorado
picture: foto
flanked by: flanqueado por
dignitaries: dignitários
guests of honor: convidados de honra
pleased to hear: encantados em ouvir
mayor: prefeito
making a speech: discursando
later: depois, mais tarde
stroll/to stroll: passeiam/passear
city parks: parques municipais
sports events: eventos esportivos,
picnics: piqueniques
featuring: com
share/to share: compartilham/compartilhar
to emphasize: para enfatizar
friendship: amizade
between: entre
countries: países

Test Your Comprehension

Luck of the Irish, page 66

1. Quando e onde ocorreram as primeiras celebrações norte-americanas do dia de São Patrício?

2. O que acontece com as pessoas que são flagradas sem estarem vestidas de verde no dia de São Patrício?

Powwows, page 68

1. A que se refere o termo do qual se deriva a palavra *powwow*?

2. Em que consiste um *powwow* tipicamente?

3. Verdadeiro ou falso? As pessoas que não são norte-americanas nativas não podem participar das festividades de um *powwow*.

Seasonal Celebrations, page 70

1. Quais são os objetivos principais dos festivais de outono na região nordeste?

2. No Lago Houghton, Michigan, um festival de inverno oferece uma competição. Para quê?

3. A a primavera no sudoeste encontra os cidadãos de Okeene, Oklahoma, fazendo o quê?

Flavor of America, page 72

1. O que acontece com os crustáceos que ganham a corrida de lagostins?

2. Onde pode ser encontrada a maior enchilada do mundo?

3. Quanto queijo é produzido a cada ano em Little Chute, Wisconsin?

Teste sua Compreensão

Parents Appreciation Day, page 75

1. Qual é a flor oficial do Dia das Mães?

2. Qual é a origem do Dia dos Pais?

Celebrating the Worker, page 79

1. Quando é o Dia do Trabalho?

2. Quando e onde o Dia do Trabalho foi celebrado pela primeira vez? Quando foi legalizado como feriado em todos os estados?

3. O Dia do Trabalho também é uma celebração não oficial. Para qual finalidade?

Shakespeare Festivals, page 80

1. Quem foi William Shakespeare?

2. O que é Shakespeare no Parque?

3. Como é possível para os grupos sem fins lucrativos apresentarem as obras de Shakespeare?

**Then join hand in hand, brave Americans all!
By uniting we stand, by dividing we fall.**

John Dickinson

People

best known: mais conhecidos
back: de volta
discovery: descobrimento
visionary project: projeto visionário
to explore: para explorar
began/to begin: começou/começar
ended/to end: terminou/terminar
traveled/to travel: viajou/viajar
over: mais de
main achievements: principais conquistas
include/to include: incluem/incluir
gained/to gain: conseguiu/conseguir
extensive knowledge: extenso conhecimento
maps: mapas
rivers: rios
mountain ranges: cordilheiras
plants: plantas
species: espécies
discovered: descobertas
described: descritas
communications: comunicação
opened/to open: abertas/abrir
army: exército
claim: reivindicação
strengthened/stregthen: reforçada/reforçar
large body: grande corpo
only woman: única mulher
birth: nascimento
son: filho
left/to leave: deixou/deixar
village: vila, aldeia
to journey: para excursionar
often: muitas vezes
credited: lhe é atribuída
guide: guia
led/to lead: conduziu/conduzir
across: através
plains: planície
contributed/to contribute: contribuiu/contribuir
significantly: significativamente
success: êxito
helped/to help: ajudou/ajudar
met/to meet: encontraram/encontrar
tribes: tribos
along the way: pelo caminho
dispelled: dissipou
war party: destacamento de guerra
wrote/to write: escreveu/escrever
party of men: grupo de homens
token of peace: símbolo de paz
retraced: reconstituída
following: seguindo
stretches/to stretch: estende-se/estender
winds/to wind: serpenteia/serpentear
high deserts: desertos altos
shores: litoral
experience/to experience: vivem a experiência/viver a experiência
learn/to learn: aprendem/aprender
first hand: primeira mão

Trail of Discovery

Meriwether Lewis and William Clark are **best known** for their expedition from the Mississippi River to the West Coast and **back**. The expedition, called the Corps of **Discovery**, was President Thomas Jefferson's **visionary project to explore** the American West. It **began** in May of 1804 and **ended** in September 1806. The expedition **traveled over** 8,000 total miles over a period of 2 years, 4 months and 10 days.

The **main achievements** of the expedition **include**:

- The U.S. **gained extensive knowledge** of the geography of the American West in the form of **maps** of major **rivers** and **mountain ranges**.
- 178 **plants** and 122 **species** of animals were **discovered** and **described**.
- Diplomatic relations and **communications** with the Indians were **opened**.
- A precedent for **Army** exploration of the West was established
- The U.S. **claim** to Oregon Territory was **strengthened**.
- A **large body** of literature about the West was established: The Lewis and Clark diaries.

Sacagawea was the **only woman** to travel with the Corps of Discovery. Two months after the **birth** of her **son**, Sacagawea **left** her **village to journey** west with Lewis and Clark. Sacagawea is **often credited** as the **guide** who **led** the Corps **across** the **plains**. She **contributed significantly** to the **success** of the journey. Simply because she was a woman, Sacagawea **helped** with the journey. The explorers **met** many **tribes along the way** and her presence **dispelled** the notion that the group was a **war party**. William Clark **wrote**, "A woman with a **party of men** is a **token of peace**."

Today, the Expedition's path can be **retraced** by **following** the Lewis and Clark National Historic Trail. The Trail **stretches** through 11 states and **winds** over mountains, along rivers, through plains and **high deserts**, and ends at the **shores** of the Pacific Oregon coast. Visitors to the Trail **experience** and **learn first hand** about the Lewis and Clark Expedition.

Mother of Civil Rights

Rosa Parks is **called** "The Mother of the Civil Rights Movement." She is **considered** one of the most important **citizens** of the 20th **century**. By **not giving up** her **seat** to a **white passenger** on a **city bus**, Rosa Parks **started** a **protest** that **redirected** the **course** of history.

In the fifties, **segregation laws** were **prevalent** in the **South**. Black and white people were segregated in **almost every aspect** of **daily life**. Buses **enforced seating policies** that **stated** there were **separate sections** for blacks and whites. White people were given **preferential treatment**.

On December 1, 1955 Rosa Parks **refused to obey** bus **driver** James Blake and would not give up her seat to a white man. She was **arrested**, **tried** and **convicted** of **violating** a city law. Her actions **prompted** the Montgomery Bus Boycott. This boycott **lasted** for **over a year** and was one of the **largest movements against** racial segregation in history. Her actions also brought Martin Luther King, Jr. to the **forefront** of the civil rights movement. In 1956 the U.S. Supreme Court **outlawed** segregation on city buses.

For the **next** forty years Rosa Parks **dedicated** her life to civil rights and **continued** to **fight** for **equal rights** for all people. She **received** many **awards**, **including** the Martin Luther King Jr. Nonviolent Peace Prize and the Presidential Medal of Freedom. Her role in American history **earned her** an **iconic status** in American culture.

Rosa Parks died on October 24, 2005 at age 92. Her life and the **positive changes** she made in America **remain** an **inspiration** to people **everywhere**.

---

called/to call: chamada/chamar
considered/to consider: considerada/considerar
citizens: cidadãos
century: século
not giving up: não ceder
seat: assento, lugar
white passenger: passageiro branco
city bus: ônibus municipal
started/to start: começou/começar
protest: protesto
redirected/to redirect: mudou/mudar
course: curso
segregation laws: leis de segregação
prevalent: prevalentes
south: sul
almost every aspect: quase todos os aspectos
daily life: vida cotidiana
enforced/to enforce: cumpriam/cumprir
seating policies: regras de localização de passageiros
stated/to state: declaravam/declarar
separate sections: seções separadas
preferential treatment: tratamento preferencial
refused/to refuse: recusou-se/recusar-se
to obey: a obedecer
driver: motorista
arrested/to arrest: presa/prender
tried/to try: julgada/julgar
convicted: condenada
violating: violar
prompted/to prompt: provocaram/provocar
lasted/to last: durou/durar
over a year: mais de um ano
largest movements: maiores movimentos
against: contra
forefront: vanguarda
outlawed/to outlaw: declarou ilegal/declarar ilegal
next: próximos
dedicated/to dedicate: dedicou/dedicar
continued/to continue: continuou/continuar
fight: lutar
equal rights: direitos iguais
received/to receive: recebeu/receber
awards: prêmios
including: incluindo
earned her: conseguiu-lhe
iconic status: estado icônico
positive changes: mudanças positivas
remain/to remain: permanecem/permanecer
inspiration: inspiração
everywhere: por toda a parte

Founding Fathers: Pais Fundadores	
also known as: também conhecidos como	
political leaders: líderes políticos	
signed/to sign: assinaram/assinar	
active: ativos	
refers to: refere-se a	
period: período	
original thirteen colonies: treze colônias originais	
gained independence: ganharam independência	
delegates: representantes	
make up/to make up: compuseram/compor	
distinguished group: grupo distinto	
represented/to represent: representavam/representar	
leadership: liderança	
everyone: todos	
extensive: extensa	
practiced/to pratice: exerciam/exercer	
wide range: ampla variedade	
occupations: ocupações	
some: alguns	
continued on: continuaram	
part of: parte de	
called/to call: chamado/chamar	
critical role: papel importante	
founding: fundação	
earned him: garantiram-lhe	
led/to lead: conduziu/conduzir	
victory: vitória	
elected/to elect: eleito/eleger	
first: primeiro	
honorable reputation: nobre reputação	
figure: figura	
among: dentre	
early: primeiros	
influential: influente	
promotion: promoção, divulgação	
ideals: ideais	
Republicanism: Republicanismo	
third: terceiro	
principal author: autor principal	
major events: eventos importantes	
during: durante	

The Founding Fathers

The **Founding Fathers** of the United States, **also known as** the Fathers of our country, are the **political leaders** who **signed** the Declaration of Independence or the United States Constitution, and were **active** in the American Revolution. The American Revolution **refers to** the **period** when the **original thirteen colonies gained independence** from the British.

The 55 **delegates** who **make up** the Founding Fathers were a **distinguished group** of men who **represented** American **leadership**. **Everyone** in the group had **extensive** political experience and **practiced** a **wide range** of **occupations**. **Some** men **continued on** to become an important **part of** American history.

GEORGE WASHINGTON

George Washington is **called** the "Father of the nation." His devotion and **critical role** in the **founding** of the United States **earned him** this title. Washington **led** America's army to **victory** over Britain in the American Revolutionary War. In 1789 he was **elected** the **first** president of the United States. He served two four-year terms from 1789 to 1797. His dedication and **honorable reputation** made him an ideal **figure among early** American politicians.

THOMAS JEFFERSON

Thomas Jefferson was an **influential** Founding Father for his **promotion** of the **ideals** of **Republicanism** in the United States. He was the **third** president of the United States and the **principal author** of the Declaration of Independence. **Major events during** his presidency include the Louisiana Purchase and the Lewis and Clark Expedition.

JAMES MADISON

James Madison is also **considered** one of the most influential Founding Fathers. He is **referred to as** the "Father of the constitution" because he **played** a **bigger role** in **designing** the **document** than **anyone else**. In 1788, he **wrote** over a third of the Federalist Papers, **still** the most **influential commentary** on the Constitution. James Madison was the **fourth** President of the United States (1809–1817). He **drafted** many **basic laws** and was responsible for the first ten **amendments** to the Constitution. For this, he is also known as the "Father of the Bill of Rights."

BENJAMIN FRANKLIN

Benjamin Franklin is one of the **best-known** Founding Fathers of the United States. He is the **only** Founding Father who is a **signatory** of all four of the major documents of the founding of the United States: the Declaration of Independence, the Treaty of Paris, the Treaty of Alliance with France, and the United States Constitution. Most people **think** of him **primarily** as a **scientist**. The famous **kite experiment**, which **verified** the **nature of electricity**, is **told** and **retold** throughout American history. It is just one of many **amazing accomplishments** made by Benjamin Franklin during his **lifetime**.

Franklin was **noted** for his **diversity** of **talents**. He was a **leading** author, politician, **printer**, scientist, **philosopher**, civic activist, and **diplomat**. Franklin was an **extraordinary inventor**. Among his many creations were the **lightning rod**, the **glass harmonica**, the Franklin **stove**, **bifocal glasses**, and **swim fins**.

In 1776, he was a **member** of the **Committee of Five** that drafted the Declaration of Independence, and made several small **changes** to Thomas Jefferson's draft.

At the signing, he is **quoted** as **stating**: "We must all **hang together**, or **assuredly** we shall all hang **separately**."

---

considered/to consider: considerado/considerar
referred to as: lembrado como
played/to play: desempenhou/desempenhar
bigger role: grande papel
designing: esquematizar
document: documento
anyone else: que qualquer outro
wrote/to write: escreveu/escrever
still: ainda
influential: influente
commentary: comentário
fourth: quarto
drafted/to draft: redigiu/redigir
basic laws: leis básicas
amendments: emendas
best-known: mais conhecidos
only: único
signatory: signatário
think/to think: pensa/pensar
primarily: principalmente
scientist: cientista
kite experiment: experiência com a pipa
verified/to verify: comprovou/comprovar
nature of electricity: natureza da eletricidade
told/to tell: contada/contar
retold: recontada
amazing: incríveis
accomplishments: conquistas
lifetime: existência
noted: famoso
diversity: diversidade
talents: talentos
leading: destacado
printer: tipógrafo
philosopher: filósofo
diplomat: diplomata
extraordinary inventor: inventor extraordinário
lightning rod: para-raios
glass harmonica: harmônica de vidro
stove: fogão
bifocal glasses: lentes bifocais
swim fins: nadadeira, pé de pato
member: membro
Committee of Five: Comitê dos Cinco
changes: mudança
quoted/to quote: citado/citar
stating/to state: declarando/declarar
hang together: permanecer unidos
assuredly: certamente
separately: separadamente

The Best of Two Worlds

Pepe Stepensky, from Mexico City, **has been living** in San Diego for the **past twenty years**. He is a **driving force** in the San Diego Latino community as the **founder** and director of the **award-winning theater group** "Teatro Punto y Coma." **In addition to** being a **published author** of **poetry** and **short stories,** Pepe, **along with** his **wife** Deborah, **own** and **operate** two **fast food** restaurants and the Cerveza Store in Seaport Village. **Maximizing** his **bilingual talents,** Pepe is a **successful voice-over** artist **performing** Hispanic characters and voiceovers for big and small companies nationwide. Deborah and Pepe have three **children**—Jessica 18, Alejandra 16 and Fernando 9 years old.

Think English (TE): **Tell us** about your **journey** to the United States.

Pepe Stepensky (PS): **I met** my wife in May of 1986 and **asked her to marry me three weeks later.** We got married in August of 1986 and **moved** to San Diego **after** our **wedding**. I was 28 years old. I had a **job offer** and **decided** to **take the chance**. I had one **brother living here** but the **rest** of my family, **including** my **parents**, **stayed** in Mexico.

TE: What were the **biggest challenges** for you **bridging** your culture with your **newly adopted** American culture? What was **most exciting** to you about bridging these cultures?

PS: **I feel** that the American culture is more individualist. Each one **cares** more for **themselves**. The Mexican culture is **about people**, friends, family. You **stay at home until** the day you get married. Your parents **are not counting** the days until you go to college so they can **remodel** your **room**! **On the other hand**, America is the **land of opportunities**. Here, the different **social classes** are not so **far away** like in Mexico. In the United States **anybody** can have the **same things** as others.

92 people

TE: **How has being** bilingual **benefitted you**?

PS: Being bilingual has **opened many doors** for me. Being a voice-over talent for the Hispanic **market** was a **great adventure** for me when I **started almost** 15 **years ago**.

TE: Are your children bilingual? How do you **maintain** and keep your Hispanic **heritage alive** with your children **growing up** in America?

PS: **We are having** a **hard time making** our kids **talk to us** in Spanish, but we are **proud** that we did it, and my kids are **perfectly** bilingual. The official language in our house is Spanish. Now that our **first daughter** is **going** to college, she **finally thanked us** because she **realized** how important it was **to know two languages**. We maintained our heritage because **every summer** we go to Mexico **to visit uncles** and **grandparents** and the kids **were able to stay** with them for a **couple of weeks**.

TE: What are your **thoughts** on the incredible **growth** of the Hispanic **population** in the US?

PS: The Hispanic market is the **fastest** growing market in the U.S. We can't **disregard** or **ignore** it. **We need to know** about it, **learn** about it and work **towards considering** them a very important part of the American culture.

TE: **What advice would you give** to a **fellow** Hispanic American **starting out** in this **country**?

PS: **Integrate. Try to understand** your new country, but **never forget** your **roots. Make sure** your children know where they **come from**, and **teach them** your language.

TE: What are you **most proud of** as a Hispanic American?

PS: I'm proud of being binational, bilingual and bicultural. **What else can I ask for**? I have the **best of two worlds**!

---

how has being: como ser
benefitted you: beneficiou você
opened/to open: abriu/abrir
many: muitas
doors: portas
market: mercado
great adventure: grande aventura
I started/to start: comecei/começar
almost: quase
years ago: anos atrás
maintain/to maintain: mantém/manter
heritage: herança
alive: viva
growing up/to grow up: crescendo/crescer
we are having: estamos tendo
hard time: dificuldade
making: em fazer
talk to us: falarem conosco
proud: orgulhosos
perfectly: completamente
first daughter: primeira filha
going/to go: (está) indo/ir
finally: finalmente
thanked us: agradeceu-nos
realized: percebeu
to know: saber
two languages: dois idiomas
every summer: todos os verões
to visit: para visitar
uncles: tios
grandparents: avós
were able to stay: puderam ficar
couple of weeks: algumas semanas
thoughts: pensamentos
growth: crescimento
population: população
fastest: mais rápido
disregard: ser indiferentes
ignore: ignorar
we need: precisamos
to know: saber
learn: aprender
towards: para
considering: considerá-los
what advice: que conselho
would you give: você daria
fellow: companheiro, compatriota
starting out/to start out: começando/começar
country: país
integrate/to integrate: integre-se/integrar
try to understand: tente entender
never forget: nunca se esqueça de
roots: raízes
make sure/to make sure: certifique-se/certificar-se
come from: (de onde) vieram
teach them/to teach: ensine-os/ensinar
most proud of: de que tem mais orgulho
what else can I ask for?: O que mais posso pedir?
best of two worlds: o melhor de dois mundos

people 93

Frank Lloyd Wright

Frank Lloyd Wright is **considered** the most **influential architect** of his time. He **influenced** the **entire course** of American architecture and he **remains**, **to this day**, America's most famous architect.

Frank Lloyd Wright **designed** about 1,000 **structures** and over 400 of these were **built**. He **described** his architecture as one that "**proceeds**, **persists**, **creates**, according to the nature of man and his **circumstances** as they both **change**."

As an independent architect, Wright **became** the **leader** of a style known as the **prairie house**. Prairie houses had **sloping roofs, clean skylines** and **extended lines** that **blend** into the **landscape**. These **designs** were considered **to complement** the land **around** Chicago where they were built. Wright **practiced** what is known as organic architecture, an architecture that is designed to naturally **fit into** the **surroundings**. Houses in **wooded regions**, **for instance**, **made heavy use** of wood. Desert houses made use of **stone**, and houses in **rocky areas** were built **mainly** of **cinder block**. He was also **well known** for making use of **innovative building materials**. Wright **often** designed furniture as well. Some of the **built-in furniture remains** in the houses today.

Wright built 362 houses, about 300 of which are still **standing**. Oak Park, Illinois, a Chicago **suburb**, has the **largest collection** of Wright houses, as well as Wright's home and **studio**. Some of the houses are **open** for **public tours**. **Walking** tours are a wonderful **way to experience** Wright's architecture and **see** the houses as they fit into the **surrounding** landscape.

Rags to Riches

Andrew Carnegie's life was a **true "rags to riches" story**. He was born to a **poor Scottish** family that immigrated to the United States. Carnegie was **devoted** to **hard work** from a **young age**. At age thirteen, Carnegie went to work in a **cotton mill**. He then **moved quickly through** a series of different jobs with Western Union and the Pennsylvania **Railroad**.

By the 1870s Carnegie had **become** a **powerful businessman** and **founded** the Carnegie Steel Company. By the 1890s, the company was the largest and most **profitable** industrial **enterprise** in the world. In 1901 he **sold** his company to JP Morgan's U.S. Steel and **retired** as the world's **richest** man. Carnegie **devoted** the **remainder** of his life to **philanthropy**.

Today, he is **remembered** as an **industrialist**, millionaire, and philanthropist. He **believed** in the "**Gospel of wealth**," which **meant** that wealthy people were **morally obligated to give** their **money back to** others in society.

In 1902 he founded the Carnegie Institution **to fund scientific research** and with a $10 million donation **established** a **pension fund** for **teachers**.

When Carnegie was a young man he **lived** near Colonel James Anderson, a rich man who **allowed** any **working boy to use** his personal **library for free**. **At that time**, free public libraries did not exist. Carnegie **never forgot** Colonel Anderson's generosity. Carnegie used his money **to support** education and **reading**. He gave money to **towns** and **cities to build** more than 2,500 public libraries. He also gave $125 million to a foundation called the Carnegie Corporation **to aid** colleges and other schools.

By 1911, Carnegie had **given away** 90 percent of his fortune. **During** his **lifetime**, he **gave away** over $350 million.

---

true: verdadeira
rags to riches: emergente, novo rico
story: história
poor: pobre
Scottish: escocesa
devoted: dedicado
hard work: trabalho pesado
young age: muito jovem
cotton mill: algodoaria
moved quickly through: avançou rapidamente por
railroad: via férrea / ferrovia
become/to become: tornado/tornar
powerful businessman: poderoso empresário
founded/to found: fundou/fundar
profitable: lucrativa
enterprise: empresa
sold/to sell: vendeu/vender
retired/to retire: aposentou-se/ aposentar-se
richest: mais rico
devoted/to devote: dedicou/dedicar
remainder: restante
philanthropy: filantropia, humanitarismo
remembered: lembrado
industrialist: industrialista
believed/to believe: acreditava/ acreditar
Gospel of wealth: Evangelho da riqueza
meant/to mean: significa/significar
morally obligated: moralmente obrigadas
to give: dar
money: dinheiro
back to: de volta
to fund: financiar
scientific research: pesquisa científica
established/to establish: estabeleceu/ estabelecer
pension fund: fundo de pensão
teachers: professores
lived/to live: viveu/viver
allowed/to allow: permitia/permitir
working boy: menino trabalhador
to use: usar
library: biblioteca
for free: de graça
at that time: naquela época
never forgot: nunca se esqueceu de
to support: patrocinar
reading: leitura
towns: povoados
cities: cidades
to build: construir
to aid: para ajudar
given away/to give away: doado/doar
during: durante
lifetime: existência
gave away/to give away: doou/doar

people

America Takes Flight

Orville and Wilbur Wright **are credited as** the two Americans to **build** the world's **first successful airplane**. On December 17, 1903, the "Wright flyer" **flew** for 12 **seconds** and 120 **feet**.

The Wright brothers **did not go** to **college**; however they had **intuitive scientific** and **technical abilities**. They **built** their own bicycles and **operated** a bicycle **repair** and **sales shop**. The **profits** from their bicycle **business funded** their **airplane-building venture**.

The brothers flew their **test planes** in Kitty Hawk, North Carolina. It was a **small town** that had **steady winds**. They could **glide** and **land safely** on the area's **sand dunes**.

The brothers continued to **develop** more **complicated** planes over the next **few years**. The Wright Company was **formed** to build and sell their airplanes.

You can see the famous airplane, the "Wright flyer," at the National Air and Space Museum in Washington, D.C.

Another famous American **aviator** is Amelia Mary Earhart. Amelia Earhart was a **renowned** American aviation **pioneer** and **women's rights activist**. **In addition to breaking** many aviation **records,** she **wrote best-selling books** about her flying experiences and **helped form** the women's pilot organization, The Ninety-Nines.

In 1928, she was the first woman to fly as a **passenger across** the Atlantic Ocean. In 1932, she became the first woman to fly solo across that **same** ocean. For this flight, she became the first woman **to receive** the Distinguished Flying Cross.

In 1937, while **attempting** a flight **around the world**, Earhart **disappeared** over the central Pacific Ocean. Her disappearance is **considered**, to this day, to be a **mystery**.

Amelia Earhart's actions have **inspired** generations of women **to follow** their **dreams** and do things **never done** by women **before**.

---

are credited as: são tidos como
build/to build: construíram/construir
first: primeiro
successful airplane: avião bem-sucedido
flew/to fly: voou/voar
seconds: segundos
feet: pés (1 pé = 30,48 cm)
did not go/to go: não foram/ir
college: universidade
intuitive: intuitivas
scientific: científicas
technical: técnicas
abilities: habilidades
built/to build: construíram/construir
operated/to operate: conduziram/conduzir
repair: conserto
sales: vendas
shop: loja
profits: lucro
business: negócio
funded/to fund: financiou/financiar
airplane-building venture: empresa de construção de aviões
test planes: aviões de teste
small town: cidade pequena
steady winds: ventos constantes
glide/to glide: plana/planar
land/to land: aterrissa/aterrissar
safely: com segurança
sand dunes: dunas de areia
develop/to develop: desenvolver/desenvolver
complicated: complicados
few years: poucos anos
formed/to form: formada/formar
aviator: aviador
renowned: famosa
pioneer: pioneira
women's rights activist: ativista dos direitos das mulheres
in addition to: além de
breaking…records: quebrar… recordes
wrote/to write: escreveu/escrever
best-selling books: livros com êxito de vendas
helped/to help: ajudou/ajudar
form: formar
passenger: passageira
across: através
same: mesmo
to receive: a receber
attempting/to attempt: tentava/tentar
around the world: ao redor do mundo
disappeared/to disappear: desapareceu/desaparecer
considered/to consider: considerada/considerar
mystery: mistério
inspired/to inspire: inspirou/inspirar
to follow: a seguir
dreams: sonhos
never done: nunca feitas
before: antes

96 people

Dr. Seuss

Dr. Seuss **helped millions** of **kids learn** how **to read**. He **entertained children** and adults **alike**. His **books** were famous for their **silly rhymes** and **whimsical characters**. Dr. Seuss **wrote** and **illustrated nearly** 50 books during his **lifetime**.

Dr. Seuss was **born,** as Thedore Geisel, in Springfield, Massachusetts, on March 2, 1904. He **graduated** from Dartmouth College in 1925 and **continued** his education at Oxford University.

During World War II, Geisel joined the Army and was **sent to** Hollywood where he wrote **documentaries** for the **military**. During this time, he also **created** a **cartoon** called Gerald McBoing-Boing. This cartoon **won him** an Oscar.

In the **spring** of 1954, a **report** was **published discussing illiteracy** among **schoolchildren**. The report **suggested** that **boring** books were **causing** children **to have trouble reading**. This **news prompted** Geisel's **publisher to send** Geisel a list of 400 **words** important for children to learn. The publisher **asked** Geisel to **shorten** the list to 250 words and **use them** to write an **entertaining** children's book. **Using** 220 of the words given to him, Geisel published *The Cat in the Hat*. The book was an **instant success**.

Winner of the Pulitzer Prize in 1984 and three Academy Awards, Theodor Geisel is **considered** the 20th century's most famous author for children.

Theodor Geisel **died** on September 24, 1991, but Dr. Seuss **lives on**, **inspiring** generations of children of **to explore the joys** of reading.

helped/to help: ajudou/ajudar
millions: milhares
kids: crianças
learn/to learn: aprenderem/aprender
to read: a ler
entertained/to entertain: entretinha/entreter
children: crianças
alike: da mesma forma
books: livros
silly: bobas
rhymes: rimas
whimsical: excêntricos
characters: personagens
wrote/to write: escreveu/escrever
illustrated/to illustrate: ilustrou/ilustrar
nearly: quase
lifetime: existência
born/to be born: nasceu/nascer
graduated/to graduate: formou-se/formar-se
continued/to continue: continuou/continuar
sent to/to send to: enviado para/enviar para
documentaries: documentários
military: exército
created/to create: criou/criar
cartoon: desenho animado
won him: o fez ganhar
spring: primavera
report: reportagem
published/to publish: publicada/publicar
discussing/to discuss: debatendo/debater
illiteracy: analfabetismo
schoolchildren: crianças em idade escolar
suggested/to suggest: sugeria/sugerir
boring: chatos
causing/to cause: causando/causar
to have trouble: ter problemas para
reading/to read: lendo/ler
news: notícias
prompted/to prompt: fizeram com que/fazer com que
publisher: editor
to send: enviasse
words: palavras
asked/to ask: pediu/pedir
shorten/to shorten: encurtar-se/encurtar
use them/to use: as usasse/usar
entertaining: divertido
using/to use: usando/usar
instant success: sucesso instantâneo
winner: ganhador
considered/to consider: considerado/considerar
died/to die: morreu/morrer
lives on: continua vivo
inspiring/to inspire: inspirando/inspirar
to explore: a explorar
the joys: as alegrias

people

Author and Preservationis

born/to be born: nasceu/nascer
immigrated/to immigrate: imigrou/imigrar
briefly: logo
attended/to attend: frequentou/frequentar
finish/to finish: terminou/terminar
instead: em vez de
walking: andando por
exploring: explorando
wilderness: áreas inabitadas
journals: diários
produced/to produce: produziram/produzir
nature writing: trabalhos escritos sobre a natureza
works: obras
include/to include: incluíam/incluir
letters: cartas
essays: ensaios
books: livros
telling of: contando sobre
have been read/to read: foram lidos/ler
still: ainda
however: contudo
not just for enjoyment: não era apenas para divertir
modern environmental activists: modernos ativistas do meio ambiente
preservationists: conservacionistas
received/to receive: recebeu/receber
helped protect: ajudaram a proteger
articles: artigos
describing/to describe: descrevendo/descrever
natural wonders: maravilhas naturais
inspired/to inspire: inspirou/inspirar
support: apoio
establishing/to establish: estabelecendo/estabelecer
another: outra
accomplishment: conquista
founded/to found: fundou/fundar
driving force: força impulsora
sleeping outside: dormir do lado de fora
under the stars: sob as estrelas
great pleasures: grandes prazeres
kept track of: manteve registro de
recording them: escrevendo-as
woke up/to wake up: acordou/acordar
watching/to watch: assistindo/assistir
daybreak: amanhecer
sunrise: nascer do sol
pale: pálido
purple: púrpura
sky: céu
changing/to change: mudando/mudar
sunbeams: raios solares
pouring/to pour: brotando/brotar
through: através
peaks: picos

John Muir was **born** in Scotland in 1838. His family **immigrated** to Wisconsin in 1849. He **briefly attended** college but did not **finish**. **Instead** he began 40 years of **walking** and **exploring** the **wilderness** of North America. His **journals produced** some of the best **nature writing** in the English language. His **works include** *The Mountains of California, Our National Parks, My First Summer in the Sierra, Steep Trails,* and others. His **letters**, **essays**, and **books telling of** his adventures in nature **have been read** by millions and are **still** popular today.

However, Muir's writing was **not just for enjoyment.** John Muir was one of the first **modern environmental activists** and **preservationists**. His direct activism and the attention his writings **received helped protect** the Yosemite Valley and other wilderness areas. His **articles** and books **describing** Yosemite's **natural wonders inspired** public **support establishing** Yosemite as the first national park in 1890.

Another great **accomplishment** is the Sierra Club, which he **founded**. The Sierra Club is one of the most important conservation organizations in the United States. His writings and philosophy were a **driving force** in the creation of the modern environmental movement.

For John Muir, **sleeping outside under the stars** was one of life's **great pleasures**. He **kept track of** his experiences by **recording them** in his journals. Here is what he wrote on July 19, 1869, when he **woke up** in the Sierra Nevada Mountains of California:

"**Watching** the **daybreak** and **sunrise**. The **pale** rose and **purple sky changing** softly to yellow and white, **sunbeams pouring through** the **peaks** and over the Yosemite domes."

Dr. Jonas Salk

Jonas Salk was born on October 28th, 1914, in New York City. His **parents** were Russian-Jewish immigrants who **fled** their **home country** for a **new life** in the United States. After **graduating high school** at the age of 15, Salk went to college **to pursue** a **law degree**. **Somewhere along the way**, he **changed his mind** and **decided** to pursue a degree in medicine. **Luckily** for the world, Jonas Salk **chose** medicine!

Salk **enrolled** in the medical school at New York University. He **began research** on the **flu virus**, **gathering knowledge** that would **lead to** his **discovery** of the **polio vaccine**. In 1947, Salk **accepted** an appointment to the Pittsburgh Medical School. He **started** working with the National Foundation for Infantile Paralysis and **saw** the opportunity to develop a vaccine **against** polio. He **devoted** the next eight years to this work.

In 1955, Jonas Salk's years of research finally **paid off**. The **summertime** was a time of **fear** and **anxiety** for many parents. Summer was the **season** when **thousands** of children became infected with the **disease** of polio. Parents' **worst** fear was **forever eliminated** when it was **announced** that Dr. Jonas Salk had developed a vaccine against the disease. Salk was **hailed** as a **miracle worker** and he **became famous overnight**. He **refused** to **patent** the vaccine, which made him even more **loved** by the people. He had **no desire to profit** personally from the discovery. His **ultimate wish** was to see the vaccine **distributed as widely as possible**, to as many people as possible. In countries where Salk's vaccine **has remained in use**, the disease has nearly been eliminated.

In 1963, Salk **founded** the Jonas Salk Institute for Biological Studies, a center for medical and scientific research. He **died** on June 23, 1995. His **legacy lives on** forever and his contributions to the world of science and health are **still utilized** today.

---

parents: pais
fled/to flee: fugiram de/fugir de
home country: país de origem
new life: nova vida
graduating/to graduate: formar-se
high school: ensino médio
to pursue: para ir atrás de
law degree: diploma de direito
somewhere along the way: em algum momento do percurso
changed/to change: mudou/mudar
his mind: de ideia
decided/to decide: decidiu/decidir
luckily: felizmente
chose/to choose: escolheu/escolher
enrolled/to enroll: matriculou-se/matricular
began/to begin: começou/começar
research: pesquisar
flu virus: vírus da gripe
gathering/to gather: reunindo/reunir
knowledge: conhecimento
lead to: levaria a
discovery: descoberta
polio vaccine: vacina antipólio
accepted/to accept: aceitou/aceitar
started/to start: começou/começar
saw/to see: viu/ver
against: contra
devoted/to devote: dedicou/dedicar
paid off/to pay off: valeram a pena/valer a pena
summertime: verão
fear: medo
anxiety: ansiedade
season: estação
thousands: milhares
disease: doença
worst: pior
forever: para sempre
eliminated: eliminado
announced/to announce: anunciado/anunciar
hailed/to hail: saudado/saudar
miracle worker: milagreiro
became famous overnight: tornou-se famoso da noite para o dia
refused/to refuse: recusou-se/recusar-se
patent: patentear
loved: amado
no desire: nenhum desejo
to profit: obter vantagem
ultimate wish: último desejo
distributed/to distribute: distribuída/distribuir
as widely as possible: o mais amplamente possível
has remained in use: continuaram em uso
founded/to found: fundou/fundar
died/to die: morreu/morrer
legacy: legado
lives on: continua vivo
still: ainda
utilized/to utilize: usadas/usar

people

Angel of the Battlefield

Clara Barton is **best known** as being the **founder** of the American Red Cross and for **serving** as a **nurse** on Civil War **battlefields**. Her **compassionate work** during the Civil War **would inspire praise** of her as "the **true heroine** of the age, the angel of the battlefield."

During the **early years** of the Civil War, she and a **few friends** began **to distribute first-aid supplies** to field hospitals, camps and battlefields. **In addition to** distributing supplies, she **worked tirelessly taking care** of **injured soldiers**.

At the **end** of the war, Barton **assisted** the government in **finding** information on **missing** soldiers. She **helped identify** and **mark almost** 13,000 **graves** at Andersonville, Georgia.

In 1881 her most **enduring** work began, the **establishment** of the American Red Cross. She **convinced** the government **to identify** the Red Cross as a governmental agency that would **provide aid** for **natural disasters**. Throughout the 1880s, victims of **fire**, **earthquake**, **drought**, tornado, and **flood** received aid and assistance from the Red Cross. Clara **learned** the importance of **educating** victims **to take care of** themselves so they would **be able to rebuild** their **lives** again after Red Cross workers had **left**. This concept of **teaching** first aid would **later** be **realized** in the formation of first-aid classes. First-aid classes are a very important part of the American Red Cross's service today.

Miss Barton continued to **work in the field** until she was **well into** her 70s. She died in 1912 at age 90 in her home. The mission of her life can be **summed up** in her **own words**, "You must **never** so much as **think** whether you like it or not, whether it is **bearable** or not; you must never think of anything except the **need**, and how **to meet it**."

Let There Be Light

Thomas Alva Edison is **considered** one of the greatest, most prolific inventors in history. He has over 1,093 U.S. **patents** in his name. His **inventions** and **devices** greatly **changed** and **influenced** life all over the world.

The invention that **first made** him famous was the **phonograph** in 1877. The cylinder phonograph was the first **machine** that could **record** and **reproduce sound**. Its invention **created** a sensation and brought Edison international **fame**.

In 1877 and 1878, Edison invented and **developed** the carbon microphone used in all **telephones along with** the Bell **receiver** until the 1980s. The carbon microphone was also used in **radio broadcasting** through the 1920s.

Edison is most famous for the **electric light bulb**. **Contrary to popular belief**, he didn't invent the light bulb, but **rather** he **improved** upon a 50-year-old idea.

The problem other inventors had **encountered** was the ability to **make it work** for **long periods** of **time**. Edison **solved** this problem and created a light bulb that **sustained** light for 40 **straight hours**. More importantly, he created a system that **allowed** homes and businesses to be **supplied** with electricity.

The **success** of electric light **brought** Thomas Edison to **new levels** of fame and **wealth**. His electric companies continued **to grow** and in 1889 they **merged** to form Edison General Electric. In 1892 Edison General Electric merged with its competitor, Thompson-Houston. Edison was **dropped** from the **name**, and the company became General Electric.

Thomas Alva Edison died in West Orange, New Jersey on October 18, 1931. **After** his death, Edison became a **folk hero** of **legendary status**. His inventions have **profoundly affected** and **shaped** the **modern society** that we **know today**.

---

considered: considerado
patents: patentes
inventions: invenções
devices: aparelhos
changed/to change: mudaram/mudar
influenced/to influence: influenciaram/influenciar
first: primeiro
made/to make: o fez/fazer
phonograph: fonógrafo
machine: máquina
record: gravar
reproduce: reproduzir
sound: som
created/to create: criou/criar
fame: fama
developed/to develop: desenvolveu/desenvolver
telephones: telefones
along with: junto com
receiver: receptora
radio broadcasting: radiotransmissão
electric light bulb: lâmpada elétrica
contrary to popular belief: contrário a crença popular
rather: mas sim
improved/to improve: aperfeiçoou/aperfeiçoar
encountered/to encounter: encontravam/encontrar
make it work: fazê-lo funcionar
long periods: longos períodos
time: tempo
solved/to solve: resolveu/resolver
sustained/to sustain: suportava/suportar
straight hours: horas seguidas
allowed/to allow: permitia/permitir
supplied/to supply: abastecidos/abastecer
success: sucesso
brought/to bring: trouxe/trazer
new levels: novos níveis
wealth: riqueza
to grow: crescer
merged/to merge: uniram/unir
dropped/to drop: tirado/tirar
name: nome
after: após, depois de
folk hero: herói popular
legendary status: distinção lendária
profoundly affected: afetaram profundamente
shaped/to shape: moldaram/moldar
modern society: sociedade moderna
know/to know: conhecemos/conhecer
today: hoje

Hispanic Americans' Famous Firsts

Hispanics **are becoming** the **largest minority group** in the United States. Hispanic Americans are **adding** great **value** to American **society** and **enriching** U.S. **government** and culture. **Throughout** this article are **listed** some of the "**famous firsts**" made by Hispanic Americans. These people have made great **contributions** to the United States and the **world**.

Hispanics **fill top positions** in the U.S. government. As of 2005, Mexican-American Alberto Gonzáles **currently serves** as U.S. **Attorney General** and **Cuban-born** Carlos Gutiérrez as **Secretary of Commerce**.

Joseph Marion Hernández was the first Hispanic American to serve in the United States **Congress**. He served from September 1822 to March 1823. From 1990 to 1993, Antonia Coello Novello served as the U.S. Surgeon General. She was first Hispanic and **the first** woman **ever to hold** this position. During her **tenure** as Surgeon General, Novello **focused** her attention on the **health** of women, children and minorities. A **workshop** that she **organized led** to the **creation** of the National Hispanic/Latino Health Initiative.

The world of **science** and **medicine** is **another** area where Hispanic Americans have greatly contributed. In 1986 Franklin Chang-Díaz became the first Costa Rican astronaut. Chang-Díaz is **also** the director of the Advanced Space Propulsion Laboratory at NASA's Johnson Space Center, where he has been **developing** a **plasma rocket**. The first **female** Hispanic astronaut was Ellen Ochoa, whose **first of four shuttle missions** was in 1991.

- **are becoming/to become:** estão se tornando/tornar-se
- **largest minority group:** maior grupo minoritário
- **adding/to add:** agregando/agregar
- **value:** valor
- **society:** sociedade
- **enriching/to enrich:** enriquecendo/enriquecer
- **government:** governo
- **throughout:** por todo
- **listed/to list:** listados/listar
- **famous firsts:** primeiros famosos
- **contributions:** contribuições
- **world:** mundo
- **fill/to fill:** ocupam/ocupar
- **top positions:** altos cargos
- **currently:** no momento
- **serves/to serve:** serve/servir
- **Attorney General:** Promotor Geral
- **Cuban-born:** nascido em Cuba
- **Secretary of Commerce:** Secretário de Comércio
- **Congress:** congresso
- **the first ... ever to hold:** primeiríssima a ocupar
- **tenure:** mandato
- **focused/to focus:** focou/focar
- **health:** saúde
- **workshop:** oficina, seminário
- **organized/to organize:** organizou/organizar
- **led/to lead:** conduziu/conduzir
- **creation:** criação
- **science:** ciência
- **medicine:** medicina
- **another:** outra
- **also:** também
- **developing/to develop:** desenvolvendo/desenvolver
- **plasma rocket:** foguete de plasma
- **female:** mulher
- **first of four:** primeira de quatro
- **shuttle missions:** missões espaciais

Luiz Walter Alvarez is the first Hispanic American **to receive** a Nobel Prize in **physics**. He received this **award** in 1968, for **discoveries** about subatomic particles.

Since the 1950s, a number of Hispanic American **musicians** and **performers** have **gained widespread popularity**, including Julio Iglesias, Jennifer López, Gloria Estefan and the group Los Lobos.

Lucrezia Bori, a Spanish soprano, became the first Hispanic American **to debut** at the Metropolitan Opera in 1912. After 1935 she was a director of the Metropolitan Opera Association. She was **distinguished** for her **stage presence** as well as her **singing voice**.

The first Hispanic American to be **inducted** into the Rock and Roll **Hall of Fame** was Carlos Santana in 1998. Santana is **considered** a **guitar-playing legend** and he has been a leader in the music industry for over 30 years.

Many Hispanic **athletes** have **made their mark** in American **sports**. In 1973 Roberto Clemente of Puerto Rico became the first Hispanic American inducted into the Hall of Fame. He was also the first Hispanic **player to serve** on the Players Association Board and to reach 3,000 **hits**. John Ruiz became the **first-ever** Hispanic **heavyweight boxing champ**. He **won** the title **defeating** Evander Holyfield in 2001.

A number of **painters** and **writers** have **further enriched** American culture, such as Hispanic artists John Valadez, Martín Ramírez, Frank Romero and Arnaldo Roche. Oscar Hijuelos is the first Hispanic to win the Pulitzer Prize for fiction. Hijuelos **earned** the Pulitzer for his book, *The Mambo Kings Play Songs of Love*. In this book he **tells the story** of Cuban musicians in New York in the early 1950s.

As more and more Hispanic Americans are **rising to the ranks** and making their mark in their **preferred fields**, the 21st century will **observe** even greater Hispanic contributions to U.S. society and culture. September 15 to October 15 is National Hispanic Heritage Month in the United States. Hispanic Heritage Month **celebrates** and **recognizes past** and **present achievements** of Hispanic Americans and **encourages future ones**.

---

to receive: a receber
physics: física
award: prêmio
discoveries: descobertas
since: desde
musicians: músicos
performers: intérpretes
gained/to gain: conseguiram/conseguir
widespread popularity: grande popularidade
to debut: a estrear
distinguished/to distinguish: reconhecida/reconhecer
stage presence: presença de palco
singing voice: vocalização
inducted: aceito
Hall of Fame: Galeria da Fama
considered/to consider: considerado/considerar
guitar-playing legend: guitarrista lendário
athletes: atletas
made their mark: deixaram sua marca
sports: esportes
player: jogador
to serve: a aparecer
hits: rebatidas
first-ever: primeiríssimo
heavyweight boxing champ: campeão de peso pesado no boxe
won/to win: ganhou/ganhar
defeating/to defeat: derrotando/derrotar
painters: pintores
writers: escritores
further enriched: enriqueceram ainda mais
earned/to earn: ganhou/ganhar
tells/to tell: conta/contar
the story: a história
as more and more: à medida que mais e mais
rising to the ranks: ascendendo às posições mais altas
preferred fields: áreas preferidas
observe: observar
celebrates/to celebrate: celebra/celebrar
recognizes/to recognize: reconhece/reconhecer
past: passados
present: presentes
achievements: conquistas
encourages/to encourage: encoraja/encorajar
future ones: conquistas futuras

people

Test Your Comprehension

Trail of Discovery, page 88

1. Por que Thomas Jefferson queria que Lewis e Clark saíssem em expedição?

2. Qual foi a única mulher a viajar com o Corpo do Descobrimento?

3. Como ela ajudou e contribuiu nesta viagem?

Mother of Civil Rights, page 89

1. O que Rosa Park se recusou a fazer?

2. Quando a segregação nos ônibus municipais foi proibida?

Founding Fathers, page 90

1. Quem são os pais fundadores?

2. Quem é chamado de Pai da Pátria?

3. Quem foi o principal autor da Declaração da Independência?

4. Benjamin Franklin ficou famoso por qual experiência cientifica?

Frank Lloyd Wright, page 94

1. Wright era famoso por qual estilo de casas?

2. Descreva este estilo.

Teste sua Compreensão

Rags to Riches, page 95

1. O que significava o "evangelho da riqueza" para Carnegie?

2. Quem inspirou Carnegie a construir e financiar as bibliotecas públicas gratuitas?

3. Quanto dinheiro Carnegie doou ao longo de sua vida?

America Takes Flight, page 96

1. Como os irmãos Wright financiaram sua empresa de construção de aviões?

2. Por que os irmãos Wright testavam seus aviões em Kitty Hawk, Carolina do Norte?

3. Por que Amelia Earhart se tornou famosa em 1928 e 1932?

Dr. Jonas Salk, page 99

1. O que Jonas Salk descobriu?

2. Qual foi o seu "maior desejo" em relação a essa vacina?

Angel of the Battlefield, page 100

1. Por que Clara Barton era chamada de o "Anjo dos Campos de Batalha"?

2. Que trabalho Clara Barton realizou no final da guerra?

The successful man will profit from his mistakes
and try again in a different way.

Dale Carnegie

Business

pay/to pay: paga/pagar
operate/to operate: administrar
needed to run: necessárias para dirigir
national parks: parques nacionais
schools: escolas
roads: estradas
military: forças armadas
government employees: funcionários públicos
system: sistema
percentage: porcentagem
income: renda
called/to call: chamado/chamar
responsible: responsável
collecting: recolher
Internal Revenue Service: Serviço da Receita Federal
enforces/to enforce: faz cumprir/fazer cumprir
laws: leis
tax returns: declaração de renda
taxes: impostos
giving: repassar
U.S. Treasury: Tesouro dos EUA
to whom: para quem
tax dollars: dinheiro arrecadado com impostos
expenses: despesas
federal budget: orçamento federal
how much: quantia
plans/to plan: planeja/planejar
spend/to spend: gasta/gastar
more: mais
raise/to raise: levanta/levantar
afford to: permitir-se
non-profit: sem fins lucrativos
report their income: informar sobre seus rendimentos
calculate/to calculate: calcula/calcular
do not have to pay: não têm que pagar
still have to report: ainda têm que informar
tax-exempt status: isenção de impostos
are taxed: cobrado impostos
earn/to earn: ganha/ganhar
interest on savings: juros sobre a poupança
profits on investments: lucros sobre os investimentos
pensions: pensão

throughout the year: ao longo do ano

Introduction to Taxes

How does the United States **pay** to **operate** our government?

The United States must pay for all of the things **needed to run** a government. The government must pay for our **national parks**, **schools**, **roads**, the **military**, **government employees**, and much more. The government has a **system** where people and companies pay a **percentage** of their **income** to the government. This is **called** the income tax.

Who is **responsible** for **collecting** the taxes?

The **Internal Revenue Service** (IRS) **enforces** the tax **laws**. The Internal Revenue Service is also responsible for processing our **tax returns**, collecting **taxes**, and for **giving** the money collected to the **U.S. Treasury**.

To whom does the Internal Revenue Service give our **tax dollars**?

The IRS gives the money collected to the U.S. Treasury, who pays various government **expenses**. The President of the United States and the Congress are responsible for the **federal budget**. The budget is **how much** the government **plans** to **spend** on various programs and services. When the government spends **more** money, it must **raise** more money through taxes. When the government spends less money, it can **afford to** lower taxes.

Who must pay taxes?

1. Every organization, person, **non-profit**, or company, must **report their income** and **calculate** their tax. Some organizations **do not have to pay** tax, but they **still have to report** to the government that they have **tax-exempt status**.

2. You **are taxed** on any money you **earn**. This includes salary from an employer, **interest on savings**, **profits on investments**, **pensions**, and other income.

108 business

3. Everyone must pay taxes **throughout the year**. This **is called** "pay as you go." This usually means your income taxes **are taken out of** your paycheck and **sent directly to** the federal government by your employer. At the **end of the year**, if you paid more than what you owe, the government **refunds** the amount paid **over what you owed**. This is called a **tax refund**. If you have not paid **enough to cover** what you owe, you must pay the **amount due by** April 15th of the **following year**. If you don't pay the taxes due, the government **will charge** you **interest** and **penalties**.

4. People who make more money have a **higher tax rate**, and people who make less money have a **lower** tax rate. Your tax rate will change **depending on** how much money you made that year. This system is called a progressive tax system.

5. People **are free to arrange** their **financial affairs in order to get tax benefits**. **For example**, you can **reduce** your **total income** if you **contribute money** to retirement accounts, such as a 401(k) or IRA plans. There are many other **types** of tax benefits. Tax benefits are how Congress **rewards** people for making **certain** types of decisions. **The goal** of **tax planning** is **to choose** which tax benefits **make the most sense** for you.

is called/to call: chamado/chamar
are taken out of: são deduzidos
sent/to send: enviados/enviar
directly to: diretamente para
end of the year: final do ano
refunds/to refund: reembolsa/reembolsar
over: sobre
what you owed: o que você devia
tax refund: reembolso tributário
enough: suficiente
to cover: para cobrir
amount: quantia
due by: com vencimento em
following year: ano seguinte
will charge/to charge: cobrará/cobrar
interest: juros
penalties: multas
higher: mais alta
tax rate: porcentagem de tributação
lower: mais baixa
depending on/to depend on: dependendo de/depender de
are free: são livres
to arrange: para organizar
financial affairs: assuntos financeiros
in order to get: a fim de receber
tax benefits: benefícios tributários
for example: por exemplo
reduce: reduzir
total income: renda total
contribute/to contribute: contribui/contribuir
money: dinheiro
types: tipos
rewards/to reward: recompensa/recompensar
certain: certos
the goal: o objetivo
tax planning: planejamento de imposto
to choose: escolher
make the most sense: faz mais sentido

move/to move: mudam-se/mudar
to work towards: para trabalhar no sentido de
better life: vida melhor
themselves: si próprios
entrepreneurship: espírito empreendedor
the route: a rota
take/to take: pegam/pegar
hope/to hope: esperam/esperar
it is often said that: sempre se diz que
starting/to start: começar/começar
business: negócio
dream: sonho
right product: produto certo
best place: melhor lugar
to launch: para lançar
new: nova
company: companhia
trouble: problema
lack/to lack: carecem de/carecer de
language: idioma, linguagem
skills: habilidades
start-up money: capital inicial
manage/to manage: gerir/gerir
grow: desenvolver
help: ajuda
to get you started: para começar
entrepreneurial drive: iniciativa empresarial
any time: a qualquer momento
worry/to worry: preocupar-se/preocupar
planning: planejamento
later: depois
need to get ... done: precisa fazer
first: primeiro
some of: alguns dos
governmental agency: agência governamental
offers/to offer: oferece/oferecer
all levels: todos os níveis
business loans: empréstimos para empresas
grants: subsídios
strong: forte
advocate: defensor
minority audiences: participação minoritária
free: grátis
online: virtual
face-to-face: presencial
counseling: orientação
low cost: de baixo custo
workshops: oficina, seminário
even easier: ainda mais fácil
is offered/to offer: é oferecida/oferecer
to advocate: defender
(to) promote: promover
(to) facilitate: facilitar
success: êxito
technical assistance: assistência técnica

110 business

Entrepreneurship

Many immigrants **move** to the United States **to work towards** a **better life** for **themselves** and their families. **Entrepreneurship** is often **the route** they **take**, or **hope** to take.

It is often said that starting a **business** is an American **dream**. With the **right product** or service, the U.S. is the **best place** in the world **to launch** a **new company**. The **trouble** is that many new entrepreneurs **lack** the **language**, business **skills**, and **start-up money** to successfully **manage** and **grow** their businesses.

STARTING OUT

Fortunately, there is **help to get you started**. There are numerous organizations helping Spanish-speaking immigrants who have an **entrepreneurial drive**.

In many other cultures, you can start a business at **any time** and **worry** about the **planning later**. In the U.S. culture, you **need to get** all the planning and permits **done first**.

Some of the best places to start are SBA, SCORE and the Hispanic Chamber of Commerce.

- Small Business Association (www.sba.gov). The SBA is a **governmental agency** that **offers all levels** of assistance, **business loans** and **grants** for small businesses. The SBA is a **strong advocate** of **minority audiences**.

- SCORE. SCORE is a subdivision of the SBA. SCORE offers **free online** or **face-to-face** business **counseling** and **low cost** seminars and **workshops**. Online you will find a list of resources specifically for minority entrepreneurs. To make it **even easier**, all of their information **is offered** in English and Spanish.

- Hispanic Chamber of Commerce (www.ushcc.com). **To advocate**, **promote** and **facilitate** the **success** of Hispanic businesses. They provide **technical assistance** to Hispanic business associations and entrepreneurs.

START-UP COSTS

Access to **capital** can be a **concern** for Hispanic business owners.

In addition to loans through governmental agencies, **more and more** banks are **setting up** divisions that **focus entirely** on loans for the Hispanic/Latino communities in the U.S.

Wells Fargo has a **long tradition** of providing **financial services** to Latinos. On their website it states: "Wells Fargo is **committed** to helping Latino owned businesses grow and **prosper**." In 1997, Wells Fargo launched Latino Business Services **to support** and **build relationships** with the Latino-owned businesses in our communities. Wells Fargo also **celebrates outstanding** Latino entrepreneurs with **award** grants.

Smaller community banks also offer small business loans for minority businesses. Do some **research** to learn about banks in your area that **pride themselves** on their relationships with the Latino community.

LOW OVERHEAD

Many people **decide** to start businesses that don't need a lot of startup money.
Miguel Peña **began selling custom boots** and **hats** after a **construction injury**. He **sold** his boots and hats at **swap meets** and to friends. Success on that level gave him the **desire to open** a **tiny store** in 1989. Today, he **operates** stores in Arizona.

Lucy Acedo **tested interest** in an **antique shop** by having frequent **garage sales** to sell her **treasures**. She **invested** around $500 **to acquire collectible dishes** and **knick-knacks** at **estate** and garage sales. She's **managed to keep** the business **running** for 4 ½ years.

The United States **truly is** a **land of opportunity**. With the **abundance** of business **resources** offered, it is possible to start your own business. If you plan to start your own business, **make the most** of what is **offered** to you and **memorize** this American **idiom**: "**Where there's a will, there's a way!**"

capital: capital (dinheiro)
concern: preocupação
in addition to: além de
more and more: mais e mais
setting up/to set up: estabelecendo/ estabelecer
focus/to focus: focalizam-se/focalizar
entirely: totalmente
long tradition: longa tradição
financial services: serviços financeiros
committed/to commit: comprometido/comprometer
prosper/to prosper: prosperar/ prosperar
to support: para apoiar
build: construir
relationships: relações
celebrates/to celebrate: homenageia/ homenagear
outstanding: sobressalente
award: recompensa
research: pesquisa
pride themselves/to pride oneself: orgulham-se/orgulhar-se
decide/to decide: decidem/decidir
began/to begin: começou/começar
selling/to sell: vendendo/vender
custom boots: botas personalizadas
hats: chapéus
construction injury: ferimento no trabalho de construção (*civil*)
sold/to sell: vendeu/vender
swap meets: bazares
desire: desejo, vontade
to open: abrir
tiny store: pequena loja
operates/to operate: administra/ administrar
tested/to test: provou/provar
interest: lucros
antique shop: loja de antiquário
garage sales: vendas de garagem
treasures: tesouros
invested/to invest: investiu/investir
to acquire: adquirir
collectible dishes: louças de coleção
knick-knacks: bugigangas
estate: patrimônio
managed/to manage: conseguiu/ conseguir
to keep... running: manter... funcionando
truly is: realmente é
land of opportunity: terra das oportunidades
abundance: abundância
resources: recursos
make the most: aproveite o máximo
offered/to offer: é oferecido/oferecer
memorize/to memorize: decore/ decorar
idiom: dito
Where there's a will, there's a way!: Querer é poder!

business 111

population: população
integrating/to integrate: integrando-se/integrar
systems: sistemas
however: contudo
say/to say: dizem/dizer
not using banks: não usam bancos
cash: pagamento à vista
preferred method: método preferido
managing/to manage: administrando/administrar
finances: finanças
remains/to remain: permanece/permanecer
lack of identification: falta de identificação
undocumented: sem documentos
banking: setor bancário
concept: conceito
laborers: trabalhadores
without: sem
income: pagamento
reluctant: relutantes
set up: abrir
account: conta
legal residency: residência legal
simply: simplesmente
unsure: inseguros
about: sobre
works/to work: funciona/funcionar
has not started/to start: não começou/começar
often come: geralmente vêm
rural areas: áreas rurais
villages: povoados
access: acesso
limited: limitado
nonexistent: inexistente
established/to establish: estabelecido/estabelecer
relationship: relação
to start: começar
new country: novo país
fully speak: falam fluentemente
language: idioma
living: viver
cash-only: pagamento somente à vista
risks: riscos
law enforcement officials: agentes da lei
criminals: criminosos
view/to view: veem/ver
easy targets: alvos fáceis
carry/to carry: carregarem/carregar

Banking in America

The nation's Hispanic **population** is **integrating** into the social and cultural **systems**. **However,** many people **say** they are **not using banks** and **cash** is the **preferred method** for **managing** their **finances**.

Cash **remains** popular because of a **lack of identification** for new or **undocumented** immigrants. Also, cultural differences make **banking** a foreign **concept** to many.

For some **laborers without** documentation, all their **income** is in cash.

Some are **reluctant** to **set up** an **account** because they might not have **legal residency**, while others are **simply unsure about** how the banking process **works**.

Another reason the Hispanic community **has not started** using banks is that they **often come** to the United States from **rural areas** in Latin American countries. In these small **villages access** to banking is **limited** or **nonexistent**. Many immigrants haven't **established** a banking **relationship** even in Mexico. It is difficult for them **to start** their banking in a **new country** where they don't **fully speak** the **language**.

Living in a **cash-only** world has its **risks**. **Law enforcement officials** say **criminals view** Hispanics as **easy targets** because they are known to often **carry** cash.

Banks **across** the nation are **welcoming** the Hispanic population and **setting up** programs specifically for Hispanics and new immigrants.

Bank of America started a **pilot program** in the Los Angeles area **late last year** that **issues credit cards** in California to non-citizens who don't have **Social Security numbers**. The **goal** of the card is **to introduce customers** to banking and **help build** a **credit history**.

Citigroup has had a similar program for years and Wells Fargo & Co. officials have said they are **considering** such a card.

Community banks are **tapping** the Hispanic **market** by **offering video tapes** that **explain topics** such as **insurance**, **investing**, **public schools** and **starting a business**.

Many banks are offering **cost effective alternatives** for **money wires** and making it **easier** and **cheaper** to wire money home. Mitchell Bank in Milwaukee **caters** to an increasingly Mexican customer base. The bank offers the first two wire transfers free, and then charges $2.50 for each additional wire. This is a **significant savings compared to** private wire services.

Many immigrants don't **realize** that you can **open** a bank account without a Social Security number. Banks nationwide **accept** identification issued by Mexican **consulates** to customers who want to open an account but don't have Social Security numbers.

All **throughout** the U.S. banks have been working very hard **in order to promote** their services and **let** the Hispanic population **know** there are many possibilities **besides** cash. The Latin American Council is working **to educate** people on the **value** of **building** a credit history, having a savings account and making investments. These are **things** that will help new immigrants **assimilate** into their **community**.

across: ao longo de
welcoming: dando as boas-vindas
setting up: estabelecendo
pilot program: programa piloto
late last year: final do ano passado
issues: emite
credit cards: cartões de crédito
Social Security numbers: número do seguro social
goal: objetivo
to introduce: introduzir
customers: clientes
help build: ajudar a construir
credit history: histórico de crédito
considering/to consider: considerando/ considerar
tapping/to tap: aproveitando/ aproveitar
market: mercado
offering/to offer oferecendo/oferecer
video tapes: fitas de vídeo
explain topics: explica temas
insurance: seguros
investing: investimento
public schools: escolas públicas
starting a business: montar um negócio
cost effective: custo-benefício
alternatives: alternativas
money wires: capital de giro
easier: mais fácil
cheaper: mais barato
caters/to cater: atende/atender
significant savings: economia significativa
compared to: comparada com
realize/to realize: percebem/perceber
open: abrir
accept/to accept: aceitam/aceitar
consulates: consulados
throughout: por todo
in order to promote: a fim de promover
let ... know: fazer... saber
besides: além de
to educate: para educar
value: valor
building: construir
things: coisas
assimilate: serem absorvidos
community: comunidade

business

job seekers: desempregados
intimidating part: parte intimidante
nerve-racking: angustiante
is unsure: está inseguro
about: sobre
rules: regras
feel/to feel: parece/parecer
uncomfortable: desconfortável
potential hires: empregados potenciais
negotiate/to negotiate: negociar
grateful: gratas
first offer: primeira oferta
fail to/to fail to: deixam de/deixar de
increase/to increase: aumentar
research/to research: pesquise/pesquisar
market value: valor de mercado
gather/to gather: recolha/recolher
current: atual
reach out: entre em contato
same: mesmo
field: campo
pay ranges: variação salarial
check/to check: verifique/verificar
allow/to allow: permite/permitir
to search: pesquisar
review/to review: analisa/analisar
remember/to remember: lembre-se/lembrar
pay/to pay: pagam/pagar
a premium: um valor superior ao nominal
bilingual employees: empregados bilíngues
depending: dependendo
earn/to earn: ganha/ganhar
as much as: até
more than: mais que
never: nunca
discuss/to discuss: discutir
always: sempre
bring up/to bring up: apresentar
broach the subject: mencionar o assunto
risk/to risk: corre o risco/correr o risco
as though: como se
job itself: trabalho em si
propose/to propose: propuser/propor
before hearing: antes de ouvir
price yourself: determinar seu preço
below: abaixo
willing: dispostos
stay silent: fique em silêncio
rush to respond: apressar-se em responder
overly enthusiastic: excessivamente entusiasmado
consider/to consider: considere/considerar

Negotiating Your Salary

For many **job seekers**, salary negotiation can be the most **intimidating part** of the employment process. It can be even more **nerve-racking** if you are a foreign professional who **is unsure about** the **rules** of salary negotiation in the United States.

While it may **feel** like an **uncomfortable** situation, U.S. employers are prepared for **potential hires** to **negotiate** compensation. People often have the tendency to be **grateful** for that **first offer** and **fail to** negotiate, says psychology professor Melanie Domenech-Rodriguez.

By using some simple negotiating techniques, you can **increase** your annual salary.

- **Research** your **market value** — Before your interview, **gather** information about the **current** market value for similar positions.
- **Reach out** to current employees at the company or colleagues in the **same field** for information on **pay ranges**.
- **Check** comparison websites like www.salary.com that **allow** you **to search** salary ranges by profession and location.
- **Review** salary information from the U.S. Bureau of Labor Statistics.

Remember, many companies **pay a premium** for **bilingual employees**. **Depending** on the industry, you could **earn as much as** 20 percent **more than** colleagues who don't speak Spanish.

Never be the first one to **discuss** salary — During the interview process, **always** let the employer be the one to **bring up** compensation. If you **broach the subject** first, you **risk** looking **as though** you are more interested in your paycheck than the **job itself**. If you **propose** an amount **before hearing** the employer's offer, you could **price yourself** well **below** what they were **willing** to pay.

Once you hear their initial offer, **stay silent** —When the employer does propose a salary amount, you shouldn't **rush to respond**. This simple tactic lets the employer know you are not **overly enthusiastic** about the offer.

114 business

Consider (and negotiate!) other types of compensation — Ask about other aspects of the offer **such as** medical and life insurance, 401(k) plans, **vacation time**, **moving expenses**, **flex time** and other benefits. These extras may effectively increase your compensation, or they can be used as **additional points** of negotiation later.

Take time to think — You shouldn't **feel pressured to accept** or **decline** an offer **on the spot**. Thank the recruiter for the offer and request a day or two to consider it.

Ask for more than you **expect to get** — Negotiators **around the world** know the concept of **meeting in the middle**. By asking for a **higher** salary **initially**, you are **creating** a win-win situation – one where **both parties** are able **to give up** something and still **win**. This **is called** a **win-win situation**.

It is always best to negotiate in person, so make an appointment **to meet with** the company representative. Briefly **remind** them:

- That you are **excited** about the opportunity
- How you **plan** on contributing to their success
- The **special skills** you bring, **including** bilingualism/biculturalism

You are then ready to make your **counter-offer**. Although you will be asking for more than you actually expect, make sure that the amount is **within the realm** of possibility based on your market research.

If you have another offer **on the table**, it's okay **to mention it**, **as long as** you are **tactful**. Never **pretend** that you have other offers if you don't.

If you have **gauged** the market **accurately**, the employer should **suggest** a "meet in the middle" figure or **at least** improve their initial offer. In cases where the salary figure is **firm**, suggest additional **perks** or benefits that would make the offer more **appealing** to you.

Get it in writing — Once you've **come to an understanding**, your **last step** is to **make sure** the company **provides** a **written employment agreement** covering not just salary, but **all the points** you negotiated. Do not **skip** this step—the person you negotiated with could leave the company or later **forget** exactly what they **agreed to verbally**.

Congratulations, you just **negotiated your way** to a higher salary!

---

such as: tais como
vacation time: período de férias
moving expenses: gastos de mudança
flex time: horário flexível
additional points: pontos extras
take time: tire um tempo
feel pressured: sentir-se pressionado
to accept: para aceitar
decline: recusar
on the spot: no momento
expect/to expect: espera/esperar
to get: conseguir
around the world: ao redor do mundo
meeting in the middle: denominador comum
higher: mais alto
initially: inicialmente
creating/to create: criando/criar
both parties: ambas as partes
to give up: desistir
win: ganhar
is called/to call: chamado/chamar
win-win situation: situação de ganho mútuo
to meet with: encontrar-se com
remind/to remind: lembre-se/lembrar
excited: entusiasmado
plan/to plan: planeja/planejar
special skills: habilidades especiais
including: incluindo
counter-offer: contraproposta
within the realm: dentro da esfera
on the table: à espera
to mention it: mencioná-la
as long as: contanto que
tactful: discreto
pretend/to pretend: finja/fingir
gauged/to gauge: calculado/calcular
accurately: com precisão
suggest/to suggest: sugerir/sugerir
at least: pelo menos
firm: estável
perks: vantagens
appealing: atraente
get it in writing: obtenha-o por escrito
come to an understanding: chegado a um entendimento
last step: último passo
make sure: certificar-se
provides/to provide: fornece/fornecer
written employment agreement: contrato de trabalho por escrito
all the points: todos os pontos
skip/to skip: pule/pular
forget/to forget: esquecer/esquecer
agreed to verbally: concordaram verbalmente
congratulations: parabéns
negotiated your way: negociou sua parte

Retirement Plans

In the United States, **many** employers **offer** a **company-sponsored retirement plan** for **employees called** a 401(k) plan. **Knowing** some basic information about the 401(k) plan **will help you** do **further research to make** the **best decision** for you and your family.

What is a 401(k) Plan?

A 401(k) plan is a company-sponsored **qualified** retirement plan for employees. Your contributions will be **deducted** from your **paycheck before** taxes are **withheld**.

You will have the option **to decide how much** you want **to contribute** to the plan each **payday**. The money you contribute to the plan is not **subject to** federal and most **state income taxes** until you **withdraw** the **funds**.

Once you are **eligible** to **start participating** in your company's 401(k) plan, **you will be given** a list of **stocks**, **bonds** and/or **money market** funds in which **you can invest**. There are limits **regarding** the **amount** you can invest.

Your contributions will be deducted from your paycheck **before** taxes are withheld. Depending on your income and **tax bracket**, this pretax deduction can **be like getting** a 25-percent **rate of return** on your **investment**. These contributions are then invested into the funds **you select**.

Your company matches your contribution to the 401(k) plan.

If you are lucky enough to work for a company that provides the benefit of a **company match**, it's like **earning free money**. **For example**, if you **choose** to contribute 2% of your **salary**, your company also contributes 2%. Your employer **will match** a maximum **amount**.

Withdrawing Money from a 401(k)

For people 70½ **years old or older**, the law currently requires that you **begin** withdrawing **money** from your 401(k). You can **defer** this withdrawal **rule** if you are **still** a **full-time** employee with the company sponsoring your 401(k). If you are 59½ or older, you may begin withdrawals **without** any **early withdrawal penalty**. You are also **exempt** from this penalty if you are over age 55 and have been **terminated** by your company or if you **become totally disabled**.

About 85 **percent** of 401(k) plans **allow** employees **to take loans against** the money in their **account**, up to a maximum of 50 percent of their **savings**. The money you **borrow is not subject to** the 10 percent penalty **as long as** you **pay it back** (with interest) **within the time established** by your employer's plan.

If you do take a loan from your 401(k), you will have up to 5 years **to repay** the loan. But if you **leave** your job, it **must be repaid within** 30 days. Any amount that you **fail to** repay is subject to the 10 percent early withdrawal penalty and taxes. And the interest? The interest you pay **goes directly** into your account—you are paying it to yourself!

Get Started

A 401(k) plan is an important part of **retirement planning**. **You should learn** everything you can from your employer about the plan that is offered. **Gather** information on **vesting**, **contribution limits**, and matching funds. Research all available information on the funds offered for investing. **Track** your investments **regularly** and **ask for assistance** if you feel your investment options **aren't performing** satisfactorily.

---

years old or older: de idade ou mais velhas
begin/to begin: comece/começar
money: dinheiro
defer/to defer: deferir/deferir
rule: regra
still: ainda
full-time: tempo integral
without: sem
early withdrawal penalty: penalização por aposentadoria antecipada (dinheiro)
exempt: isento
terminated/to terminate: despedido/despedir
become/to become: tornar-se/tornar
totally: totalmente
disabled: incapacitado
about: a respeito de
percent: porcento
allow/to allow: permitem/permitir
to take: tomar
loans: empréstimos
against: contra
account: contas
savings: economias
borrow/to borrow: toma emprestado/tomar emprestado
is not subject to: não é sujeito a
as long as: desde que
pay it back: devolva
within the time established: dentro do prazo estabelecido
to repay: para devolver (dinheiro)
leave/to leave: deixas/deixar
must be repaid within: deve ser devolvido dentro de
fail to/to fail to do something: não conseguir/não conseguir fazer algo
goes/to go: vai/ir
directly: diretamente
retirement planning: plano de aposentadoria
you should learn: deveria aprender
gather/to gather: junta/juntar
vesting: aquisição de direito a pensão
contribution limits: limites de contribuição
track/to track: controla/controlar
regularly: regularmente
ask for/to ask for: peça/pedir
assistance: assistência, ajuda
aren't performing/to perform: não estão rendendo/render

subtle: sutis
not-so-subtle: nem tão sutis
between: entre
the way: a forma
employment interviews: entrevistas de emprego
conducted/to conduct: conduzidas/conduzir
top ten tips: dez melhores dicas
avoid: evitar
misconceptions: ideias equivocadas
pitfalls: armadilhas
job: trabalho
acing: conseguir resultados fenomenais, triunfar
take credit/to take credit: receba o mérito/receber o mérito
accomplishments: resultados
expects you: espera que você
"toot you own horn": literalmente: "toque sua própria buzina"/fale dos seus resultados
can be awkward: pode resultar incômodo ou embaraçoso
group-oriented: com orientacão grupal
crucial part: parte crucial
discussing: discutir
viewed/to view: visto/ver
arrogant: arrogante
egotistical: egoista
in fact: de fato
point out/to point out: indica/indicar
solo successes: resultados próprios
will assume/to assume: assumirão/assumir
to talk about: para falar sobre
eye contact: contato visual
picturing you as: imaginarão você como
co-worker: colega de trabalho
expect/to expect: esperam/esperar
look them in the eye: olhe-os nos olhos
act: atuar
shows confidence: mostra confiança
failing: falhar
could be interpreted: poderia ser interpretado
sign: sinal, indicação
untruthful: mentiroso
get to the point: ir direto ao ponto
focus/to focus: foque/focar
relevant facts: feitos relevantes
busy: ocupados
time is short: há pouco tempo
to shine: brilhar
brief time: breve tempo
in front of them: frente a eles
personal issues: questões pessoais
to break the ice: para romper o gelo
tell me: diga-me
are not asking/to ask: não estão perguntando/perguntar
childhood: infância
to hear: escutar
the jobs you've had: os trabalhos que você teve
past: passado

118 business

Mastering the Interview

There are some **subtle**—and some **not-so-subtle**—differences **between the way employment interviews** are **conducted** in the United States and in Latin America.

Here are the **top ten tips** from Hispanic job board LatPro.com to help you **avoid** possible **misconceptions** and cultural **pitfalls** so you can get the **job** you want!

Top Ten Tips for **Acing** your U.S. Job Interview

1. Take Credit for your Professional Accomplishments
An employer **expects you** to "**toot your own horn,**" says Graciela Kenig, founder and president of LatinoWorkforce.com. This **can be awkward** for Latinos, who are more community and **group-oriented**, but it's a **crucial part** of the U.S. interview.

Discussing your individual accomplishments won't be **viewed** as **arrogant** or **egotistical**. **In fact**, if you don't **point out** your **solo successes**, employers **will assume** you don't have significant contributions **to talk about**.

2. Make Eye Contact
Interviewers will be **picturing you** as a potential **co-worker** during the interview. They **expect** you **to look them in the eye** and **act** like a colleague. In the U.S. making good eye contact **shows confidence**; **failing** to look your interviewer in the eye will not only make them uncomfortable, it **could be interpreted** as a **sign** that you are being evasive or **untruthful**.

3. Be Direct
In the U.S. interview you should **get to the point** quickly and **focus** only on the **relevant facts**. Getting directly to the matter at hand may seem rude or abrupt to a Latino, but it won't to the person doing the interview. They are **busy**, **time is short**, and you need **to shine** during the **brief time** you have **in front of them**.

4. Focus on Professional, not Personal Issues
Interviewers may ask a question just **to break the ice,** says Nelson De Leon, bilingual recruiting consultant and the owner and founder of America At Work.com. When an interviewer asks you to "**tell me** something about yourself," they **are not asking** about your **childhood**, your dogs or your family. They want **to hear** about you in relation to **the jobs you've had** in the **past** and the job you want.

5. Get Rid of the "Yes Syndrome"
The Yes Syndrome is something De Leon identifies as an idiosyncrasy of Hispanic culture. As an interviewer is talking, the recruit may be **nodding his head**, saying yes **over and over**, but that doesn't necessarily mean they've **understood** everything. It does mean they've **heard**; they are **listening**, and they won't interrupt for fear of seeming rude. "**It's okay** to **ask questions**," says De Leon. It **does not make you look stupid**, as some **fear**. It makes you look and **sound engaged** in the interview.

6. Don't Be Passive
If you are **too humble** or too reserved, you may appear **uninterested** in the job, warns De Leon. Once you start asking questions, it shows you have a **good grasp** of the job **at hand**. The **smartest** people don't give the best answers, they ask the best questions, showing potential employers they can **identify** problems.

7. Beware Tu versus Usted
Latinos are **aware** of the **formality** of "usted," but because English only uses "you," be **conscious** that you **don't get too familiar** with your interviewer. While a recruit should not be subservient, there should still be respect. If you **happen to be** interviewing in Spanish, **stick with** "usted" during the interview. Don't lapse into using "tú" for the entire corporate culture.

8. Dress Conservatively
Even if the **day-to-day dress** of regular employees **is casual**, you should **choose** conservative **business attire** for your interview. A professional appearance **shows** that you **respect** the interviewer and **are serious about** the available position. Avoid anything that **will detract** from the interview, **including** too much **jewelry**, perfume or **aftershave**.

9. Don't be Discouraged if the Interviewer Seems Impersonal
Employers who don't ask about **your background**, your family, your kids and your church **are not being rude**, and it **does not mean** they **don't like you** as a potential employee. In the U.S., many personal questions like these are **prohibited** during an interview.

10. Research the company before your interview – and don't forget your Hispanic connections!
It's a **big world**, but cultural connections can make the world **seem smaller**. **In addition to** more traditional research methods, reaching out to fellow Latinos can **give you valuable insight** into a company. Within the **close-knit** Hispanic community, **chances are good** that you can **find** someone who has already interviewed with or **worked for** a particular company. **All you have to do** is ask!

---

get rid of: livre-se de
nodding his head: concordando com a cabeça
over and over: várias vezes
understood/to understand: entendido/entender
heard/to hear: escutado/escutar
listening/to listen: escutando/escutar
it's okay: está bem
ask questions: perguntar
does not make you look stupid: não faz você parecer estúpido
fear/to fear: temem/temer
sound/to sound: soe/soar
engaged: interessado
passive: passivo
too humble: muito humilde
uninterested: desinteressado
good grasp: boa compreensão
at hand: em mão (este trabalho)
smartest: mais inteligentes
identify: identificar
beware: tome cuidado
aware: conscientes
formality: formalidade
conscious: consciente
don't get too familiar: não trate... com excessiva confiança
happen to be: se por acaso estiver
stick with: manter junto
dress conservatively: vista-se de forma tradicional
day-to-day dress: vestimenta diária
is casual: é informal
choose/to choose: escolhe/escolher
business attire: traje de negócios
shows/to show: mostra/mostrar
respect/to respect: respeita/respeitar
are serious about: tem intenções sérias sobre
will detract: desmerecer
including: incluindo
jewelry: joias
aftershave: loção pós-barba
don't be discouraged: não se desanime
seems/to seem: parecer
your background: sua origem
are not being rude: não estão sendo grosseiros
does not mean: não significa
don't like you: não gostam de você
prohibited: proibidas
research/to research: investigue/investigar
don't forget: não esqueça
connections: conexões
big world: mundo grande
seem smaller: parecer menor
in addition to: além disso
give you valuable insights: dá-lhe uma valiosa perspectiva
close-knit: muito unida
chances are good: as chances são boas
find/to find: encontrar/encontrar
worked for: trabalhou para
all you have to do: tudo o que você tem de fazer

business 119

Test Your Comprehension

Introduction to Taxes, page 108

1. Quem é o responsável pelo recolhimento dos impostos?

2. Para quem a Receita Federal repassa o dinheiro dos impostos?

3. O que acontece se você não pagar os impostos?

Entrepreneurship, page 110

1. O que muitos empresários novos precisam para desenvolver seus negócios?

2. Além dos empréstimos obtidos através de agências governamentais, onde mais se pode conseguir um empréstimo?

3. O que são os gastos gerais baixos?

Banking in America, page 112

1. Por que muitos imigrantes preferem pagamento à vista em vez de usarem um banco?

2. Por que é arriscado viver num mundo de pagamentos à vista?

3. O Banco da América começou um programa que emite cartões de crédito na Califórnia a não cidadãos que não têm número do seguro social. Qual é o objetivo deste cartão?

Negotiating Your Salary, page 114

1. Dependendo da indústria, quanto mais uma pessoa poderia ganhar como empregado bilíngue?

2. O que o artigo sugere que você faça após o empregador ter feito a oferta inicial de salário?

3. Uma vez que tenha concordado com o salário, qual é o último passo que não pode faltar?

Teste sua Compreensão

Retirement Plans, page 116

1. O que é o Plano 401(k)?

2. Ao que não está sujeito o dinheiro atribuído ao plano?

3. Qual é a parte importante do planejamento para a aposentadoria?

Mastering the Interview, page 118

1. Verdadeiro ou falso? Discutir suas conquistas pessoais será visto como arrogância e egoísmo.

2. O que significa fazer um bom contato visual?

3. O que acontece quando se faz perguntas durante a entrevista?

4. Se a entrevista for feita em português, usar "você" ou "senhor"?

5. Por que não são feitas muitas perguntas pessoais durante uma entrevista?

Informações Importantes!

Os artigos *Negotiating Your Salary* e *Mastering the Interview* foram fornecidos pelo **LatPro.com**, o site mais visitado pelos hispânicos e profissionais bilíngues a procura de trabalho. Desde 1997 o LatPro tem ajudado os hispânicos desempregados a encontrar emprego nas melhores companhias por todos os Estados Unidos e América Latina. Além dos avisos de trabalhos atuais, este site de emprego (vencedor de vários prêmios e disponível em inglês, espanhol e português) oferece amplo assessoramento para os hispânicos que estão procurando emprego. Visite o **LatPro.com** para ler mais artigos relacionados com a sua carreira, conselhos para seu currículo e recursos para profissionais hispânicos.

The future belongs to those
who believe in the beauty of their dreams.

Eleanor Roosevelt

Empowerment

Citizenship

With the exception of Native Americans, the United States is a nation of people who **left** their **home country looking for** a **better life**. The **population** of the United States is **made up of** a **mixture** of people from different countries and is **sometimes called** a "melting pot." **Although** your **neighbor** or **co-worker** may have been **born** in the United States, **at some point**, that person's family left their home country and **came** to the United States.

Living in the United States doesn't **automatically** make one an American citizen. Residents of the United States can be **aliens**, **nationals**, or **citizens**.

- Aliens: Aliens are people **who have left** a foreign country to live in the United States. They have **some of the same freedoms** and **legal rights** as U.S. citizens, but they **cannot vote** in **elections**.

- Nationals: American nationals are **natives** of American territorial possessions. They have all the legal protections which citizens have, but they **do not have** the full **political rights** of U.S. citizens.

- Citizens: Persons born in the U.S. are citizens of the United States. Persons born in other countries who **want to become** citizens must **apply for** and **pass** a **citizenship test**. Those who become citizens **in this manner** are **naturalized** citizens.

Over time, most immigrants become U.S. citizens. The process, **however**, is not an **easy** one. It **involves learning** how **to speak, read**, and **write ordinary** English; learning about the history and government of the United States and **patiently wading through** a bureaucratic process.

Community-based organizations and local government agencies have **developed** materials and **techniques** to help immigrants become **full participants** in our **society**.

---

with the exception of: com exceção de
left/to leave: deixaram/deixar
home country: país de origem
looking for/to look for: buscando/buscar
better life: vida melhor
population: população
made up of: composta
mixture: mistura
sometimes: às vezes
called/to call: chamada/chamar
although: embora
neighbor: vizinho
co-worker: colega de trabalho
born: nascido
at some point: em algum momento
came/to come: veio/vir
living: viver
automatically: automaticamente
aliens: estrangeiros
nationals: nacionais
citizens: cidadãos
who have left: que deixaram
some of the same: algumas das mesmas
freedoms: liberdades
legal rights: direitos legais
cannot vote: não podem votar
elections: eleições
natives: nativos
do not have: não têm
political rights: direitos políticos
want/to want: querem/querer
to become: tornar-se
apply for: requerer
pass: passar em
citizenship test: teste de cidadania
in this manner: desta maneira
naturalized/to naturalize: naturalizados/naturalizar
over time: com o tempo
however: contudo
easy: fácil
involves/to involve: envolve/envolver
learning: aprender
to speak: falar
read: ler
write: escrever
ordinary: básico
patiently: pacientemente
wading through: abrir caminho através de
developed/to develop: desenvolveram/desenvolver
techniques: técnicas
full participants: participantes com plenos direitos
society: sociedade

Civic Participation

Participation in America's **civic life** is something that **may at first seem** like a **luxury** for immigrants. As people **become rooted** in their **adopted country**, most immigrants become citizens. **Beyond that, voter registration**, voting, and other forms of civic participation **vary**. Even **as they become** a **larger portion** of our population, new Americans are **under-represented** in our civic life.

This **is beginning to change**! There are a **number** of groups **around** the **country** who **help** immigrants **understand** our civic culture and help them **get involved**. Some groups **regularly** hold voter registration **drives**. In the process, they are helping to **transform** our civic culture. As the number of new citizens **continues to grow**, our civic culture will grow **as well**—**adapting** to **desires** and **needs** of immigrants who have become Americans by **choice**.

The **following** organizations **provide outstanding** civic participation programs and information:

- National Association of Latino Elected Officials: www.naleo.org
- Democracy Collaborative: www.democracycollaborative.org

QUICK FACTS
Hispanic Immigrants and the Electorate
- **Over** 5.9 million Latinos participated in the presidential election in 2000.
- In the **last decade**, the number of **voting-age** Latinos **rose** by 47%. Latinos **as a percentage** of the voters **nationwide** went from 5% in 1996 to 7% in 2000.

Immigrants as **Volunteers** and **Philanthropists**
- Hispanic Americans 45 and **older** volunteer the **most hours** per month. They are the **most likely** to provide help to immigrants in this country and **send** money to help people in other countries.
- In 2001 Hispanic Americans sent **remittances** to Latin America and the Caribbean totaling $23 billion.

Immigrants in the **Military**
- 1.1 million—the number of Latino **veterans** of the U.S. **armed forces**.
- **About** 63,000 people of Hispanic origin were on **active duty** in 2002 in the U.S.

---

civic life: vida civil
may at first seem: pode parecer a princípio
luxury: luxo
become rooted: tornaram-se enraizadas
adopted country: país adotivo
beyond that: além disto
voter registration: título de eleitor
vary/to vary: variam/variar
as they become: à medida que se tornam
larger portion: porção maior
under-represented: pouco representados
is beginning to change: começando a mudar
number: número
around: ao redor
country: país
help/to help: ajudam/ajudar
understand: entender
get involved/to involve: envolver-se/envolver
regularly: regularmente
drives: campanhas
transform: transformar
continues/to continue: continua/continuar
to grow: a crescer
as well: também
adapting/to adapt: adaptando-se/adaptar
desires: desejos
needs: necessidades
choice: escolha
following: seguintes
provide/to provide: fornecem/fornecer
outstanding: excelentes
over: mais de
last decade: última década
voting-age: em idade de votar
rose/to rise: aumentou/aumentar
as a percentage: como uma porcentagem
nationwide: por todo o país
volunteers: voluntários
philanthropists: filantropos
older: mais velhos
most hours: maior número de horas
most likely: mais prováveis
send: enviar
remittances: quantias
military: forças armadas
veterans: veteranos
armed forces: forças armadas
about: cerca de, aproximadamente
active duty: serviço militar obrigatório

empowerment 125

Empowerment with Education

Latinos are one of our nation's **largest** ethnic minorities and the **fastest-growing segment** of our population.

Between 2000 and 2005 the Hispanic population in the United States **grew from** 12.5 percent of the **overall** population **to about** 14 percent. **All indications** are that this **trend will continue**. **As of** 2005, there were over 42 million Hispanics living in the United States. The U.S. Census Bureau **estimates** that number **will increase** to 63 million by 2030.

As the Hispanic population continues to increase, education is a **key issue**. **Although** a growing segment of the Hispanic population is achieving **educational excellence**, reports from the U.S. Census Bureau **reveal** a **startling discrepancy** in the educational **attainment** of Hispanics **compared to** other groups:

- In 2000, 36 percent of Hispanic high school graduates ages 18 to 24 **enrolled in colleges** and universities, compared to 44 percent of non-Hispanic whites.
- In 2000, Hispanic students **accounted for** 7 percent of students enrolled at **4-year institutions**.
- About 12 percent of Hispanic adults **currently** have a **bachelor's degree**, **compared with** 30.5 percent of non-Hispanic whites.

There are **several** organizations that **might help you** in your **search** for **scholarships** or **financial aid**. **In order to most effectively plan** your search, you should **contact** the necessary organizations **up to a year in advance**. Your **first step** should be **to decide** on a **few schools** and contact their financial aid **offices, asking about** any scholarships or financial aid they offer to **minority students**.

Be sure to explore all financial aid and scholarship possibilities, **not just** those opportunities **targeted specifically** towards minorities. The federal government has several major financial aid **packages**, **work-study programs**, and **grants**. You may contact their educational **hotline** at 1-(800) 433-3243.

The Hispanic Scholarship Fund (HSF) is the nation's **leading organization** supporting Hispanic higher education. HSF **was founded** in 1975 with a vision of **strengthening the country** by **advancing** college education among Hispanic Americans. **In support of** its mission **to double the rate of** Hispanics **earning** college degrees, HSF provides the Latino community with **more** college scholarships and educational **outreach support than any other** organization in the country. **In addition**, HSF **launched** the Hispanic Scholarship Fund Institute **to create public partnerships** in support of its work. **During** its 31-year history, HSF **has awarded** more than 78,000 scholarships to Latinos from all 50 states, Puerto Rico, the U.S. Virgin Islands and Guam. HSF **scholars have attended** more than 1,700 colleges and universities. To read more, go to www.hsf.net.

The Hispanic College Fund **provides talented** and **underprivileged** Hispanic **youth** with mentors, **resources** and scholarships. For more information, go to www.hispanicfund.org.

The Hispanic Bar Association of D.C. is a separate **non-profit entity**. First- and second-year law students attending D.C.-area law schools are **eligible to apply** for the fellowship. To read more, go to www.hbadc.org.

The Association of Latino Professionals in Finance and Accounting (ALPFA) provides many programs and **benefits** to **aspiring** Latino students interested in **accounting**, **finance** or related **career** professions. **To learn more**, go to www.alpfa.org.

---

be sure to: certifique-se de
explore: explorar
not just: não apenas
targeted specifically: dirigidas especificamente
packages: pacotes
work-study programs: programas de trabalho e estudo
grants: auxílios
hotline: linha de acesso direto
leading organization: organização líder
was founded/to found: foi fundada/fundar
strengthening: fortalecimento
the country: do país
advancing: progredindo
in support of: em apoio a
to double the rate of: para duplicar a taxa de
earning: que conseguem
more... than any other: mais... que qualquer outra
outreach: alcance
support: apoio
in addition: além disso
launched/to launch: lançou/lançar
to create: para criar
public: públicas
partnerships: parcerias
during: durante
has awarded/to award: recompensou/recompensar
scholars: bolsa
have attended/to attend: auxiliou/auxiliar
provides/to provide: fornece/fornecer
talented: talentosos
underprivileged: desfavorecidos
youth: jovens
resources: recursos
non-profit entity: entidade sem fins lucrativos
eligible: qualificados
to apply: para solicitar
benefits: benefícios
aspiring: aspirantes
accounting: contabilidade
finance: administração de finanças
career: carreiras
to learn more: para aprender mais

empowerment

world of opportunity: mundo de oportunidades
across: por todo
specialty: especialização
credit classes: matérias obrigatórias na grade
non-credit: eletivas
a host of: um monte de
options: opções
there are over: há mais de
open admissions policies: políticas de admissão abertas
low tuitions: matrículas com custo mais baixo
represent/to represent: representam/representar
rich diversity: rica diversidade
include/to include: incluem/incluir
mix of ages: mistura de idades
variety: variedade
ethnic: etnias
backgrounds: origens
numerous: numerosos
entire: completos
focused: focados
are provided/to provide: são fornecidas/fornecer
service: serviço
low cost: baixo custo
free: grátis
for example: por exemplo
are offered/to offer: são oferecidas/oferecer
all levels: todos os níveis
morning: manhã
evening: anoitecer
as an added bonus: como um bônus extra
free babysitting: serviços gratuitos de babá
in addition: além disso
job training: capacitação trabalhista
finding a job: conseguir um trabalho
also: também
offers/to offer: oferece/oferecer
to assist: para ajudar
filling out/to fill out: preenchimento/preencher
application forms: formulários de requerimento
passing/to pass: passar/aprovar
citizenship: cidadania
test: teste
interview: entrevista

Community Colleges

There is a **world of opportunity** at community colleges **across** the United States. You can choose from **specialty** career training, college-**credit classes**, English as a Second Language, **non-credit** classes, and **a host of** fun personal enrichment **options**.

There are over 1200 public and independent community colleges in the United States educating over 11.6 million students. Through **open admissions policies** and **low tuitions**, the students **represent** the **rich diversity** of the United States. Classes **include** a **mix of ages** along with a **variety** of **ethnic** and socioeconomic **backgrounds**.

English as a Second Language (ESL)

Numerous community colleges have **entire** departments **focused** on English as a Second Language. These classes **are provided** as a **service** to the community for a **low cost**, or **free**.

For example, in the San Diego Community College District all ESL classes are free. Classes **are offered** in **all levels** from **morning** to the **evening**. **As an added bonus**, they also provide **free babysitting** through the Community-Based English Tutoring Program. **In addition**, a Vocational English as a Second Language (VESL) series is offered for **job training** or **finding a job**. The San Diego district **also offers** citizenship classes **to assist** in **filling out application forms** and **passing** the **citizenship test** and **interview**.

128 empowerment

College and Workforce Training Credits

Attaining credits **that transfer** for a **baccalaureate degree** continues to be the goal for a **large segment** of the community college population. Many **success stories** got their **start** at community colleges, including **members of Congress**, **astronauts**, actors, scientists, **business leaders** and philanthropists.

Many others receive an **Associate Degree**, which is a **two-year certificate**. The five **hottest** community college programs are **registered nursing**, **law enforcement**, **licensed practical nursing**, **radiology**, and **computer technologies**.

Personal Enrichment

Have you ever **wanted to learn** about **photography** or **wines**? **How about** mastering using your **personal home computer**, or **feeling more savvy** with your personal **finances**? Community colleges offer an **exciting range** of non-credit classes **to enrich** your life and world.

So what are you **waiting for**? **Contact** your local community college today, and ask them **to mail** their course listing to find your **personal goldmine** of opportunity.

Go to www.aacc.nche.edu or call 202-728-0200 **to find a location** in your **neighborhood**.

---

attaining: obter
that transfer: que sejam transferidos
baccalaureate degree: bacharelado
large segment: grande segmento
success stories: histórias de sucesso
start: começo
members of Congress: membros do Congresso
astronauts: astronautas
business leaders: líderes empresariais
many others: muitos outros
associate degree: título de sócio
two-year certificate: certificado de dois anos
hottest: mais populares
registered: diplomada
nursing: enfermeira
law enforcement: aplicação da lei
licensed: licenciada
practical nursing: auxiliar de enfermagem
radiology: radiologia
computer technologies: tecnologias da computação
wanted to learn: quis aprender
photography: fotografia
wines: vinhos
how about: que tal
personal home computer: computador pessoal
feeling: sentir-se
more savvy: mais experiente
finances: finanças
exciting range: emocionante variedade
to enrich: enriquecer
so: então
waiting for/to wait for: esperando/esperar
contact/to contact: entre em contato/entrar em contato
to mail/to mail: enviem por correio/enviar por correio
personal goldmine: mina de ouro pessoal
to find: encontrar
a location: um lugar
neighborhood: bairro

empowerment

Helping Children Succeed

When **parents** are **involved** in their **children's education**, kids **do better** in **school**. In **numerous studies, researchers report** the importance for parents **to be actively involved** in their child's education. Why is **parental involvement** important?

- The family makes **critical contributions** to **student achievement** from preschool through high school. A home **environment** that **encourages** learning is **more important** to student achievement than **income**, **education level** or cultural **background**.

- **Reading aloud** to children is the most important activity that parents can do **to increase** their child's **chances** of **reading success**.

- When children and parents **talk regularly** about school, children **perform** better **academically**.

- Three kinds of parental involvement at home are **consistently associated with** higher student achievement: actively organizing and **monitoring** a child's time, helping with **homework** and **discussing school matters**.

- **The earlier** that parent involvement begins in a child's educational process, **the more powerful** the effects.

- **Positive results** of parental involvement **include improved** student achievement, **reduced absenteeism**, and improved **behavior**.

COMMUNICATING WITH TEACHERS

Good communication **between** parents and **teachers** has many **benefits**. When parents and teachers **share information**, children learn more and parents and teachers **feel more supported**. Good communication **can help create** positive **feelings** between teachers and parents.

---

parents: pais
involved: envolvidos
children's education: educação dos filhos
do better: têm mais êxito
school: escola
numerous studies: muitos estudos
researchers: pesquisadores
report/to report: informam/informar
to be actively involved: estarem ativamente envolvidos
parental involvement: participação dos pais
critical contributions: contribuições fundamentais
student achievement: realizações do estudante
environment: ambiente
encourages/to encourage: encoraja/encorajar
more important: mais importante
income: rendimentos
education level: nível educacional
background: origem
reading aloud: ler em voz alta
to increase: para aumentar
chances: probabilidades
reading success: êxito na leitura
talk/to talk: conversam/conversar
regularly: regularmente
perform/to perform: desempenham-se/desempenhar
academically: academicamente
consistently: constantemente
associated with: associados com
monitoring: controlar
homework: dever de casa
discussing: discutindo
school matters: assuntos da escola
the earlier... the more powerful: quanto mais cedo... mais poderosos
positive: positivos
results: resultados
include/to include: incluem/incluir
improved: aperfeiçoado
reduced absenteeism: redução de ausências
behavior: comportamento
between: entre
teachers: professores
benefits: benefícios
share/to share: compartilham/compartilhar
information: informação
feel/to feel: sentem-se/sentir-se
more supported: mais apoiados
can help: pode ajudar
create/to create: criar/criar
feelings: sentimentos

Parent-teacher communication can be **hard** when parents feel **uncomfortable** in school and **don't speak** English well. **Fortunately**, both parents and teachers have **developed ways** to make communication **easier**.

Here are some ideas to help **overcome** the language **barrier**.

- **Spend time** at the school. A mother **speaks** Spanish and her child's teacher does not. The mother feels **comfortable** at the school, but uncomfortable working in the **classroom**. She **still helps** with school events by doing things like **decorating** the school. Helping out in the school **lets everyone see** that **she cares about** her child and the school. She **stays involved** and **knows what is going on.**

- **Find someone** who speaks your language. Find another parent or teacher in the school who speaks Spanish and is bilingual. They can **listen** to parents' **concerns** or **translate** during parent-teacher conferences. **Another option** is **to bring** a bilingual friend or family member to school to help with translation.

- **Ask** about **language classes** at the school. **Sometimes** schools can help parents learn the new language. One parent **took** English as a Second Language (ESL) lessons **right in her** child's school.

- **Volunteer** at home. At some schools, you can help with a **class project** at home. Teachers **will appreciate** your involvement and your children **will see** that you care about their school.

Teachers **agree** with the importance of parent's participation with their schools. Teachers **have suggested** that **greater support** from parents and the community would make education a **high priority**.

One teacher **said**, "If every family **valued** education and **let their children know** that, there would be a **completely** different **attitude** towards education. Parents are their child's **first teachers** and **should never stop playing that role**."

---

hard: difícil
uncomfortable: desconfortáveis
don't speak: não falam
fortunately: felizmente
developed ways: desenvolveram formas
easier: más fácil
overcome: superar
barrier: barreira
spend time: passe um tempo
speaks/to speak: fala/falar
comfortable: confortável
classroom: sala de aula
still helps: ainda ajuda
decorating: decorar
lets everyone see: deixa que todos vejam
she cares about: ela se importa
stays/to stay: fica/ficar
involved: envolvida
knows/to know: sabe/saber
what is going on: o que está acontecendo
find someone: encontre alguém
listen: escutar
concerns: preocupações
translate/to translate: traduzir/traduzir
another option: outra opção
to bring: trazer
ask/to ask: pergunte/perguntar
language classes: aulas de idiomas
sometimes: às vezes
took/to take: recebeu/receber
right in her: na sua própria escola
volunteer: voluntarie-se
class project: projeto de aula
will appreciate/to appreciate: apreciarão/apreciar
will see/to see: verão/ver
agree: concordam
have suggested/to suggest: tem sugerido/sugerir
greater support: maior apoio
high priority: alta prioridade
said/to say: disse/dizer
valued/to value: valorizasse/valorizar
let their children know: deixasse seus filhos saberem
completely: completamente
attitude: atitude
first teachers: primeiros professores
should never stop: nunca deveriam parar de
playing that role: desempenhar este papel

empowerment 131

requests: pedidos
bilingual employees: empregados bilíngues
growing/to grow: crescendo/crescer
greatest need: maior necessidade
consumer services industry: indústria de prestação de serviços ao consumidor
such areas as: áreas como
retailing: varejo
communications: meios de comunicação
banking: setor bancário
to fill positions: preencher cargos
call center staff: pessoal de central de atendimento
medical: (pessoal) médico
legal: legal
administrative staff: pessoal administrativo
receptionists: recepcionistas
the need: a necessidade
can vary: pode variar
depending on: dependendo de
in general: em geral
most highly requested: mais solicitado
language: idioma
million-plus: mais de... milhões
still growing: ainda crescendo
however: contudo
there is: há
increasing need: crescente necessidade
usually: geralmente
first choice: primeira escolha
will continue to be: continuará sendo
Spanish-speaking: falantes de espanhol
to find: para encontrar
business: negócios
background: história
fluent: fluente
recruiters: recrutadores
resourceful: rico em recursos
employers: empregadores
have joined/to join: uniram-se/unir
now: agora
participate/to participate: participam/participar
all of these: todas estas

Maximizing Your Talents

Requests for **bilingual employees** are **growing** in the United States. The **greatest need** for bilingual employees is in the **consumer services industry** in **such areas as retailing**, **communications**, and **banking**. Bilingual employees are needed **to fill positions** as **call center staff**, **medical** and **legal administrative staff**, and **receptionists**.

The need for bilingual employees **can vary depending on** what area of the country a company serves. **In general**, Spanish is the **most highly requested language**, **due to** the 40 **million-plus** Hispanic population, which is **still growing**. **However, there is** an **increasing need** for Chinese and Vietnamese on the West Coast and for French and Portuguese on the East Coast, due to increasing populations from these immigrant groups.

Spanish is **usually** the **first choice** for companies requesting a bilingual employee. As the Hispanic population grows, there is, and **will continue to be**, a need for **Spanish-speaking** employees.

FINDING THE BILINGUAL EMPLOYEE

To find employees who have a **business background** and are **fluent** in Spanish, some **recruiters** have become **resourceful**. **Employers have joined** and **now participate** in such organizations as the Latin American Association, the Hispanic Chamber of Commerce and the National Society of Hispanic MBAs.

All of these organizations are a **valuable** resource **since** they not only have fluent Spanish speakers, but also **candidates** with the **required** educational background and **business skills** needed.

TESTING FOR LANGUAGE AND CULTURAL UNDERSTANDING

Many employees **say** they are bilingual, **but** are they bilingual in **financial transactions** or **technical terminology**? **To verify** that a bilingual employee **not only** speaks a second language fluently **but also** speaks with knowledge of the **proper vocabulary** for the **position**, many recruiters **test** candidates **during** the **interview** process.

Even though a **prospective** employee **might be fluent** in the language needed, **it does not mean** they have the **necessary skills** required for the position. Prospective employees not only have to be fluent in Spanish, but they also must speak English, **along with** having **previous work experience**.

THE FUTURE

As the **purchasing power** of immigrants across the United States grows, companies **are recognizing** that they must have a **workforce** that **reflects** their **consumer bases**. Bilingual employees **must have both** language and **cultural awareness**. Employers are **looking for** the **best talent** they can for any position **that is open**, and **they know** that the employee that is fluent in a second language **does create an advantage**.

---

valuable: valiosas
since: desde
candidates: candidatos
required: requeridos
business skills: habilidades empresariais
testing: testes
understanding: compreensão
say/to say: dizem/dizer
but: mas
financial transactions: transações financeiras
technical terminology: terminologia técnica
to verify: para verificar
not only...but also: não só... como também
proper vocabulary: vocabulário adequado
position: posto
test/to test: testam/testar
during: durante
interview: entrevista
even though: embora
prospective: potencial, provável
might be fluent: possa ser fluente
it does not mean: isto não significa
necessary skills: habilidades necessárias
along with: junto com
previous work experience: experiência de trabalho prévia
purchasing power: poder de compra
are recognizing/to recognize: estão reconhecendo/reconhecer
workforce: mão de obra
reflects/to reflect: reflete/refletir
consumer bases: bases de consumidores
must have: devem ter
both: ambos
cultural awareness: consciência cultural
looking for/to look for: procurando/procurar
best talent: melhor talento
that is open: que esteja aberto
they know/to know: eles sabem/saber
does create an advantage: criam uma vantagem

empowerment

during: durante
immigration process: processo de imigração
someone: alguém
may need help: pode precisar de ajuda
understanding: para entender
laws: leis
while: enquanto que
can feel: pode parecer
overwhelming: opressivo
daunting: amedrontador
proper research: pesquisa adequada
will find/to find: descobrirá/descobrir
abundance: abundância
along the way: durante o processo
lawyer: advogado
graduated/to graduate: graduou/graduar
licensed: licenciado/a
to practice law: para praticar a advocacia
regulated/to regulate: regulado/regular
obtain: obter
legal status: estado legal
represent you: representá-lo
court: tribunal
following ways: seguintes formas
analyze: analisar
facts of your case: fatos do seu caso
explain: explicar
benefits: benefícios
you may be eligible: você possa ter direito
recommend: recomendar
best ways: melhores maneiras
complete: completar
submit: apresentar
applications: requerimentos
stay current: ficar atualizado
that affect you: que afetam você
avoid: evitar
delays: atrasos
discuss: discutir
status: situação
speak for you: falar por você
file: propor em juízo
appeals: apelações
waivers: renúncias
utilize: usar
how do you find: como encontrar
online: virtual
directory: diretório
who are members: que são membros
free legal services: serviços legais gratuitos
self-help: autoajuda

Legal Resources

During the **immigration process,** you or **someone** in your family **may need help understanding** the many immigration **laws. While** the process **can feel overwhelming** and **daunting,** with the **proper research** you **will find** there is an **abundance** of legal resources and organizations to help you **along the way.**

An immigration **lawyer** has studied the immigration laws of the United States and has **graduated** from law school. He or she is **licensed to practice law** and is **regulated** by the State and Federal Government. He or she can help you **obtain legal status** from the Department of Homeland Security or **represent you** in Immigration **Court.**

An immigration lawyer can help you in the **following ways:**

- **Analyze** the **facts of your case** thoroughly.
- **Explain** all the **benefits** for which **you may be eligible**.
- **Recommend** the **best ways** to obtain legal status.
- **Complete** and **submit** your **applications** properly.
- **Stay current** on the new laws **that affect you**.
- **Avoid delays** and problems with your case.
- **Discuss** the **status** of your case with you.
- **Speak for you** and represent you in court.
- **File** necessary **appeals** and **waivers**.
- **Utilize** the system to your advantage.

How do you find an immigration lawyer or the necessary resources to assist you?

Visit www.ailalawyer.com, the **online directory** of attorneys **who are members** of the American Immigration Lawyers Association.

On this web site you will find **free legal services** provided by state. You will also find national and community resources and **self-help** materials. http://www.usdoj.gov/eoir/probono/probono.htm

Used with the permission of the American Immigration Law Foundation

134 empowerment

Public Benefits

Many immigrants, **even when eligible** for **public benefits**, **do not apply** for **fear** that **accepting** benefits **will have consequences** for their immigration **status** or that of **someone** in their family. Even when immigrants are **aware of** their **rights**, local agencies **sometimes mistakenly deny** benefits to immigrants **who are entitled** to them, or **ask for** information that **may discourage** an **applicant** from **obtaining** the benefit. Immigrants **with limited** English **proficiency face additional barriers** when service provider agencies **fail to make** appropriate **language translation services available** to their clients.

National and local organizations and **advocacy groups** have been **filling the gap** in **assisting** immigrants **to navigate** the **various** and **continuously changing** public benefits laws and policies. Immigrants come to this country **ready to work**, and many work in **low-wage**, **undesirable jobs**. Immigrants **should have access to** public benefits that **they pay for** with their **taxes**.

Today and **throughout history**, immigrants **contribute far more** to the American **economy** and culture than **they receive** in benefits.

The **following** organizations **provide outstanding** public benefit programs, activities, and information.

- Center for Public Policy Priorities: www.cppp.org
- Coalition on Human Needs: www.chn.org/issuebriefs/immigrants.asp
- Center on Budget and Policy Priorities: www.cbpp.org/pubs/immpub.htm
- The Finance Project: www.financeprojectinfo.org
- National Immigration Law Center: www.nilc.org

Used with the permission of the National Immigration Forum

---

even when eligible: mesmo quando qualificados
public benefits: benefícios públicos
do not apply/to apply: não os requerem/requerer
fear: medo
accepting: aceitar
will have/to have: terá/ter
consequences: consequências
status: situação
someone: alguém
aware of: conscientes de
rights: direitos
sometimes: às vezes
mistakenly: erroneamente
deny/to deny: negam/negar
who are entitled: que têm direito
ask for/to ask for: pedem/pedir
may discourage: pode desencorajar
applicant: requerente
obtaining/to obtain: recebendo/receber
with limited ... proficiency: com limitada... fluência
face/to face: enfrentam/enfrentar
additional barriers: barreiras adicionais
fail: falham
to make...available: em tornar... disponível
language translation services: serviços de tradução de idiomas
advocacy groups: grupos de apoio
filling the gap: preenchendo a lacuna
assisting/to assist: ajudando/ajudar
to navigate: a percorrer
various: várias
continuously changing: constante mudança
ready to work: prontos para trabalharem
low-wage: baixo salário
undesirable: indesejáveis
jobs: trabalhos
should have access to: deveriam ter acesso a
they pay for: eles pagam
taxes: impostos
throughout history: através da história
contribute/to contribute: contribuem/contribuir
far more: muito mais
economy: economia
they receive: o que recebem
following: seguintes
provide/to provide: fornecem/fornecer
outstanding: notáveis

empowerment

Owning Your Own Home

Since a **large number of** immigrants have **come to** the United States **in the last** 10 years and because many of them **begin** their **working careers** in **low-paying jobs**, many **do not yet own** homes. The **cost of housing** presents a **significant financial barrier** for many people. Yet, as a group, immigrants **steadily pursue** homeownership.

Financial institutions are beginning to **realize** the **huge potential** immigrants **represent** for the housing market. In the last few years, many **have made commitments** to reach out to immigrant populations and are **providing** immigrants with the skills they need **to gain access to** the housing market.

These efforts are beginning to **pay off**, as immigrants are **increasingly achieving** the American **dream** of homeownership.

According to recent reports, Hispanics **still face** significant barriers to achieving the American dream of owning a home. **In response to** this problem, the Congressional Hispanic Caucus Institute (CHCI) **launched** the National Housing Initiative (NHI).

The NHI **benefits** areas with large Hispanic populations and **will employ up to** 4 **mid-career** professionals **to create** and **implement specialized housing initiatives** for the purpose of increasing homeownership opportunities for Latinos **across the country**.

Homeownership is one of the best ways **we have to help empower** families to achieve financial security and help communities **attain greater stability**. For this reason, CHCI reports that they are **proud** to launch this exciting and important **endeavor** to help address the housing **needs** of Latinos everywhere. It is through an initiative such as this that Hispanics **will continue to assume** greater **leadership roles** in all **sectors of society**.

For more information on CHCI and its leadership **development** programs and scholarship awards, please visit www.chciyouth.org or call toll-free 1-800 EXCEL DC.

Parent-Teacher Association

As the largest **volunteer child advocacy association** in the nation, the **National Parent-Teacher Association** (PTA) **reminds** our country of its obligations to children. The PTA **provides** parents and families with a **powerful voice to speak on behalf of** every child **while** providing the **best tools** for parents **to help** their children be **successful students**.

The National PTA **does not act alone**. Working in cooperation with many national education, **health**, **safety**, and child advocacy groups and federal agencies, the National PTA **collaborates** on projects that **benefit children** and that bring **valuable resources** to its **members**.

The PTA is the nation's original parent group in schools, **influencing** millions of parents, **past and present**, to get involved in their children's education. A national, nonprofit organization, **neither** the organization **nor** its leaders **receive any financial benefit** from PTA activities. The PTA is **composed of** 6 million volunteers in 23,000 local units. **Run by** volunteers and **led by** volunteers, the PTA is **accountable to** parents and schools. The PTA gives parents what they want—a **way to help** their children succeed.

JOIN THE PTA

The PTA is **open to all** adults who **care** about children and schools. The **main thing** parents want from schools is to help their child **succeed academically**, emotionally, and personally. The PTA **bridges** the gap **between** homes and schools. **By getting involved** with the PTA, the child **who benefits most** is one's own. **They work hard** to bring mothers, fathers, teachers, school administrators, grandparents, mentors, **foster parents**, other **caregivers**, and **community leaders** into the association.

Talk with the **school principals** in your town **to find out** how you may **partner** with the schools and be one of the members of a **powerful** organization that **makes a difference every day**.

---

volunteer child advocacy association: associação voluntária de auxílio infantil
National Parent-Teacher Association: Associação Nacional de Pais e Mestres
reminds/to remind: lembra/lembrar
provides/to provide: fornece/fornecer
powerful voice: poderosa voz
to speak on behalf of: para falar em nome de
while: enquanto
best tools: melhores ferramentas
to help: para ajudar
successful students: estudantes bem-sucedidos
does not act alone: não age sozinho
health: saúde
safety: segurança
collaborates/to collaborate: colabora/colaborar
benefit children: beneficiam as crianças
valuable resources: recursos valiosos
members: membros
influencing/to influence: influenciando/influenciar
past and present: ontem e hoje
neither... nor...: nem... nem
receive/to receive: recebem/receber
any financial benefit: nenhum benefício financeiro
composed of: composto de
run by: administrado por
led by: dirigido por
accountable to: responde a
way to help: forma de ajudar
open to all: aberta a todos
care/to care: preocupam-se/preocupar-se
main thing: principal coisa
succeed academically: tenham êxito acadêmico
bridges/to bridge: supera/superar
between: entre
by getting involved: ao envolver-se
who benefits most: quem mais se beneficia
they work hard: eles trabalham duro
foster parents: pais adotivos
caregivers: profissionais da saúde
community leaders: líderes comunitários
talk with/to talk with: fale com/falar com
school principals: diretores escolares
to find out: para descobrir
partner: associar-se a
powerful: poderosa
makes a difference: faz diferença
every day: todos os dias

You and Your Community

Being involved in your community has **benefits** on **many levels**. On a local level it **allows you to get to know** your **neighbors** and **integrate** better **into your immediate surroundings**. It **also** helps you **identify** and **utilize** the many **resources** available for you and your family. On a national level your involvement **helps to build** a **society** that **values diversity** and **respects** the **dignity** and **rights of all people**.

Local Communities

- **Libraries** — Many libraries **offer free internet access** and **computer classes**. They also offer ESL classes, **wonderful** children's programs, **magazines** and **books** in Spanish, **as well as** citizenship **test preparation** books and resources.

- **Church** — Local churches often offer free **ESL classes** as well as other classes **designed** to help immigrants **adjust** to life in the United States.

- **Community Centers** — Community Centers, also called Parks and Recreation departments, are **found** in most **medium-sized cities** and offer an abundance of resources for you and your family. **Here** you can find adult and children's programs, **child care**, **summer programs**, local **concerts** and community festivals.

---

being involved: estar envolvido
benefits: benefícios
many: muitos
levels: níveis
allows you to: permite-lhe
get to know: conhecer
neighbors: vizinhos
integrate: integrar-se
into your immediate surroundings: em sua vizinhança próxima
also: também
identify: identificar
utilize: usar
resources: recursos
helps/to help: ajuda/ajudar
to build: a construir
society: sociedade
values/to value: valoriza/valorizar
diversity: diversidade
respects/to respect: respeita/respeitar
dignity: dignidade
rights: direitos
of all people: de todas as pessoas
libraries: bibliotecas
offer/to offer: oferecem/oferecer
free: grátis, gratuito
internet access: acesso à internet
computer classes: aulas de informática
wonderful: maravilhosos
magazines: revistas
books: livros
as well as: bem como
test preparation: preparatórios para testes
church: igreja
ESL classes: aulas de inglês como segunda língua *(ESL=English as a Second Language)*
designed/to design: projetadas/projetar
adjust: acomodarem-se
community centers: centros comunitários
found: que se encontram
medium-sized cities: cidades medianas
here: aqui
child care: cuidado infantil
summer programs: programas de verão
concerts: shows

- **Volunteer** — A **great way to meet new people** and make a difference in your community is to volunteer. **Even if you are not yet fluent** in English, this is a great way **to practice** your English. Volunteer **options** include: working at local **homeless shelters**, **assisting** adults or children to **learn to read** with **literacy programs**, **litter patrol** with **environmental programs**, or helping out at local festivals or **fundraisers**.

National Communities

- National Council of La Raza is a **nonprofit** organization **established** in 1968 **to reduce poverty** and discrimination and **improve life opportunities** for Hispanic Americans.

- LULAC — The Mission of the League of United Latin American Citizens is **to advance** the **economic condition**, educational **attainment**, political **influence**, **health** and civil **rights** of the Hispanic population of the United States.

There are many options for community involvement **right outside your door**. **Take a class**, **listen to** a concert in the park, **help organize** the **next** Cinco De Mayo festival. **Take the time** to **be involved** and **make the most** of your community.

volunteer: voluntario
great way: excelente maneira
to meet new people: conhecer novas pessoas
even if: até se
you are not yet fluent: você ainda não é fluente
to practice: de praticar
options: opções
homeless shelters: abrigos
assisting: ajudando
learn to read: aprender a ler
literacy programs: programas de alfabetização
litter patrol: patrulhas sanitárias
environmental programs: programas ambientais
fundraisers: para arrecadar fundos
nonprofit: sem fins lucrativos
established: fundada
to reduce: para reduzir
poverty: pobreza
improve life opportunities: melhorar as oportunidades de vida
to advance: fazer avançar
economic condition: condição econômica
attainment: qualificação
influence: influência
health: saúde
rights: direitos
right outside your door: do lado de fora
take a class: tenha uma aula
listen to/to listen to: escute/escutar
help organize: ajude a organizar
next: próximo
take the time: tire um tempo
be involved: estar envolvido
make the most: aproveite ao máximo

empowerment 139

because: porque
growing: crescendo
opportunities: oportunidades
graduates: graduados
across many fields: através de muitos campos
recognizing the need to hire: reconhecendo a necessidade de contratar
understand/to understand: entendem/entender
language: idioma
unfortunately: infelizmente
heritage: herança
overcome negative stereotypes: superar estereótipos negativos
job search: busca de emprego
highlight/to highlight: destacar
unique benefits: benefícios únicos
background: história pessoal
language skills: habilidades em idiomas
insight: melhor compreensão
make the most: aproveitar ao máximo
minority recruiting efforts: esforços para recrutar minorias
diligently work: trabalham aplicadamente
promote/to promote: promover
reaching out: estendendo a mão
sponsoring/to sponsor: patrocinando/patrocinar
career fairs: feiras de trabalho
recruiting events: eventos de recrutamento
scholarships: bolsas de estudos
connecting with/to connect with: conectando-se com/conectar-se com
professional societies: sociedades profissionais
searching/to search: procurando/procurar
job boards: anúncios de emprego
niche boards: anúncios especializados
either...or: tanto... quanto
diversity job board: anúncio de trabalho para minorias, diversidade
are under-represented: têm pouca representação
despite: apesar de
advances: avanços
fields: campos
hear/to hear: ouvimos/ouvir
mentioning/to mention: mencionando/mencionar
engineering: engenharia
healthcare: assistência médica
nurses: enfermeiros/as
physicians: médicos
complex: complexas
are not entering: não estão entrando

140 empowerment

Hispanics in the Workplace

Because the Hispanic population is **growing** so rapidly in the U.S., there are **opportunities** for **graduates across many fields**. Employers are **recognizing the need to hire** individuals who **understand** the **language** and culture of this growing segment of the population, and there are opportunities in many professions. **Unfortunately**, individuals of Hispanic **heritage** may still have to **overcome negative stereotypes** during their **job search,** but it is important to remember that being bicultural is a definite competitive advantage. Job seekers should **highlight** the **unique benefits** their **background** can provide to an employer, including international experience, **language skills** and cultural **insight**.

What Are Employers Doing?

To **make the most** of their **minority recruiting efforts**, the most successful employers use a variety of methods and **diligently work** to **promote** these initiatives on campus.

Many employers are **reaching out** to Hispanic students by **sponsoring career fairs** and other events on campus, attending **recruiting events** and even offering **scholarships** to Hispanic students. Companies are also **connecting with** students through **professional societies** such as the Society of Hispanic Professional Engineers and the Association of Latino Professionals in Finance and Accounting.

Where to Look for Your First Job

Students should be **searching** the Internet **job boards**, both the big ones as well as **niche boards** that match **either** their career functions, locations **or** ethnic background. LatPro.com, for example, is a niche **diversity job board** for Hispanic and bilingual professionals.

Industries Where Hispanics Are Under-Represented

Despite promising **advances** in many areas, Hispanics continue to be under-represented in a variety of professions. The **fields** we **hear** employers **mentioning** most include science, information technology, **engineering** and **healthcare** (especially **nurses** and **physicians** with Spanish language skills).

The reasons are varied and **complex,** but multicultural students **are not entering** these fields in **great enough numbers**. We can **encourage** students **to pursue** these fields by increasing scholarships **to ease** the **financial burden** of advanced education, **as well as** promoting **mentorship** opportunities **to expose** young Latinos/Latinas to these career options **early on**.

What are employers looking for?

Many employers **want to see that** students are **involved** in organizations related to their profession, especially those **focused on** supporting Hispanic professionals **within a specific field**. **For example**, accounting students and graduates **should consider joining** the Association of Latino Professionals in Finance and Accounting. Other organizations include the Society of Hispanic Professional Engineers, the National Association of Hispanic Nurses, and many others. These organizations are an excellent **source** for **networking** opportunities and **job leads**. An **online listing** can be found at: http://www.latpro.com/network.

Another source of networking opportunities would be Hispanic Chambers of Commerce. Every resource should be used, especially for **newly** graduating students **in search of** their first jobs.

It is important for Hispanic students to learn how organizations value a diverse workforce. Employers **can better inform** students about **corporate diversity initiatives** by using multiple **strategies** such as promoting **employee referral programs** and **affinity** organizations within the company, sponsoring scholarships for Hispanic students, **advertising** on diversity job boards, and **supporting** Hispanic professional organizations **within their field**.

Recruiting Hispanic employees requires the employer to understand the benefit that a diverse workforce brings to the business **bottom line**. Minority **candidates** want to know that they are being recruited for their skills and the value they will bring to an organization, versus being a **number** in a **diversity hiring effort**.

---

great enough numbers: quantidade suficiente
encourage: encorajar
to pursue: seguir
to ease: para facilitar
financial burden: carga econômica
as well as: bem como
mentorship: aconselhamento, consultoria
to expose: para expor
early on: desde o começo
want to see that: querem ver que
involved: envolvidos
focused on: focados em
within: dentro
specific field: campo específico
for example: por exemplo
should consider joining: deveriam considerar unirem-se
source: fonte
networking: rede de contatos
job leads: ofertas de emprego
online listing: lista virtual
newly: recém
in search of: em busca de
value/to value: valorizam/valorizar
can better inform: podem informar melhor
corporate diversity initiatives: iniciativa empresarial sobre a diversidade
strategies: estratégias
employee referral programs: programa de recomendação de empregados
affinity: afinidade
advertising/to advertise: noticiando/noticiar
supporting/to support: apoiando/apoiar
within their field: dentro de sua área
bottom line: ponto principal
candidates: candidatos
number: número
diversity hiring effort: esforço para empregar grupos diversos

---

Este artigo foi escrito pelos colaboradores da LatPro.com, o site de busca de trabalho mais visitado por hispânicos e profissionais bilíngues. Desde 1997, LatPro tem ajudado os hispânicos em busca de trabalho, a encontrar emprego nas melhores empresas dentro dos Estados Unidos e na América Latina. Este site de anúncios de emprego, vencedor de vários prêmios e disponível em inglês, espanhol e português, oferece avisos de trabalhos atuais, artigos com assessoramento para sua carreira, conselhos para o seu curriculum vitae, um calendário de eventos profissionais, informação sobre imigração para os Estados Unidos e diversos recursos para os hispânicos.

empowerment

Test Your Comprehension

Citizenship, page 124

1. Os residentes dos Estados Unidos podem ser estrangeiros, nacionais ou cidadãos. Quem são os estrangeiros e quais são os seus direitos?

2. Quem são os nacionais e quais são os seus direitos?

Empowerment with Education, page 126

1. Qual é a minoria étnica mais numerosa da nação e o segmento com crescimento populacional mais rápido?

2. Qual deve ser o seu primeiro passo quando for procurar ajuda financeira ou bolsas de estudo?

3. Quantas bolsas as HSF concederam aos hispânicos em seus 31 anos de história?

Community Colleges, page 128

1. Quantas universidades públicas existem nos Estados Unidos?

2. O que é um "associate degree"?

3. Quais são os programas de universidades públicas mais populares?

Helping Children Succeed, page 130

1. Verdadeiro ou Falso? Os filhos se saem melhor na escola quando seus pais estão envolvidos em sua educação?

2. O que acontece quando os pais e os professores compartilham informações?

3. Quais são algumas ideias para ajudar a superar a barreira do idioma e participar de maneira mais ativa na escola de seu filho?

Teste sua Compreensão

Bilingual Resources, page 132

1. Quais indústrias têm uma maior necessidade de empregados bilíngues?

2. Como o empregador faz para verificar se o empregado bilíngue tem fluência e conhece o vocabulário adequado para o posto?

3. Que outra coisa os possíveis empregados precisam além de falar espanhol com fluência?

Legal Resources, page 134

1. O que é um advogado de imigração?

2. Como um advogado de imigração pode ajudar a um novo imigrante nos EUA?

Owning Your Own Home, page 136

1. Qual é a taxa de propriedade de habitação para os hispânicos nos Estados Unidos?

2. Ter casa própria é considerado uma das melhores formas de ajudar a possibilitar o quê?

You and Your Community, page 138

1. Quais são alguns dos benefícios de estar envolvido com a sua comunidade?

2. O que pode ser encontrado nos Departamentos de Parques e Recreação?

3. Qual é uma excelente forma de fazer novas amizades e criar uma mudança em sua comunidade?

A page of history is worth a pound of logic.

Oliver Wendell Holmes

History

states: estados
first: primeiros
last: últimos
to join: a unir-se
voted/to vote: votou/votar
to become independent: tornar-se independente
however: contudo
we celebrate/to celebrate: nós celebramos/celebrar
took/to take: levou/levar
to accept: para aprovar
written/to write: escrito/escrever
edited/to edit: editado/editar
explained/to explain: explicava/explicar
separating/to separate: separando-se/separar
ruler: governante, soberano
now: agora
considered/to consider: considerado/considerar
birthday: aniversário
parades: desfiles
fireworks: fogos de artifício
songs: músicas
live readings: leituras ao vivo
decision to break from: decisão de separar-se de
easy choice: escolha fácil
however: contudo
repeated injuries: repetidas lesões
against: contra
convinced/to convince: convenceram/convencer
to join: a unirem-se
rebellion: rebelião
difficult fighting: luta difícil
to win: ganhar
freedom: liberdade

Independence Day

There are 50 **states** in the Union. The **first** 13 states were Connecticut, New Hampshire, New York, New Jersey, Maryland, Virginia, Pennsylvania, Rhode Island, Massachusetts, Georgia, Delaware, North Carolina, and South Carolina. The **last** state **to join** the Union was Hawaii.

Congress **voted** for the United States **to become independent** from Great Britain on July 2, 1776. **However**, **we celebrate** Independence Day on July 4th. This is because it **took** two days for Congress to vote **to accept** an official Declaration of Independence. This document was **written** by Thomas Jefferson and **edited** by Congress. It **explained** why the American colonies were **separating** from their British **ruler**. The 4th of July is **now considered** the **birthday** of America. We celebrate with **parades, fireworks**, patriotic **songs**, and **live readings** of the Declaration of Independence.

The **decision to break from** the British was not an **easy choice** for many colonists. **However**, Great Britain's "**repeated injuries**" **against** the Americans **convinced** many **to join** the **rebellion**. After years of **difficult fighting**, the colonists went on **to win** their **freedom**.

Stars and Stripes

We call the American **flag** the "**Stars** and **Stripes**." Congress **chose** the stars and stripes **design** for our flag on June 14, 1777. Congress **explained** the colors: **red stands for hardiness** and valor, **white** for **purity** and **innocence**, and **blue** for **vigilance**, **perseverance**, and **justice**.

The white stars on the flag **represent** the United States as **being like** "a **new constellation**" in the **sky**. The nation was **seen** as a new constellation because the **republican system** of government was new and different in the 1770s. In the republican system of government, leaders **work to help** all of the country's people. They **do not act** to help only a **few** special citizens. **Since** the people **choose** these leaders, the people **hold the power** of government.

Each star represents a **state**. This is why the number of stars **has changed over the years** from 13 to 50. The number of stars **reached** 50 in 1959. In that year, Hawaii **joined** the United States as the 50th state.

The stars represent the Founding Fathers' **view** of the American **experiment** in democracy. To them, the **goal** of a republic **based** on **individual freedom** was a noble idea. Stars are **considered** a symbol of the **heavens** and the **high**, ambitious vision of the Founding Fathers.

In 1818, Congress **decided** that the number of red and white stripes on the flag **should always be** 13. This would **honor** the original states, **no matter how many** new states would join the United States later.

we call/to call: nós chamamos/chamar
flag: bandeira
stars: estrelas
stripes: listras
chose/to choose: escolheu/escolher
design: desenho
explained/to explain: explicou/explicar
red: vermelho
stands for/to stand for: representa/representar
hardiness: persistência
white: branco
purity: pureza
innocence: inocência
blue: azul
vigilance: vigilância
perseverance: perseverança
justice: justiça
represent/to represent: representam/representar
being like: sendo como
new: nova
constellation: constelação
sky: céu
seen: vista
republican system: sistema republicano
work to help: trabalham para ajudar
do not act: não agem
few: alguns, poucos
since: desde que
choose/to choose: escolheram/escolher
hold the power: mantém o poder
state: estado
has changed over the years: mudou com o passar dos anos
reached/to reach: alcançou/alcançar
joined/to join: uniu-se/unir
view: visão
experiment: experimentou
goal: objetivo
based: baseada
individual freedom: liberdade individual
considered/to consider: consideradas/considerar
heavens: céus
high: altura
decided/to decide: decidiu/decidir
should always be: deveria ser sempre
honor: honrar
no matter how many: não importa quantos

history

place: lugar
school: escola
process: processo
designed: projetado
writers: autores
to select: para escolher
came from/to come from: veio de/vir de
compromise: compromisso
between: entre
being elected: sendo eleito
chosen: escolhido
combining: combinando
vote/to vote: votam/votar
meet/to meet: reúnem-se/reunir
to choose: para escolher
today: hoje
officially: oficialmente
first in line: primeiro na fila
to take over: suceder
happened/ to happen: aconteceu/acontecer
times: vezes
died in office: morreram estando no poder
killed/to kill: mortos/matar
resigned/to resign: renunciou/renunciar

The Electoral College

The Electoral College is not a **place** or a **school.** The Electoral College is a **process** that was **designed** by the **writers** of the Constitution **to select** presidents. It **came from** a **compromise between** the President **being elected** directly by the people and the President being **chosen** by Congress. **Combining** these ideas, the American people **vote** for a "college" of electors, who then **meet to choose** the President. **Today**, the people of each of the 50 states and the District of Columbia vote for the electors in November. The electors then **officially** vote for the President in December.

The Vice President is **first in line to take over** as President. This has **happened** nine **times** in U.S. history. Four presidents **died in office**, four presidents were **killed** in office, and one president, Richard Nixon, **resigned** from office.

Supreme Law of the Land

The U.S. Constitution **has lasted longer** than any **other country's** constitution. It is the **basic legal framework establishing** the U.S. government. **Every** person and every agency and department of government must **follow** the Constitution. This is why it is **called** the "**supreme law of the land**." **Under** this system, the **powers** of the national government are **limited** to those **written** in the Constitution. The **guiding principle behind** this system is **often called** the **rule** of law.

It **is not easy** for the Constitution to be **changed**. Changes to the constitution are called Amendments. **First, two-thirds** of the Senate and two-thirds of the House of Representatives must vote **to approve** an amendment. Then**, three-fourths** of the states must approve the amendment.

The first amendments to the Constitution were **added** in 1791. These original ten amendments are called the Bill of Rights. Since the Bill of Rights **passed**, 17 more amendments **have been added**. The 27th amendment is the **most recent addition**. It was added in 1992 and **addresses** how Senators and Representatives are **paid**. **Interestingly**, Congress **first discussed** this Amendment **back in** 1789.

has lasted longer: durou mais tempo
other: outro
country's: de ... país
basic legal framework: marco legal básico
establishing/to establish: que estabelece/estabelecer
every: todas
follow: seguir
called/to call: chamada/chamar
supreme law of the land: lei suprema do país
under: sob
powers: poderes
limited/limit: limitados/limitar
written/to write: escritos/escrever
guiding principle: princípio guia
behind: por trás de
often called: geralmente chamado de
rule: domínio (da lei)
is not easy: não é fácil
changed/to change: mudada/mudar
first: primeiro
two-thirds: dois terços
to approve: para aprovar
three-fourths: três quartos
added/to add: adicionadas/adicionar
passed/to pass: foi aprovada/aprovar
have been added: foram adicionadas
most recent addition: mais recente adição
addresses/to address: indica/indicar
paid/to pay: pagos/pagar
interestingly: de forma interessante
first discussed: discutiu pela primeira vez
back in: em *(referindo-se a um tempo anterior)*

history 149

Divisions of Power

The **writers** of the Constitution **created** a process that **divides** the government's **power among** three **branches**: Executive, Judicial, and Legislative. These branches **operate under** a **system** of **checks** and **balances**. This **means** that each branch can **block**, or **threaten to** block, the action of **another** branch. This way, no one branch can **grow too powerful** and **harm** the **liberties** of **citizens**.

Congress is a legislative branch. The **main job** of Congress is **to make federal laws**. Congress is divided into two parts—the **Senate** and the House of Representatives. By dividing Congress into two parts, the Constitution **put** the checks and balances idea **to work within** the legislative branch. Each part of Congress **makes sure** that the other does not **become** too powerful. These two "check" each other because **both** must **agree** for a law to be **made**.

Specific powers are **assigned** to each of these **chambers**. **Only** the Senate has the power **to reject** a **treaty signed** by the President. Only the House of Representatives has the power **to begin considering** a **bill** that makes Americans **pay taxes**. **Also**, only the House of Representatives has the power to make a President **go to trial** for a **crime against** the United States.

A federal law is a **rule** that all people **living** in the United States **must follow**. Every law begins as a **proposal** made by a member of Congress. Tax proposals must begin in the House of Representatives. Other types of proposals can be made by any senator or representative. When the Senate or House begins **to debate** the proposal, it is **called** a bill. If the President **signs** the bill, it becomes a federal law.

The nation is **divided** into 435 Congressional **districts**. The people of each district are **represented** by a **member** of the House of Representatives.

The **people** of each state also **vote** for two U.S. senators. There are 100 senators (two **from each** state). The **term of office** for members of the House of Representatives is two years. The term for senators is six years.

One reason the Senate was **created** was **to make** states with **fewer** people **equal** in power to states with many people. With two senators representing each state, states with **small populations** have the same Senate representation as states with **large** populations.

The writers of the Constitution **wanted** senators to be **independent** of **public opinion**. A **longer**, six-year term **would give them** this **protection**. The Constitution **puts no limit** on the number of terms a senator may **serve**.

rule: regra
living: vivendo
must follow: devem seguir
proposal: proposta
to debate: a debater
called/to call: chamado/chamar
signs/to sign: assina/assinar
divided/dividir: dividida/dividir
districts: distritos
represented/to represent: representadas/representar
member: membro
people: pessoas
vote: votar
from each: de cada
term of office: duração do mandato
one reason: um motivo
created/to create: criado/criar
to make: para fazer
fewer: poucas
equal: iguais
small populations: populações pequenas
large: grandes
wanted/to want: queriam/querer
independent: independentes
public opinion: opinião pública
longer: mais extenso
would give them: lhes daria
protection: proteção
puts no limit: não limita
serve: servir

official home: residência oficial
built/to build: construída/construir
between: entre
helped choose: ajudou a escolher
exact location: localização exata
supervised/to supervise: supervisionou/supervisionar
never actually lived: na verdade nunca morou
to live: viver
burned/to burn: queimada/queimar
troops: tropas
during: durante
war: guerra
destructive fire: incêndio destruidor
took place/to take place: ocorreu/ocorrer
established/to establish: estabeleceu/estabelecer
did not exist/to exist: não existia/existir
at that time: naquela época
soon began discussing: logo começou a discutir
permanent: permanente
within: dentro de
fought/to fight: lutaram/lutar
bitterly: asperamente
against: contra
southern: sulistas
wanted/to want: queria/querer
to be in: fosse em
finally: finalmente
North: Norte
agreed to let: concordou em deixar
in return: em troca
relieved/to relieve: liberado/liberar
debt: dívida
owed/to owe: deviam/dever
building: construção
known as: conhecida como
until: até
before then: antes disso
current look: aparência atual
renovation: reforma
happened/to happen: ocorreu/ocorrer

History of the White House

The President's **official home** is the White House. The first White House was **built between** 1792 and 1800 in Washington, D.C. President George Washington **helped choose** its **exact location** and **supervised** its construction, but **never actually lived** there. America's second president, John Adams, was the first **to live** in the White House. Fourteen years after construction, the White House was **burned** by British **troops during** the **War** of 1812. Another **destructive fire took place** there in 1929, when Herbert Hoover was president.

When the Constitution **established** our nation in 1789, the city of Washington, D.C. **did not exist**. **At that time**, the capital was New York City. Congress **soon began discussing** the location of a **permanent** capital city. **Within** Congress, representatives of northern states **fought bitterly against** representatives of **southern** states. Each side **wanted** the capital **to be in** their region. **Finally**, with the Compromise of 1790, the **North agreed to let** the capital be in the South. **In return**, the North was **relieved** of some of the **debt** that they **owed** from the Revolutionary War.

The **building** was not officially **known as** the White House **until** 1901, when Theodore Roosevelt was president. **Before then**, it was also called the "President's Palace," the "President's House," and the "Executive Mansion." The **current look** of the White House comes from a **renovation** that **happened** when Harry Truman was president.

The Bill of Rights

Freedom of speech is a very important **civil liberty**. The **first** section of the Bill of Rights, the First Amendment, **guarantees** this freedom. Speech **can mean writing**, **performing**, or other ways of **expressing yourself**. Americans have the basic right **to express** their **views** on any **subject**. This is **true even if** the government **disagrees** with these views.

When the Constitution was **first written**, it did not **focus** on individual **rights**. The **goal** was **to create** the system and **structure** of government. Many Americans wanted a specific list of **things** the government **could not do**. James Madison **responded** with a list of individual rights and limits of government. Some of these **included** citizens' rights **to practice** their religion **freely**, to speak and **publish** freely, and to **complain publicly** about anything they wanted. The list was in the form of changes, or amendments, to the Constitution. These amendments were **ratified** in 1791. They soon **became known as** the Bill of Rights.

The Bill of Rights guarantees the rights of individuals and **limits** government **power**. The first eight amendments **set out** individual rights, such as the freedom of expression; the **right to bear arms**; freedom from **search without warrant**; freedom to not be **tried** twice for the **same crime**; the right to not **testify against yourself**; the right **to trial by a jury** of **peers**; the right to an **attorney**; and protection against **excessive fines** and **unusual punishments**.

One **reason** that millions of immigrants **have come to** America is this guarantee of rights. The Fifth Amendment guarantees everyone in the United States **equal protection under** the law. This is **true no matter** what color your **skin** is, what **language** you speak, or what religion you practice.

---

freedom of speech: liberdade de expressão
civil liberty: liberdade civil
first: primeira
guarantees/to guarantee: garante/garantir
can mean: pode significar
writing: escrever
performing: atuar
expressing yourself: expressar-se
to express: de expressar
views: opiniões
subject: tema
true: genuíno
even if: mesmo se
disagrees/to disagree: discordar/discordar
first written: inicialmente escrita
focus/to focus: focava/focar
rights: direitos
goal: objetivo
to create: criar
structure: estrutura
things: coisas
could not do: não podia fazer
responded/to respond: respondeu/responder
included/to include: incluíam/incluir
to practice: de praticar
freely: livremente
publish: anunciar
complain publicly: reclamar publicamente
ratified/to ratify: ratificadas/ratificar
became known as: ficaram conhecidas como
limits/to limit: limita/limitar
power: poder
set out/to set out: expuseram/expor
right to bear arms: direito de portar armas
search without warrant: mandado de busca e apreensão
tried/to try: julgado/julgar
same crime: mesmo crime
testify against yourself: produzir provas contra si mesmo
to trial by a jury: julgado por um júri
peers: pares
attorney: advogado
excessive fines: multas excessivas
unusual punishments: punições incomuns
reason: motivo
have come to: vieram para
equal protection under: igualdade de proteção perante
true: verdade
no matter: não importa
skin: pele
language: idioma

United States Presidency

The **writers** of the Constitution **argued over** how much **power** the **new** President should have. They **decided** that the President's powers should be **limited** in many ways, but that the President should be Commander-in-Chief of the **military**. **During** the Revolutionary War, George Washington, **known as** the "**father of our country**" had been **Supreme Commander** of the military. From this position, he **led** the U.S. **forces to victory**. This **helped make him** a **unanimous choice** to be the **first** President and Commander-in-Chief.

Washington was a **brave** military general, a **respected** leader of the American Revolution, and our first President. His leadership was very important **during** America's transition from **war** and revolution to **stability under** the new government. **After** his victory **over** the British army, Washington **retired**. He **reluctantly left retirement** and helped lead the **effort to create** a Constitution for the United States.

The President is **both** the head of state and the head of the Executive branch of the government. Presidential powers **include** the **ability** to **sign treaties** with other countries and **select** ambassadors to represent the United States **abroad**. As **head** of the executive branch, the President **names** the top leaders of the federal departments. **However**, the Senate has the power to **reject** the President's choices. This **limit** on the power of the President is an example of **checks and balances**.

Early American leaders **felt** that the head of the British government, the **king**, had too much power. Because of this, they limited the powers of the head of the new U.S. government. They decided that the President would have to be **elected** by the people **every four years**.

The writers of the Constitution wanted the President to be an **experienced** leader with a **strong connection** to the United States. The **eligibility requirements make sure** that this **happens**. A **candidate** for president must be a **native-born**, not a **naturalized citizen,** be **at least** 35 **years old**, and have **lived** in the U.S. for at least 14 years. The **youngest** person in American history to become president was Theodore Roosevelt. Roosevelt **entered** the White House when he was 42 years old.

The first U.S. President, George Washington, only **ran** for president **twice**. Washington felt that one person **should not serve** as president for a very **long time**. **Following** this tradition, no future president served for **more than** two terms until Franklin Roosevelt. Roosevelt was elected to four terms. **Not long after** he **died**, the Constitution was **amended** so that a president could only serve two full terms.

early: primeiros
felt/to feel: sentiram/sentir
king: rei
elected/to elect: eleito/eleger
every four years: a cada quatro anos
experienced: experiente
strong connection: forte conexão
eligibility requirements: requerimentos para ser eleito
make sure: garantem
happens/to happen: ocorra/ocorrer
candidate: candidato
native-born: nascido no país
naturalized citizen: cidadão naturalizado
at least: pelo menos
years old: anos de idade
lived/to live vivido/viver
youngest: mais jovem
entered/to enter: ingressou/ingressar
ran/to run: concorreu/concorrer
twice: duas vezes
should not serve: não deveria trabalhar
long time: muito tempo
following/to follow: seguindo/seguir
more than: mais de
not long after: não muito depois que
died/to die: morreu/morrer
amended/to amend: emendada/emendar

history 155

The American Revolution

European **countries began taking control** of areas of America in the 1500s. These European-controlled areas were **called** colonies. England's **first successful** American colony was Virginia. Virginia began in 1607 as a **small camp** at Jamestown. Later, Pennsylvania was **founded** as a **home** for a **religious group**, the Quakers. The Dutch colony of New Netherlands was **captured** by British **forces** in 1664 and **renamed** New York. The 13 American colonies **would later unite** into one country, but the history of **each one** was **quite distinct**.

The Mayflower **left** from Plymouth, England, on September 6, 1620. After 65 days **crossing** the **ocean**, the **ship landed** in **what is now** the state of Massachusetts. **Soon after**, the Pilgrims **signed** an **agreement** called the Mayflower Compact. In it, the Pilgrims **agreed to unite** into a "Civil Body Politic." The Compact did not **set up** a governing system, as the Constitution later would. It **did contain** the idea that the people **freely agreed to live under** the government. The **power** of this government **came directly** from the people.

In 1774, representatives from 12 of the colonies **met** in Philadelphia, Pennsylvania, for the First Continental Congress. They **protested** British **laws** that **treated them unfairly**. They also began to **organize** an **army**. After **fighting began between** the colonists and the British army, a Second Continental Congress met. This group **appointed** Jefferson and others **to create** the Declaration of Independence.

This document **stated** that if a government **does not protect** the **rights** of the people, the people can create a **new** government. **Following** this idea, the colonists **broke from** their British rulers and **formed** a new country.

---

countries: países
began/to begin: começaram/começar
taking control: a tomar o controle
called/to call: chamadas/chamar
first successful: primeira bem-sucedida
small camp: pequeno acampamento
founded/to found fundada/fundar
home: lar
religious group: grupo religioso
captured/to capture: capturada/capturar
forces: forças
renamed/to rename: renomeada/renomear
would later unite: se uniriam mais tarde
each one: cada uma
quite distinct: bastante diferente
left/to leave: saiu/sair
crossing/to cross: cruzando/cruzar
ocean: oceano
ship: navio
landed/to land: aportou/aportar
what is now: no que é hoje
soon after: logo depois
signed/to sign: assinaram/assinar
agreement: acordo
agreed to unite: concordaram em unir-se
set up/to set up: estabeleceu/estabelecer
did contain/to contain: continha/conter
freely agreed to live under: concordaram livremente em viver sob
power: poder
came directly: vinha diretamente
met/to meet: encontraram-se/encontrar
protested/to protest: protestaram/protestar
laws: leis
treated them: os tratavam
unfairly: injustamente
organize: organizar
army: exército
fighting: luta
began/to begin: começou/começar
between: entre
appointed/to appoint: designou/designar
to create: para criar
stated/to state: afirmava/afirmar
does not protect: não proteger
rights: direitos
new: novo
following: seguindo
broke from: separaram-se de
formed/to form: formaram/formar

The Declaration of Independence, **adopted** July 4, 1776, is **based on** ideas about freedom and basic individual rights that all men and women are created **equal** and have the **right to life**, **liberty**, and the **pursuit** of **happiness**. Thomas Jefferson and the Founding Fathers **believed** that people are **born** with natural rights that no government can **take away**. Government **exists** only **to protect** these rights. Because the people **voluntarily give up** power to a government, they can **take back** that power. The British government **was not protecting** the rights of the colonists, so they took back their power and **separated** from Great Britain.

The American colonists' **anger** had been **building** for **years** before the Revolutionary War began. The Americans **fought** this war because they **wanted** freedom from British **rule**. The fighting of the war **ended** in 1781, **after** the Battle of Yorktown. The Americans, with French **help**, **won** this battle. It was not **until** 1783 that the British **fully accepted** United States independence.

Patrick Henry was a **fiery leader** of the American Revolution. Before U.S. independence, he **spoke out for** colonial rights within the Virginia legislature. He is famous for his **commitment** to the **cause** when he said **"Give me liberty or give me death."** Henry **represented** Virginia in **both** the First and Second Continental Congresses. He **helped push** the colonies **toward** independence. In 1775, when the Revolutionary War began, Henry **convinced** Virginia **to join** the colonists' **side**. **Later** he became the **first governor** of Virginia.

adopted/to adopt: adotada/adotar
based on: baseada em
equal: iguais
right to life: direito à vida
liberty: liberdade
pursuit: busca
happiness: felicidade
believed/to believe: acreditavam/acreditar
(people) born: (pessoas) nascem
take away: tirar
exists/to exist: existe/existir
to protect: para proteger
voluntarily: voluntariamente
give up/to give up: renunciam/renunciar
take back: recuperar
was not protecting: não estava protegendo
separated/to separate: separaram-se/separar
anger: raiva
building/to build: crescendo/crescer
years: anos
fought/to fight: lutaram/lutar
wanted/to want: queriam/querer
rule: domínio
ended/to end: terminou/terminar
after: após
help: ajuda
won/to win: ganharam/ganhar
until: até
fully accepted: aceitou completamente
fiery leader: líder exaltado
spoke out for/to speak out for: manifestou-se a favor de/manifestar-se
commitment: compromisso
cause: causa
give me liberty or give me death: dê-me a liberdade ou dê-me a morte
represented/to represent: representou/representar
both: ambos
helped/to help: ajudou/ajudar
push: impulsionar
toward: para
convinced/to convince: convenceu/convencer
to join: a unir-se
side: lado
later: mais
first: primeiro
governor: governador

history 157

The Underground Railroad

noted/to note: percebeu/perceber
train: trem
ran without tracks: andava sem rastros
railroad: ferrovia
transported slaves: transportava os escravos
network: rede
led by secret: guiada por secretos
growing: crescente
called: chamados
thousands: milhares
found/to find: encontraram/encontrar
runaway: fugitivos
sought refuge: pediram refúgio
hide/to hide: escondiam/esconder
escaped: fugitivos
teach them: ensinavam-lhes
codes: códigos
phrases: frases
to help: para ajudar
find: encontrar
next safe house: próxima casa segura
continued/to continue: continuou/continuar
reached/to reach: alcançou/alcançar
born into: nascido em
strength of character: força de caráter
able to: capaz de
herself: a si mesma
hundreds: centenas
obtain: obter
after living: após viver
learned/to learn: soube/saber
separated/to separate: separada/separar
sold/to sell: vendida/vender
planned/to plan: planejou/planejar
neighbor: vizinho
told her: contou-lhe
traveled/to travel: viajou/viajar
back: parte de trás
wagon: vagão
covered/to cover: coberta/cobrir
sack: saco
made her way: abriu seu caminho
described/to describe: descreveu/descrever
heaven: paraíso
cooked/to cook: cozinhou/cozinhar
sewed/to sew: costurou/costurar
to save: para juntar
money: dinheiro
to rescue: para resgatar
gain: ganhar
to alert: para alertar
danger: perigo
nurse: enfermeira
sick: doentes
wounded: feridos
taught/to teach: ensinou/ensinar
newly freed: recém-libertos
care: cuidar
ship: navio
honored/to honor: homenageou/homenagear
accomplishments: conquistas
postage stamp: selo postal

In 1786, George Washington **noted** the existence of an invisible **train** that **ran without tracks**. This **railroad transported slaves** to freedom through a **network** of "stations" **led by secret** "conductors." By 1831, this **growing** freedom network was **called** the "Underground Railroad." **Thousands** of slaves **found** freedom through this human train in the 1800s.

Runaway slaves from the South **sought refuge** in states where slavery was prohibited. Conductors on the railroad would **hide escaped** slaves in their homes and **teach them** secret **codes** and **phrases to help** them **find** the **next safe house** along the railroad. This **continued** until they **reached** freedom.

One of the most famous conductors along the Underground Railroad was Harriet Tubman. Harriet was **born into** slavery, but through her **strength of character**, she was **able to** help **herself** and **hundreds** of others **obtain** freedom. **After living** in Maryland for 25 years as a slave, Harriet **learned** she was going to be **separated** from her family and **sold**, so she **planned** her escape. A **neighbor told her** of two houses where she would be safe. She **traveled** to the first house in the **back** of a **wagon covered** with a **sack**, and then **made her way** to Philadelphia on her own. Harriet **described** freedom as "**heaven**."

In Philadelphia, Harriet **cooked** and **sewed to save** enough **money to rescue** her family. She eventually helped 300 slaves **gain** freedom. Harriet used music, Bible verses, and folklore **to alert** escaped slaves of **danger** and give them directions to safe houses.

During the Civil War, Harriet was a **nurse** to **sick** and **wounded** Union soldiers. She also **taught newly freed** men and women how to **care** for themselves. In World War II, a **ship** was named in her memory, and in 1995, the federal government **honored** her **accomplishments** with a **postage stamp**.

A Time of Crisis

October 29, 1929, "Black Tuesday," was a **dark day** in history, **officially setting off** the Great Depression. The **stock market crashed** and **unemployment skyrocketed**. Many people **became homeless**. In 1932, Franklin Delano Roosevelt was **elected** president and he **promised** a "New Deal" for the American people. Congress **created** The Works Progress Administration (WPA), which **offered** work **relief** for **thousands** of people.

The **end** to the Great Depression **came about** in 1941 with America's **entry** into World War II. America **sided with** Britain, France and the Soviet Union **against** Germany, Italy, and Japan. The **loss of lives** in this war was **staggering**.

President Franklin Roosevelt **called** December 7, 1941, "a **date** which **will live in infamy**." On that day, Japanese **planes attacked** the United States Naval Base at Pearl Harbor, Hawaii. The **bombing killed more than** 2,300 Americans. The attack **took the country by surprise**.

"**AIR RAID** ON PEARL HARBOR THIS IS NOT A **DRILL**."

The **ranking** United States **naval officer** in Pearl Harbor **sent** this **message** to all major Navy commands and **fleet units**. Radio stations **receiving** the **news interrupted** regular **broadcasts to announce** the tragic news to the American public. Most people **knew** what the attack **meant** for the U.S. even before Roosevelt's official announcement the next day. The U.S. **would declare** war on Japan.

The U.S. was **already close** to joining the war, but had **committed** to **neutrality**, only committing to **sending** war **supplies on loan** to Great Britain, France, and Russia. Within days, Japan, Germany, and Italy declared war on the United States. December 7, the "date which will live in infamy," **brought us into** World War II.

---

dark day: dia sombrio
officially: oficialmente
setting off: provocando
stock market crashed: bolsa de valores quebrou
unemployment: desemprego
skyrocketed: disparou
became homeless: ficaram sem casa
elected/to elect: eleito/eleger
promised/to promise: prometeu/prometer
created/to create: criou/criar
offered/to offer: oferecia/oferecer
relief: alivio
thousands: milhares
end: final
came about/to come about: ocorreu/ocorrer
entry: entrada
sided with: aliou-se
against: contra
loss of lives: perdas de vida
staggering: espantosa
called/to call: chamou/chamar
date: data
will live in infamy: viverá na vergonha
planes: aviões
attacked/to attack: atacaram/atacar
bombing: bombardeio
killed/to kill: matou/matar
more than: mais de
took the country by surprise: pegou o país de surpresa
air raid: ataque aéreo
drill: treino
ranking: responsável
naval officer: oficial da marinha
sent/to send: enviou/enviar
message: mensagem
fleet units: unidades da frota
receiving/to recieve: que estavam recebendo/receber
news: notícias
interrupted/to interrupt: interromperam/interromper
broadcasts: transmissões
to announce: para anunciar
knew/to know: sabia/saber
meant/to mean: significava/significar
would declare/to declare: declarariam/declarar
already close: já estava perto
committed/to commit: comprometido/comprometer
neutrality: neutralidade
sending: enviar
supplies: suprimentos
on loan: como empréstimo
brought us into: levou-nos a

Spanish-American War

When Cuban **rebels began** a **violent revolution against** Spanish **rule** in 1895, and a **mysterious** explosion **sunk** the *U.S.S. Maine* in the Havana **harbor**, the U.S. **entered** into a **war** with Spain. The war **took place** from April to August 1898. **Only** 113 days after the **outbreak** of war, the Treaty of Paris, which **ended** the **conflict,** gave the United States **ownership** of Puerto Rico, the Philippines, and Guam.

The war **served** to **further cement relations** between the American North and South. The war gave **both sides** a common **enemy** for the **first time** since the **end** of the Civil War in 1865. Many **friendships** were **formed** between **soldiers** of both northern and southern states during their **tours of duty**. This was an important **development** since many soldiers in this war were the **children** of Civil War **veterans** on **both sides**.

The Spanish–American War is **significant** in American history because it **enabled** the United States **to emerge** as a **power** on the **world stage**. The war **marked** American **entry** into world **affairs**. **Over the course** of the **next century**, the United States **had** a large **hand in** various conflicts **around** the world. The United States entered a **lengthy** and **prosperous period** of rapid **economic growth**, population growth, and **technological innovation** which **lasted through** the 1920s.

Women's Right to Vote

Presidents Andrew Jackson, James Polk, and John Tyler, **like many** Americans of the Western Expansion **era** (1829 – 1859), **embraced** the notion of **enlarging** the "**empire for liberty**." **In other words**, they wanted **to expand** the **borders** of America **westward**.

While some **pioneers headed** west to California, others **attempted** to expand the idea of what "liberty" in America **meant**. Abolitionists **opposed laws** that **kept** African Americans **enslaved**, and **advocates** of **women's suffrage argued** that **wives**, **mothers** and **daughters** should **play** a more significant role in **society** by **voting**, **holding office**, and **working outside the home**.

During this **time**, the **right** of women in the United States to vote was **debated.**

Today, women in the United States can vote, **own property**, and hold political office, but it was not always this way. 150 years ago, women **did not have** the same privileges as men in many ways, and they had **to fight** for their rights. In July of 1848, a group of women and men **interested** in **discussing** the position of women in American society **met** at the Seneca Falls Convention in New York.

The assembled group also **considered** and voted on a **number** of resolutions. The number one **point** that was met with **strong opposition**, but was eventually **passed**, was the **following**: "**Resolved**, That it is the **duty** of the women of this country **to secure** to **themselves** their **sacred right to vote**."

The fight for women's **equal** rights was a **long, hard battle**. After the **signing** of "The Declaration of Rights and Sentiments" in 1848, it **took** 72 years of **organized struggle** before most women **won** the right to vote when the Nineteenth Amendment to the U.S. Constitution was passed in 1920.

---

like many: como muitos
era: época
embraced/to embrace: adotaram/adotar
enlarging: aumentar
empire for liberty: império para a liberdade
in other words: em outras palavras
to expand: expandir
borders: limites
westward: para o oeste
while: enquanto
pioneers: pioneiros
headed/to head: dirigiram-se/dirigir-se
attempted/to attempt: tentaram/tentar
meant/to mean: significava/significar
opposed laws: opuseram-se às leis
kept/to keep: mantinham/manter
enslaved/to enslave: escravizados/escravizar
advocates: defensores
women's suffrage: direito de voto de uma mulher
argued/to argue: argumentavam/argumentar
wives: esposas
mothers: mães
daughters: filhas
play: atuar
society: sociedade
voting: votando
holding office: ocupando cargos
working outside the home: trabalhando fora de casa
during: durante
time: período
right: direito
own property: ter propriedades
did not have: não tinham
to fight: que lutar
interested: interessados
discussing: discutir
met/to meet: reuniram-se/reunir-se
considered/to consider: considerou/considerar
number: número
point: ponto
strong opposition: forte oposição
passed/to pass: foi aprovada/aprovar
following: seguinte
resolved: resolvido
duty: dever
to secure: assegurar
themselves: a si mesmas
sacred: sagrado
right to vote: direito ao voto
equal: iguais
long, hard battle: batalha longa e dura
signing: assinatura
took/to take: levou/levar
organized struggle: luta organizada
won/to win: ganhou/ganhar

Test Your Comprehension

Independence Day, page 146

1. Quantos estados há nos Estados Unidos?

2. O que é celebrado no dia 4 de Julho?

Stars and Stripes, page 147

1. Quais são as cores da bandeira norte-americana?

2. O que significam as estrelas da bandeira?

3. Quantas estrelas há na bandeira norte-americana?

4. Quantas listras há na bandeira norte-americana e quais são as cores?

5. O que representam as listras da bandeira?

Electoral College, page 148

1. Quem elege o presidente dos Estados Unidos?

2. Quem se torna presidente no caso de morte ou renuncia?

Supreme Law of the Land, page 149

1. O que é a Constituição?

2. Como são chamadas as mudanças feitas na Constituição?

Teste sua Compreensão

Divisions of Power, page 150

1. Quais são os três ramos do governo norte-americano?

2. Qual é o ramo legislativo no governo norte-americano?

3. Quem faz as leis federais nos Estados Unidos?

4. Quem elege os membros do Congresso?

5. Quantos senadores há no Congresso?

United States Presidency, page 154

1. Qual o presidente chamado de "Pai da Pátria"?

2. Qual é a duração do mandato do presidente?

3. Quais são alguns dos pré-requisitos para ser candidato a presidente?

4. Quantos mandatos completos um presidente pode exercer?

The Bill of Rights, page 153

1. Qual é a origem da liberdade de expressão?

2. O que é a Declaração de Direitos?

3. De quem são os direitos que estão garantidos pela Constituição e pela Declaração de Direitos?

**The clearest way into the universe
is through a forest wilderness.**

John Muir

Geography

specific site: lugar específico
listed: listado
works/to work: trabalha/trabalhar
to conserve: para preservar
places: lugares
importance: importância
future generations: gerações futuras
natural geographical areas: áreas geográficas naturais
particular interest: interesse particular
limestone caves: cavernas de calcário
deepest: mais profunda
built/to build: construíram/construir
multistory stone villages: aldeias de pedra com vários andares
impressive: impressionantes
road system: sistema rodoviário
houses/to house: abriga/abrigar
densest: mais densa
example: exemplo
architecture: arquitetura
inhabited/to inhabit: habitada/habitar
active community: comunidade ativa
formed by: compostas por
inches: polegadas
deep: de profundidade
miles: milhas
wide: de largura
flows/to flow: fluem/fluir
slowly: lentamente
across: através de
marshes: pântanos
pine forests: florestas de pinheiros
mangrove islands: ilhas de mangues
species: espécies
birds: pássaros
live/to live: vivem/viver
as well as: assim como
alligators: aligátores (*espécie de jacaré*)
manatees: peixe-boi
panthers: panteras
ranges/to range: varia/variar
width: largura
attains/to attain: atinge/atingir
depth: profundidade
smoke: fumaça
name: nome
given/to give: dado/dar
exudes/to exude: goteja/gotejar
oily residues: resíduos oleosos
create/to create: criam/criar
smoke-like haze: nevoeiro como fumaça
surrounds/to surround: rodeia/rodear
peaks: picos
fills/to fill: enchem/encher
valleys: vales

World Heritage Sites

A UNESCO World Heritage Site is a **specific site** that is **listed** by the international World Heritage Program. The program **works to conserve places** of cultural or natural **importance** and preserve each site for **future generations**.

In the United States, there are 22 world heritage sites. Seventeen of these are **natural geographical areas** of **particular interest** or importance.

CARLSBAD CAVERNS, NEW MEXICO: Carlsbad Caverns National Park is home to more than 80 **limestone caves**. The nation's **deepest** cave, at 1,597 feet, is found here.

CHACO CULTURE, NEW MEXICO: The Anasazi, or "Ancient Ones," **built** large **multistory stone villages** and an **impressive** 400-mile **road system** in Chaco canyon. Chaco canyon **houses** the **densest** and most exceptional concentration of pueblos in the American Southwest.

TAOS PUEBLO, NEW MEXICO: Pueblo de Taos is the best preserved of the pueblos in the U.S. Taos is a great **example** of the traditional **architecture** of the pre-Hispanic period. Today Taos is **inhabited** by the Taos Pueblo Indians, and it is still an **active community**.

EVERGLADES NATIONAL PARK, FLORIDA: The Everglades are **formed by** a river of fresh water 6 **inches deep** and 50 **miles wide** that **flows slowly across marshes, pine forests**, and **mangrove islands**. More than 300 **species** of **birds live** in the park **as well as alligators**, **manatees**, and Florida **panthers**.

GRAND CANYON, ARIZONA: The Grand Canyon, created by the Colorado River, is 277 miles long, **ranges** in **width** from 0.25 to 15 miles and **attains** a **depth** of more than a mile.

SMOKY MOUNTAINS, NORTH CAROLINA/TENNESSEE: "Place of Blue **Smoke**" was the **name given** by the Cherokee Indians to these Appalachian Highlands. The forest here **exudes** water vapor and **oily residues** which **create** a **smoke-like haze** that **surrounds** the **peaks** and **fills** the **valleys**.

HAWAII VOLCANOES NATIONAL PARK: It is thought that the Hawaiian islands were **created** when **molten rock pushed through** Earth's **crust, forming** volcanoes. The park's two most impressive volcanoes are Kilauea and Mauna Loa.

MAMMOTH CAVE, KENTUCKY: Mammoth Cave is the world's most extensive cave system, with 345 miles of **passages**. Water **seeping into** the cave creates stalactites, stalagmites, and white crystal formations. **Rare** and **unusual** animals are found here, such as **blind fish** and **colorless spiders**. They **demonstrate** adaptation to the total **darkness** and **isolation**.

CAHOKIA MOUNDS STATE HISTORIC SITE, ILLINOIS: The Cahokia site was the **regional center** for the Mississippian Indian culture. Cahokia **features** the largest prehistoric **earthen constructions** in the Americas. This site is a testament to the **sophisticated engineering skills** of Mississippian culture.

MESA VERDE NATIONAL PARK, COLORADO: The Anasazi **established** villages on the **high, flat land** of southwestern Colorado. In the late 1100s they began constructing multistory stone apartment houses, **tucked on ledges** and **under** rock **overhangs**.

OLYMPIC NATIONAL PARK, WASHINGTON: The park **encompasses not only snow-capped** Mount Olympus, glaciers, **alpine meadows**, and **rocky** Pacific Mountain **coastline, but also** one of the few **temperate rain forests** in the world.

WATERTON-GLACIER INTERNATIONAL PEACE PARK, MONTANA: The two parks **sustain** a **surprisingly** diverse habitat, **including wolves, bears**, and **mountain lions**. It features a **wide variety** of wild flowers and **wildlife**.

REDWOOD NATIONAL PARK, CALIFORNIA: Redwood National Park **contains** the **tallest living** things on Earth: **evergreen trees** that **grow** to 350 feet.

GLACIER BAY NATIONAL PARK AND PRESERVE, ALASKA: The park is made up of a **huge chain** of **tidewater** glaciers and a dramatic **range** of **landscapes**, from rocky terrain **covered** by ice to **lush** temperate rain forest. Brown and black bears, **mountain goats, whales, seals**, and eagles can be **found within** the park.

---

it is thought/to think: acredita-se/acreditar
created/crear: criadas/criar
molten rock: rocha derretida
pushed/to push: empurrada/empurrar
through: através
crust: crosta
forming: formando
passages: passagens
seeping into: penetrando em
rare: raros
unusual: incomuns
blind fish: peixes cegos
colorless spiders: aranhas incolores
demonstrate/to demonstrate: demonstram/demonstrar
darkness: escuridão
isolation: isolamento
regional center: centro regional
features/to feature: tem como atração principal/ter como atração principal
earthen constructions: construções de terra
sophisticated: sofisticadas
engineering skills: habilidades de engenharia
established/to establish: fundaram/fundar
high: alta
flat land: terra plana
tucked on ledges: dobradas nas bordas
under: sob
overhangs: salientes
encompasses/to encompass: abrange/abranger
not only...but also: não apenas... como também
snow-capped: (pico de montanha) coberto de neve
alpine meadows: prados alpinos
rocky: rochosas
coastline: costa
temperate rain forests: florestas pluviais temperadas
sustain/to sustain: sustentam/sustentar
surprisingly: surpreendente
including: incluindo
wolves: lobos
bears: ursos
mountain lions: pumas
wide variety: ampla variedade
wildlife: vida selvagem
contains/to contain: acomoda/acomodar
tallest: mais altos
living: seres vivos
evergreen trees: árvores de folhas perenes
grow/to grow: crescem/crescer
huge chain: enorme cadeia
tidewater: maré
range: variedade
landscapes: paisagens
covered: coberto
lush: rica/exuberante
mountain goats: cabras montanhesas
whales: baleias
seals: focas
found within: encontrados dentro

geography

highest: mais altas
located/to locate: localizadas/localizar
home: lar
peaks: picos
reaches/to reach: atinge/atingir
height: altura
approximately: aproximadamente
ocean floor: fundo do oceano
above sea level: acima do nível do mar
generally given: geralmente dadas
hiker's paradise: paraíso dos excursionistas
trails: trilhas
ranging/to range: que variam/variar
short: curtas
walks: caminhadas
strenuous treks: exaustivas caminhadas
long enough: compridas o suficiente
to require: para requerer
overnight camping: acampamento pela noite
bears: ursos
live/to live: vivem/viver
park: parque
as well as: assim como
deer: cervos
elk: alces
tall: de altura
largest known: maior conhecida
free-standing: solta
exposed granite: granito exposto
top: topo
allows/to allow: permite/permitir
spectacular views: vistas espetaculares
nature: naturais
prominent: proeminente
range: cadeia de montanhas
glaciers: geleiras
main feature: característica principal

Majestic Mountains

The **highest** mountains in the U.S. are **located** in four states: Alaska, California, Colorado and Washington. Alaska is **home** to 19 of the 20 highest **peaks** in the U.S. and Colorado is home to 16 of the 50 highest peaks in the U.S.

Mount McKinley or Denali in Alaska is the highest mountain peak in North America. At its peak it **reaches** a **height** of **approximately** 20,320 feet.

The United States is home to the world's highest mountain, from its base on the **ocean floor**. Mauna Kea, on Hawaii is 33,474 feet high but only 13,796 feet are **above sea level**. Heights of mountains are **generally given** as heights above sea level.

The Great Smoky Mountains are a **hiker's paradise** with over 800 miles of **trails ranging** from **short walks** to **strenuous treks** that are **long enough to require overnight camping**. Sixteen-hundred **bears live** in the **park as well as deer** and **elk**.

Stone Mountain Park is Georgia's most popular attraction. The mountain is 825 feet **tall**. It is the world's **largest known free-standing** piece of **exposed granite**. The 1.3-mile trail to the **top** of the mountain **allows spectacular views**. There are also 15 miles of **nature** trails for hiking.

At 7962 feet, Mount Olympus is the tallest and most **prominent** mountain in the Olympic Mountain **range** of Western Washington. Mount Olympus has eight **glaciers** and is the **main feature** of Olympic National Park.

MOUNTAINS AND YOU

Mountains **play** an important role in our lives! **Climbers** and tourists **visit** mountains for the **scenery**. **Farmers graze** their animals on them. Water **authorities** make **reservoirs** and **pump** the water to towns and cities. Forestry companies **grow** coniferous forests and **harvest wood** from them.

Tourism has many **advantages**; however, it can have a **serious impact** on the **environment**. As more and more people visit the mountains, the **chances** of the environment being permanently **damaged** become ever greater.

When hiking, **check** to **make sure** the trail you have **chosen** is **open** for use. Make sure it is dry and you always **stay** on the trail. **Mountain biking** and even hiking on **wet** trails **causes damage** that can be irreparable. You should also have **proper footwear** so you can hike through **puddles**. **Walking around** a puddle **widens** the trail and causes erosion.

If you are camping **on or near** a mountain, camp on a **durable surface** such as **rock**, **sand** or **dry grass**. This **minimizes** impact and doesn't **scare** away wildlife.

Finally, don't **pick** the **flowers**! **Leaving** flowers and plants **in place** is very important for **seeding**. If it's **blooming**, and you **take** the **seed away** it won't get **pollinated**, it's no longer a **food source** for **bees**. **Draw** it, **photograph** it or **smell** it, but don't pick it!

play/to play: desempenham/desempenhar
climbers: alpinistas
visit/to visit: visitam/visitar
scenery: paisagem
farmers: fazendeiros
graze: pastoreiam
authorities: autoridades
reservoirs: reservatórios
pump/to pump: bombeiam/bombear
grow/to grow: cultivam/cultivar
harvest/to harvest: colhem/colher
wood: madeira
advantages: vantagens
serious impact: grave impacto
environment: meio ambiente
chances: chances
damaged: danificado
check/to check: certifique-se/certificar
make sure/to make sure: assegurar que
chosen/to choose: escolheu/escolher
open: aberta
stay/to stay: fique/ficar
mountain biking: ciclismo de montanha
wet: molhadas
causes/to cause: causam/causar
damage: danos
proper footwear: calçado adequado
puddles: poças *de lama*
walking around: caminhar ao redor
widens/to widen: amplia/ampliar
on or near: sobre ou próximo
durable surface: superfície durável
rock: rocha
sand: areia
dry grass: grama seca
minimizes/to minimize: minimiza/minimizar
scare/to scare: espanta/espantar
pick/to pick: colha/colher
flowers: flores
leaving: deixe
in place: em seus lugares
seeding: semeadura
blooming: florescendo
take...away/to take away: tira/tirar
seed: semente
pollinated/to pollinate: polinizado/polinizar
food source: fonte de alimento
bees: abelhas
draw/to draw: desenhe/desenhar
photograph/to photograph: fotografe/fotografar
smell/to smell: cheire/cheirar

geography

desert regions: regiões desérticas
make up/to make up: compõem/compor
largest: maior
covers/to cover: cobre/cobrir
over: mais de
square: quadradas
northern: do norte
three-quarters: três quartos
western: do oeste
southern: do sul
southeastern: do sudoeste
corner: ângulo
third: terço
considered/to consider: considerado/considerar
cold: frio
daytime: horas do dia
below freezing: abaixo de zero
sagebrush: artemísia
vast: vastas
shrub: arbustos
cacti: cactos
compared with: comparado com
range: variedade
richest: mais rico
receives/to receive: recebe/receber
moisture: umidade
summer: verão
season: estação
making/to make: tornando-o/tornar
freezing: geladas
expected/to expect: esperadas/esperar
winter: inverno
broken up/to break up: dividido/dividir
mountain ranges: cadeias de montanhas
referred/to refer: referidas como/referir
sky islands: ilhas do céu
isolation: isolamento
smallest: menor
occupies/to occupy: ocupa/ocupar
large portion: grande porção
named after: leva o nome de
boundaries: limites
defined/to define: definidos/definir
presence: presença
well known: bem conhecida

North American Deserts

Four **desert regions make up** the North American Deserts: the Great Basin, the Mojave, the Sonoran, and the Chihuahuan.

GREAT BASIN DESERT

The Great Basin Desert is the **largest** desert in the U.S. and **covers over** 190,000 **square** miles. It covers the **northern three-quarters** of Nevada, **western** and **southern** Utah, the **southeastern corner** of Oregon and the southern **third** of Idaho.

The Great Basin is **considered** a **cold** desert. A cold desert is one with **daytime** temperatures **below freezing** for part of the year. **Sagebrush** covers **vast** areas of the Great Basin Desert. This is mainly a **shrub** desert with few **cacti**. **Compared with** the other deserts of North America, the Great Basin Desert has a limited **range** of plants and animals.

SONORAN DESERT

The Sonoran desert is considered the biologically **richest** desert in the world. It **receives** much of its **moisture** during the **summer** "monsoon" **season**, **making** it a subtropical desert. **Freezing** conditions can be **expected** for a few nights in **winter**.

The northern part of this desert is in Arizona and California, but it pushes far down into Mexico on both sides of the Gulf of California. It is **broken up** by numerous **mountain ranges**. In the Southwest these mountain ranges are **referred** to as "**sky islands**" due to their **isolation** by valleys.

MOJAVE DESERT

The Mojave is the **smallest** of the North American deserts. It **occupies** a **large portion** of southern California and smaller parts of southwestern Utah, southern Nevada, and northwestern Arizona. It is **named after** the Mojave tribe of Native Americans. The Mojave Desert's **boundaries** are usually **defined** by the **presence** of Joshua Trees. These are the most popular and **well known** plant of the Mojave Desert.

The Mojave Desert receives **less than** 6 inches of rain a year, which makes it the **driest** of the North American deserts. A small California **community** located in the Mojave Desert once went 767 days **without rain**! The Mojave Desert is home to the Mojave National Preserve and the **hottest** place in North America: **Death Valley**. The **all-time record high** was **recorded** here at 134 **degrees**.

ANIMALS OF THE DESERT

Animals that live in the desert have **to adapt** to **lack** of water, extreme temperatures, and **shortage** of food. **To avoid daytime** heat, many desert animals are nocturnal. They **burrow** beneath the surface or **hide** in the **shade**. Many desert animals do not **drink** water at all; they get water from their food or the **moisture** in the plants. The most commonly known animals in North American deserts are the coyote and the **jackrabbit**.

The coyote is a **member** of the dog family and **closely related** to the wolf. The coyote is a fast-running carnivore and **feeds** mainly on small **mammals**. The coyote is one of the **few wild** animals whose communication is frequently **heard**. At night, coyotes **howl** and **emit** a series of short, **high-pitched** yips. Howls are **used** to **keep in touch** with other coyotes in the area.

Jackrabbits are large, **long-legged**, **long-eared hares**. Hares are **similar to rabbits**, but larger. The fur on their long **ears** is **marked** with black **spots**. They are very **fast-moving** mammals and can **run** up to 45 **miles per hour**. Jackrabbits are strict vegetarians. They eat a great variety of **herbs** and shrubs. It is **estimated** that nearly 2 million jackrabbits are **hunted** each year in California.

Other animals **found** in American deserts include **rattlesnakes**, **bighorn sheep**, **roadrunners**, and antelope.

---

less than: menos de
driest: mais seco
community: comunidade
without rain: sem chuva
hottest: mais quente
Death Valley: Vale da Morte
all-time record high: a mais alta temperatura de todos os tempos
recorded/to record: registrada/registrar
degrees: graus
to adapt: adaptar
lack: falta
shortage: escassez
to avoid: para evitar
daytime: horas do dia
burrow/to burrow: cavam/cavar
hide/to hide: escondem-se/esconder
shade: sombra
drink/to drink: bebem/beber
moisture: umidade
jackrabbit: lebre
member: membro
closely related: parente próximo
feeds/to feed: alimenta-se/alimentar
mammals: mamíferos
few: poucos
wild: selvagens
heard/to hear: ouvida/ouvir
howl/to howl: uivam/uivar
emit/to emit: emitem/emitir
high-pitched: agudos
used/to use: usados/usar
keep in touch: ficar em contato
long-legged: pernas longas
long-eared: de orelhas compridas
hares: lebres
similar to: parecidas com
rabbits: coelhos
ears: orelhas
marked: manchadas
spots: pintas
fast-moving: movem-se rápido
run/to run: corre/correr
miles per hour: milhas por hora
herbs: ervas
estimated/to estimate: estima-se/estimar
hunted/to hunt: caçados/caçar
found/to find: encontrados/encontrar
rattlesnakes: cascavéis
bighorn sheep: carneiro montês
roadrunners: pássaros papa-léguas

geography **171**

The Great Lakes

The **Great Lakes**—Superior, Michigan, Huron, Erie, and Ontario—are a group of five lakes on the U.S.-Canadian **border**. They are the largest **fresh water** system on Earth.

Covering more than 94,000 square miles, the Great Lakes **hold** about **one-fifth** of the **world's** fresh water **supply** and **nine-tenths** of the U.S. supply.

The geography of the Great Lakes **shoreline flourishes** with diverse plant and animal life. The shoreline systems include **sandy beaches**, **sand dunes** and **wetlands**.

The most common shoreline in the Great Lakes region is the sand beach. The beaches are a great **place** for humans to **swim** and a great place for **birds** and other small other animals to **find food**. Beaches are **rich feeding grounds** for **shorebirds**. A variety of **beetles**, **spiders**, and birds like to feed upon the **driftwood** and other debris that **collects** on the beach.

The sand dunes of the Great Lakes are the largest freshwater coastal dunes in the world. The Indiana Dunes National Lakeshore ranks **seventh among** national parks in plant diversity. Dunes are also the **home of** many **endangered** animals and plants. The piping plover, a small shorebird, **nests** in the shoreline dunes.

The freshwater wetlands of the Great Lakes are ecologically **unique**. They **range from** small wetlands in bays **to extensive** wetlands along the shoreline. Wetlands are an important part of **duck** and **geese** migration. They **provide** food, **resting stops** and habitats. Wetlands also **improve water quality** by **slowing runoff**, and **processing organic waste** before it **reaches open** water. This process **protects aquatic life** and sources of **drinking** water.

The shorelines of The Great Lakes are threatened by human impacts, such as **housing developments**, tourism, and erosion. **We need** to **ensure** that we don't **destroy** this diverse and beautiful area that took nature **years to create**.

Great Lakes: Grandes Lagos
border: fronteira
fresh water: água doce
covering: cobrindo
hold/to hold: guardam/guardar
one-fifth: um quinto
world's: do mundo
supply: suprimento
nine-tenths: nove décimos
shoreline: costa
flourishes/to flourish: floresce/florescer
sandy beaches: praias arenosas
sand dunes: dunas de areia
wetlands: pântanos
place: lugar
swim: nadar
birds: pássaros
find food: encontrar comida
rich feeding grounds: terrenos ricos em alimentos
shorebirds: aves costeiras
beetles: besouros
spiders: aranhas
driftwood: madeira flutuante
collects/to collect: juntam-se/juntar
seventh: sétimo
among: entre
home of: casa de
endangered: em risco de extinção
nests: ninhos
unique: únicas
range from...to: variam de... a
extensive: extensos
duck: patos
geese: gansos
provide/to provide: fornecem/fornecer
resting stops: paradas para descansar
improve/to improve: melhoram/melhorar
water quality: qualidade da água
slowing/to slow: reduzindo/reduzir
runoff: escoamento
processing/to process: processando/processar
organic waste: lixos orgânicos
reaches/to reach: alcance/alcançar
open: aberta
protects/to protect: protege/proteger
aquatic life: vida aquática
drinking: potável
housing developments: complexos habitacionais
we need/to need: nós precisamos/precisar
ensure: assegurar
destroy/to destroy: destruímos/destruir
years: anos
to create: para criar

Protecting Our Environment

The **natural resources available** to people—for food and other production, **maintaining healthy lives**, and the **pleasure** of a beautiful **landscape**—can seem **boundless**. But **growing populations** are **placing increasing pressure** on the resources. Many of these resources, **once used**, are not **renewable**.

Fresh water **supplies** are essential for agricultural production, for **drinking**, and for **maintenance** of important habitats of animals. Fresh water supplies are **projected** to be inadequate to **meet the needs** of one-third of the world's population by 2025, unless better **use** is made of this precious resource. In many **coastal areas**, pollution has **reduced** the **quality** of the water, **affecting** the quality of water and **aquatic life**. **Forests** are being **cut down** faster than they are being **regenerated** or **planted**.

USAID takes an **integrated approach** to natural resources **management**. Land and water must be **managed skillfully** so that they are able to maintain our **basic ability** to **produce** food. Water supplies must be used more efficiently—and water quality must be maintained or even **improved**—if people are to **remain healthy**.

Forests must be **protected** by those who live in or **close** to them. New approaches to involving these people in the wise management of a resource important to everyone in the world are being developed and applied in many areas. **Sound methods** for **harvesting** trees for **timber** and management of forest trees are being **implemented**. These kinds of programs **promise to slow** the **rate** of deforestation. However, illegal and destructive **logging** remains a **threat** to biodiversity conservation. **Once lost**, it will be impossible for the world **to recover** that diversity of our natural resources.

USAID is an **outstanding** organization that works to protect the environment in more than 100 countries **worldwide**. The work they do provides a **better future** for all.

For more information visit: www.usaid.gov.

---

natural resources available: recursos naturais disponíveis
maintaining/to maintain: mantendo/manter
healthy lives: vidas saudáveis
pleasure: prazer
landscape: paisagens
boundless: sem limites
growing populations: populações em crescimento
placing/to place: colocando/colocar
increasing pressure: crescente pressão
once used: uma vez usados
renewable: renováveis
fresh: doce
supplies: suprimentos
drinking: beber
maintenance: manutenção
projected/to project: projetadas/projetar
meet the needs: satisfazer às necessidades
use: uso
coastal areas: áreas costeiras
reduced/to reduce: reduzido/reduzir
quality: qualidade
affecting/to affect: afetando/afetar
aquatic life: vida aquática
forests: florestas
cut down/to cut down: derrubadas/derrubar
regenerated/to regenerate: restauradas/restaurar
planted/to plant: plantadas/plantar
integrated approach: abordagem completa
management: administração
managed/to manage: administrados/administrar
skillfully: habilmente
basic ability: habilidade básica
produce: produzir
improved/to improve: melhoradas/melhorar
remain healthy: manterem-se saudáveis
protected/to protect: protegidas/proteger
close: próximos
sound methods: métodos seguros
harvesting: colher
timber: madeira
implemented/to implement: implementados/implementar
promise/to promise: prometem/prometer
to slow: frear
rate: ritmo
logging: derrubada de árvores
threat: ameaça
once lost: uma vez perdida
to recover: recuperar
outstanding: notória
worldwide: por todo o mundo
better future: futuro melhor

geography

Land of Waterfalls

America's **outstanding waterfalls** can **be found hiking through forests, alongside rivers** or **even** in **scorching deserts**. Whether a **trickle**, a **stream** or a **cascade**, the **delight** and **serenity** of a waterfall is **enjoyed** by people of **all ages**.

NIAGARA FALLS, NEW YORK

Niagara Falls is a group of **massive** waterfalls **located** on the Niagara River on the **border between** the United States and Canada. The Falls are **comprised** of three separate waterfalls: Horseshoe Falls, American Falls, and the smaller, adjacent Bridal Veil Falls. Niagara Falls is very **wide**, and the most voluminous waterfall in North America. Niagara Falls is **not only renowned** for its **beauty**. The Falls are a **valuable source** of hydroelectric **power** for **both** Ontario and New York.

CALF CREEK FALLS, UTAH

The Calf Creek Recreation Area in **south central** Utah offers a **little-known treasure** in one of the American deserts, the Calf Creek Falls. **While** a **year-round creek** is **relatively rare** in the desert, a year-round 126-foot waterfall is rare and **stunning**. It is 5.5 miles **roundtrip** to hike into the falls. Most of the trail is **sandy** and the **walk** can **become** very **tiring**, especially in **warm weather. However**, **once** you **reach** the falls you will **find** a **cool**, **shady haven** well **worth the effort**.

YOSEMITE FALLS, CALIFORNIA

Yosemite Falls is the **highest** waterfall in North America. Located in Yosemite National Park in California, it's a major attraction in the park, especially in **late spring** when the water **flow** is at its **peak**. At 2425 feet, Yosemite Falls is the **sixth**-highest waterfall in the world.

MULTNOMAH FALLS, OREGON

Multnomah Falls is the **tallest** waterfall in Oregon and also the second-highest year-round waterfall in the United States. The water of the falls **plummets** 620 feet from its origin on Larch Mountain. **Unusually cold** weather can **turn** this waterfall into a **frozen icicle**! The frozen falls are a **sight to behold**.

AMICALOLA FALLS, GEORGIA

Amicalola Falls is **derived** from a Cherokee **word meaning** "tumbling waters." The falls reach the **height** of 729 feet, which makes it the highest waterfall east of the Mississippi. **In addition,** the falls are just a hike away from Springer Mountain, famous for being the **southern end** of the Appalachian Trail.

NORTH CLEAR CREEK FALLS, COLORADO

The **unusual setting** for these waterfalls **sets them apart** from others and makes them even more spectacular. North Creek Falls are **surrounded** by **flat lands covered** with **prairie grasses**. Located **above** the Rio Grande, these falls **crash** more than 100 feet to the **canyon below** and are **believed** to be the most **photographed** waterfall in Colorado.

SHOSHONE FALLS, IDAHO

Shoshone Falls are the **most well known** falls in Idaho, and the most **powerful** falls in the Northwest. The falls are **controlled** by the Milner **Dam** and they are **turned off during** the **agricultural season** by **diverting** the water to the **farmlands**. They **let them flow freely** in the **winter** and spring, **completely covering** the **cliff**. These falls are 212 feet high and 1200 feet wide.

PUNCH BOWL FALLS, OREGON

Punch Bowl Falls is spectacular and is the most photographed waterfall in the Pacific Northwest. The falls **occur** where Eagle Creek **cuts through** a **narrow channel flanked** by cliffs, and **drops powerfully** into a large **bowl**. The falls' **name comes from** the **resemblance** of the area to an **actual punch** bowl.

---

tallest: mais alta
plummets/to plummet: mergulham/mergulhar
unusually cold: excepcionalmente fria
turn: transformar
frozen: gelada
icicle: ponta de gelo
sight: vista
to behold: digna de ser contemplada
derived/to derive: derivada/derivar
word: palavra
meaning/to mean: que significa/significar
tumbling waters: quedas d'água
height: altura
in addition: além de
southern end: extremo sul
unusual: incomum
setting: entorno
sets them apart: as distingue
surrounded/to surround: rodeadas/rodear
flat lands: terras planas
covered/to cover: cobertas/cobrir
prairie: pradaria
grasses: pastos
above: acima
crash/to crash: chocam-se/chocar
canyon: cânion, desfiladeiro
below: abaixo
believed/to believe: tidos como/ter
photographed: fotografados
most well known: mais conhecidas
powerful: poderosas
controlled/to control: controladas/controlar
dam: represa
turned off/to turn off: desligadas/desligar
during: durante
agricultural season: época agrícola
diverting/to divert: desviando/desviar
farmlands: terras cultivadas
let them flow freely: deixam-na correr livremente
winter: inverno
completely: completamente
covering/to cover: cobrindo/cobrir
cliff: penhasco
occur/to occur: ocorrem/ocorrer
cuts through: atravessa
narrow channel: canal estreito
flanked/to flank: ladeado/ladear
drops/to drop: cai/cair
powerfully: poderosamente
bowl: cavidade, tigela
name: nome
comes from/to come from: origina-se/originar
resemblance: semelhança
actual: verdadeiro
punch: ponche

geography

Tropical Rain Forests

true: verdadeira
tropical rain forest: floresta tropical pluvial
diversity: diversidade
isolation: isolamento
resulted/to result: resultou/resultar
fungi: fungos
mosses: musgos
snails: caracóis
birds: pássaros
wildlife: vida selvagem
places: lugares
wettest: mais úmido
averages/to average: atinge a média/atingir a média
rainfall: precipitações
live/to live: vivem/viver
developed/to develop: desenvolvido/desenvolver
bills: bicos
formed: formados
feeding: alimentar
wet: úmidas
rare: raros
caterpillars: lagartas
triggered/trigger: provocadas/provocar
touch: toque
snatch/to snatch: arrebatam/arrebatar
prey: presa
mimic/to mimic: imitam/imitar
twigs: ramos
grab/to grab: agarram/agarrar
comes too close: aproximam-se muito
found/to find: encontradas/encontrar
in turn: em troca
defenseless against: indefesas contra
pigs: porcos
brought/to bring: trazidos/trazer
over the years: com o passar dos anos
escaped/to escape: escaparam/escapar
turned/to turn: tornaram-se/tornar-se
feral: selvagens
wild: violentos
soil erosion: erosão do solo
spread/to spread: espalharam/espalhar
weeds: ervas daninhas
diseases: doenças
polluted/to pollute: contaminaram/contaminar
supplies: suprimentos
crowding out/to crowd out: expulsando/expulsar
lost/to loose: perdeu/perder
two-thirds: dois terços
clearing: limpeza
fire: incêndios
half: metade
habitat loss: perda de habitat
disease: doenças
saving: salvar
remaining: restantes
a race against time: corrida contra o tempo

Hawaii is the only state with a **true tropical rain forest**. Hawaiian tropical forests are home to a large **diversity** of species. The **isolation** of the Hawaiian Islands from the rest of the world has **resulted** in an incredible diversity of **fungi**, **mosses**, **snails**, **birds**, and other **wildlife**. This diversity makes Hawaii's tropical forests some of the most spectacular **places** on Earth.

The world's **wettest** rain forest is found in Hawaii on Mount Waialeale. This forest **averages** 450 inches of **rainfall** per year.

An incredible variety of plants and animals **live** in the tropical forests of Hawaii. Birds native to the forest are hawks, crows, thrushes, and honeycreepers. The honeycreepers have **developed** diverse **bills formed** for **feeding** on the different plants in these **wet** forests. **Rare** carnivorous **caterpillars** are native to Hawaii. When **triggered** by **touch**, these caterpillars **snatch** their **prey**. The caterpillars **mimic twigs** and **grab** prey that **comes too close**.

The native plants in the Hawaiian islands are **found** nowhere else on Earth. **In turn**, most native plants are **defenseless against** introduced species such as **pigs**. Pigs were **brought** to Hawaii from Polynesia and Europe. **Over the years** the pigs have **escaped** and **turned feral**. These **wild** pigs are very destructive to the Hawaiian forests. They have destroyed vegetation, caused **soil erosion**, **spread weeds** and **diseases**, and **polluted** water **supplies**. Other introduced plants and animals are **crowding out** the native plants and animals. Hawaii has **lost two-thirds** of its original forests to agriculture, **clearing**, and **fire**, and **half** its native birds through **habitat loss** and **disease**. **Saving** Hawaii's **remaining** native species is now **a race against time**.

Temperate Rain Forests

Temperate rainforests are **much younger** than tropical rainforests. The **soil** in temperate forests **contains** more **nutrients** than that of the tropics. Temperate rainforests are **located along** the Pacific coast of the United States. Temperate rainforests are much more **scarce** than tropical rainforests. Some of the best forests are found in Olympic National Park, Mount Rainier National Park, Tongass National Forest, Mount St. Helens National Monument and Redwood National Park.

Olympic National Park is located on the Olympic Peninsula of Washington state. The **western side** of the park is **home to** a temperate rain forest and the **wettest** area in the continental United States. **Because** this is a temperate rainforest it contains **dense timber**, **including** spruce and fir.

The Tongass National Forest in southeastern Alaska is the **largest** national forest in the United States. It **spans** over 17 **million acres**. It is a **northern** temperate rain forest, home to rare flora and fauna that are **endangered elsewhere**. The Tongass National Forest is also home to about 70,000 people who **depend** on the national forest for their **livelihood**. Several Alaska Native **tribes live throughout** Southeast Alaska. 31 **communities** are located within the forest; the largest is Juneau, the state capital, with a **population** of 31,000. The forest is **named** for the Tongass group of the Tlingit people, who **inhabited** the Alaska **panhandle**.

temperate: temperadas
much younger: muito mais jovens
soil: solo
contains/to contain: contém/conter
nutrients: nutrientes
located/to locate: localizadas/localizar
along: ao longo de
scarce: escassas
western side: lado oeste
home to: casa para
wettest: mais úmidas
because: porque
dense timber: árvores densas
including: incluindo
largest: maior
spans/to span: abrange/abranger
million acres: milhões de acres
northern: do norte
endangered: em risco de extinção
elsewhere: em outro lugar
depend/to depend: dependem/depender
livelihood: sustento
tribes: tribos
live/to live: vivem/viver
throughout: por toda
communities: comunidades
population: população
named/to name: chamada/chamar
inhabited/to inhabit: habitaram/habitar
panhandle: faixa estreita de terra

geography

all: todos
are found/to find: são encontrados/ encontrar
including: incluindo
designated/to designate: designados/ designar
high threat: grave ameaça
located/to locate: localizadas/localizar
most: a maioria
erupted/to erupt: entrou em erupção/ entrar em erupção
time: tempo
far back: há muito tempo
listed/to list: listados/listar
below: abaixo
considered/to consider: considerado/ considerar
monarch: rei, monarca
single: única
any kind: de qualquer tipo
miles: milhas
long: de comprimento
wide: de largura
rises/to rise: eleva-se/elevar-se
base: base
sea floor: fundo do mar
last: última
eruption: erupção
ended/to end: terminou/terminar
period: período
silence: silêncio
remains/to remain: continua/ continuar
extremely: extremamente
dangerous: perigoso
historically: historicamente
once: uma vez
decade: década
recorded: registrada
slowed/to slow: freado/frear
pace: ritmo
scientists: cientistas
constantly: constantemente
monitor/to monitor: monitoram/ monitorar
anticipation: antecipação
next: próxima

Volcanoes of the United States

All of the volcanoes in the United States **are found** in the western states, **including** Alaska and Hawaii. There are 169 volcanoes in the United States. Eighteen of them have been **designated** as "very **high threat**" volcanoes. These high-threat volcanoes are **located** in Hawaii, Oregon, Washington and Alaska. **Most** of them haven't **erupted** for a very long **time**, as **far back** as the 1700s.

Listed below are some of the most famous volcanoes in the United States.

Mauna Loa is **considered** the "**monarch** of mountains." It is the largest volcano and the largest **single** mountain of **any kind** in the world. It is 60 **miles long**, 30 miles **wide**, and **rises** 28,680 feet from its **base** on the **sea floor**. Mauna Loa's **last** major **eruption** was in 1984. It **ended** a 9-year **period** of **silence**. Mauna Loa **remains** an **extremely dangerous** volcano that can erupt in many different directions.

Historically, Mauna Loa has erupted at least **once** in every **decade** of **recorded** Hawaiian history. It has, however, **slowed** its **pace** with eruptions in 1950, 1975 and 1984. **Scientists** and residents of the Big Island **constantly monitor** Mauna Loa in **anticipation** of its **next** eruption.

Kilauea Volcano, on the **southeast side** of the Big Island, is one of the most active on earth. Its **current** eruption **started** in January 1983 and **continues** to this day. During this eruption over 500 acres have been **added** to the Big Island's **shoreline**. In the course of the eruption, lava flows have **destroyed** a famous 700 year-old Hawaiian **temple**, **overrun** many houses, and permanently **blocked highways**.

There are no indications that the current eruption **will come to an end anytime soon**. Visitors to Hawaii Volcanoes National Park have a **unique opportunity** to see lava in action. Near the southwestern **edge** of the caldera is the "**fire pit**," known as Halemaumau (House of **Everlasting Fire**), which has **at times contained** a **lake** of **boiling** lava.

Mount St. Helens is an active volcano in Skamania County, Washington. It is most famous for its **disastrous** eruption on May 18, 1980. This was the **deadliest** and most **economically** destructive volcanic **event** in the history of the United States. Fifty-seven people were **killed**, and 250 homes, 47 **bridges**, 15 miles of **railways** and 185 miles of highway were destroyed. The eruption caused a massive **debris avalanche, reducing** the **elevation** of the mountain's **summit** from 9,677 feet to 8,365 feet and **replacing** it with a mile-wide **horseshoe-shaped** crater. The debris avalanche was the largest in recorded history.

southeast: sudoeste
side: lado
current: atual
started/to start: começou/começar
continues/to continue: continua/continuar
added/to add: adicionados/adicionar
shoreline: costa
destroyed/to destroy: destruíram/destruir
temple: templo
overrun/to overrun: invadiu/invadir
blocked/to block: bloqueou/bloquear
highways: estradas
will come to an end: terminará
anytime soon: futuro próximo
unique: única
opportunity: oportunidade
edge: margem
fire pit: "escavação no solo para manter o poço de fogo"
everlasting fire: fogo eterno
at times: às vezes
contained/to contain: conteve/conter
lake: lago
boiling: fervente
disastrous: desastrosa
deadliest: fatal
economically: economicamente
event: evento
killed/to kill: mortas/matar
bridges: pontes
railways: ferrovias
debris avalanche: avalanche de escombros
reducing/to reduce: reduzindo/reduzir
elevation: elevação
summit: pico
replacing/to replace: substituindo/substituir
horseshoe-shaped: forma de ferradura

Test Your Comprehension

World Heritage Sites, page 166

1. Qual o objetivo de um lugar ser considerado Patrimônio Histórico da UNESCO?

2. Onde está localizada a caverna mais profunda do país?

3. Quais são os animais raros e incomuns encontrados no Parque Nacional da Caverna do Mamute?

4. O que há no parque Nacional Redwood?

Majestic Mountains, page 168

1. Qual é o pico de montanha mais alto na América do Norte?

2. Qual é a atração mais popular na Geórgia e por que é famosa?

North American Deserts, page 170

1. O que é um deserto frio?

2. Que deserto é considerado deserto biologicamente o mais rico do mundo?

3. Qual é o lugar mais quente da América do Norte?

4. Por que os coiotes uivam à noite?

The Great Lakes, page 172

1. Qual é o tipo de costa mais comum na região dos Grandes Lagos?

2. Por que os alagadiços são importantes?

3. O que está ameaçando as costas dos Grandes Lagos?

Teste sua Compreensão

Land of Waterfalls, page 174

1. As Cataratas do Niágara são conhecidas por sua beleza e pelo que mais?

2. Qual é a catarata mais alta da América do Norte?

3. Onde estão as cataratas mais poderosas do noroeste?

Temperate Rain Forests, page 177

1. O que faz com que as florestas pluviais temperadas sejam diferentes das florestas pluviais tropicais?

2. Qual floresta pluvial é a área mais úmida dos Estados Unidos continental?

3. Qual é a maior floresta nacional dos Estados Unidos?

Tropical Rain Forests, page 176

1. Qual foi o resultado do isolamento entre as ilhas do Havaí e o resto do mundo?

2. Onde está localizada a floresta pluvial mais úmida do mundo?

3. O que está destruindo ou danificando as florestas havaianas?

Volcanoes of the U.S., page 178

1. Quantos vulcões norte-americanos são considerados de risco muito alto?

2. Qual é o maior vulcão e montanha, de qualquer tipo, no mundo?

3. O que foi destruído no fluxo da erupção do Vulcão Kilauea?

One cannot think well, love well, sleep well, if one has not dined well.

Virginia Woolf

Gastronomy

American Apple Pie

You may have heard the expression, **"as American as apple pie,"** in conversation. Apple pie **has remained** an iconic part of American culture **through** the **years**. Apple pie is **considered** a **"comfort food"** for many from **coast to coast**. The **dessert** has also been used in the **phrase**, "for mom and apple pie," said to be the popular **answer** that **World War II** American **soldiers used** when **they were asked why** they were **going to** war.

APPLE EXPRESSIONS

Apples have been a **favorite fruit** for **generations** of Americans and **have become part of** many **common sayings**.

1. The Big Apple: **Nickname** for New York City

2. Apple **of my eye: Object** of my **affection** or my **darling.**

3. The apple **doesn't fall far from the tree**: A **child** is **displaying similar traits** to his or her **parents.**

4. **Bad** Apple: **troublemaker.**

5. An apple **a day keeps** the doctor **away: Eating** fruits like apples **will keep you healthy.**

6. **It's like** apples and **oranges: Comparing two things** that are **completely different** and **difficult** to compare.

7. Apples for the **teacher**: Apples are **associated with going back to school** and children **giving** apples to the teacher as a **present**.

BASIC APPLE PIE RECIPE
8 servings

CRUST:
2½ cups **white flour**
2 tablespoons **sugar**
¼ teaspoon **salt**
½ cup cold **butter**
5 tablespoons cold **vegetable shortening**
8 tablespoons **ice water**

Measure flour, sugar and salt. **Stir** to combine. **Add** the **chilled** butter pieces and shortening to the **bowl**. **Cut them in** with a **pastry cutter** or **knife**. Do not **overmix**. Add ice water. Mix until the **dough** holds together. **Turn** dough onto a **lightly floured surface**, **knead** together, and then **divide in half**. **Flatten** each half into a **disk**, **wrap** in **plastic wrap** and chill for **at least** half an hour.

Roll out one of the disks on a floured surface until you have a **circle** that is 12 inches in **diameter**. Place the circle of dough into a 9" **pie plate**, **trimming** any extra dough from the edges with a sharp knife. **Return it to** the refrigerator **until** you are ready to make the pie. Add **filling (see below)**. Roll out the **second ball** of dough and **cover**. **Pinch** the edges of the crust together. Cut two or three **slits** on top.

FILLING
⅓ to ⅔ cup sugar
¼ cup all-purpose flour
½ teaspoon **ground nutmeg**
½ teaspoon ground **cinnamon**
Pinch of salt
8 medium-sized apples (a medium apple = about 1 cup)
2 tablespoons margarine

Heat oven to 425 degrees. **Peel** and **slice** the apples. Mix sugar, flour, nutmeg, cinnamon, and salt in a bowl. Stir in apples. **Pour into pastry-lined pie plate** and **dot** with margarine. Cover with top crust and **seal the edges**. Cut slits in the top. **Bake** 40 to 50 minutes or until **crust is brown** and juice begins **to bubble** through slits in crust.

Serve warm with **ice cream** for "apple pie a la mode"!

---

white flour: farinha de trigo
sugar: açúcar
salt: sal
butter: manteiga
vegetable shortening: gordura vegetal
ice water: água gelada
measure/to measure: meça/medir
stir/to stir: mexa/mexer
add/to add: adicione/adicionar
chilled: frios
bowl: tigela
cut them in: corte-os
pastry cutter: cortador de massa
knife: faca
overmix: misture muito
dough: massa
turn/to turn: gire/girar
lightly floured surface: superfície ligeiramente enfarinhada
knead/to knead: amasse/amassar
divide in half: divida ao meio
flatten/to flatten: alise/alisar
disk: disco
wrap/to wrap: embale/embalar
plastic wrap: filme plástico
at least: pelo menos
roll out/to roll out: estenda/estender
circle: círculo
diameter: diâmetro
pie plate: tabuleiro de torta
trimming/to trim: recortando/recortar
return it to: coloque de volta
until: até
filling: recheio
see below: veja abaixo
second ball: segunda bola
cover/to cover: cubra/cobrir
pinch/to pinch: belisque/beliscar
slits: fendas
ground nutmeg: noz moscada moída
cinnamon: canela
heat/to heat: aqueça/aquecer
oven: forno
peel/to peel: descasque/descascar
slice/to slice: fatie/fatiar
pour into/to pour: despeje/despejar
pastry-lined pie plate: tabuleiro de tortas
dot/to dot: salpique/salpicar
seal/to seal: feche/fechar
the edges: as bordas
bake/to bake: asse/assar
crust is brown: crosta esteja marrom
to bubble: borbulhar
serve/to serve: sirva/servir
warm: quente
ice cream: sorvete

gastronomy 185

diverse:	diversificada
is found/to find:	encontrada/encontrar
places:	lugares
food:	comida
a land of:	uma terra de
regional cuisine:	culinária regional
coast to coast:	de costa a costa
neighborhoods:	vizinhanças
pride themselves:	orgulham-se
have been made famous:	tornaram-se famosos
beans:	feijões
slow-baked:	assados em fogo baixo
molasses:	melaço
dish:	prato
colonial days:	dias coloniais
was nicknamed/to nickname:	foi apelidado/apelidar
Pilgrims:	peregrinos
learned/to learn:	aprenderam/aprender
to make:	fazer
substituted/to substitute:	substituíram/substituir
pork fat:	gordura de porco
maple syrup:	xarope de bordo
bear fat:	gordura de urso
navy bean:	feijão branco
declared it/to declare:	o declarou/declarar
key lime pie:	torta de limão
best-loved:	mais amada
fabulous:	fabulosa
is described as:	é descrita como
lime-flavored:	com sabor de limão
custard:	manjar
sour:	azedas
custard:	creme
nestled in:	aninhado em
graham-cracker:	biscoito Graham
crust:	crosta
tart:	azedo
has been called:	foi chamado
greatest contribution:	maior contribuição
cuisine:	cozinha
can be found/to find:	pode ser encontrado/encontrar
at its best:	em sua melhor forma
settlers:	colonos
fish soup:	sopa de peixe
missing/to miss:	estavam sem/estar sem (*faltar*)
normally:	normalmente
of the area:	da área
offered/to offer:	ofereceram/oferecer
stew:	cozido
no longer:	já não
recognizable:	reconhecido

186   gastronomy

Taste of America

The United States is a **diverse** and multicultural nation. Diversity **is found** among people, **places** and **food**. America is **a land of** good eating. Delicious **regional cuisine** is found from **coast to coast**. **Neighborhoods**, cities and states **pride themselves** on their regional food and some locations **have been made famous** by the food they best prepare.

BOSTON BAKED BEANS

Beans slow-baked in **molasses** have been a favorite Boston **dish** since **colonial days**. The beans are so popular that Boston **was nicknamed** "Beantown." The **Pilgrims learned** how **to make** baked beans from the Native Americans. They **substituted** molasses and **pork fat** for the **maple syrup** and **bear fat** used by the Natives. The **navy bean** is the official vegetable of Massachusetts, and in 1993 the state **declared it** the original bean of Boston baked beans

FLORIDA KEY LIME PIE

Key West, Florida, is famous for its **key lime pie**, one of America's **best-loved** regional dishes. Every restaurant in the Florida Keys serves this **fabulous** pie. Key lime pie **is described as** "An American pie containing a **lime-flavored custard** topped with meringue." Key limes are very **sour**, and key lime juice is used to make a perfect custard filling. **Nestled in** a sweet **graham-cracker crust**, this official desert of the Florida Keys is **tart**, refreshing and delicious.

NEW ORLEANS GUMBO

Gumbo **has been called** Louisiana's **greatest contribution** to American **cuisine**. Gumbo is classic Cajun food and **can be found** throughout the South but is served **at its best** in Louisiana. When the first French **settlers** came to Louisiana, they brought their love for bouillabaisse, a **fish soup**. They substituted local ingredients because they were **missing** ingredients they **normally** used at home. The Spanish, Africans, and natives **of the area offered** their contributions of food and the **stew** was **no longer recognizable** as bouillabaisse. It became gumbo.

HOT DOGS

Hot dogs **are considered by some** the favorite American food. Charles Feltman, a German **butcher**, **opened** up the first Coney Island hot dog stand in Brooklyn, New York in 1867. Harry Magely **is credited for putting** the hot dog into a **bun** and **topping it** with condiments. He **reportedly instructed** his **vendors to shout**, "Red hots! Get your red hots!"

Some people say there is one place where a hot dog always **tastes best**—at a baseball game! The National Hot Dog and Sausage Council **reports that** baseball fans **will consume** over 27 million hot dogs at major-league parks just this year!

PHILLY CHEESE STEAK

Philadelphia **is home to** the cheese steak. The cheese steak is a **sandwich** prepared on a **long roll** and filled with **sliced pieces** of **steak** and **melted cheese**. The cheese steak is a **comfort food** for natives of Philadelphia. **It was invented** in the city in 1930 and is considered a city icon. According to Philadelphians, **you cannot make** an authentic Philadelphia cheese steak sandwich without an authentic Philadelphia roll. The rolls must be **long and thin**, **not fluffy** or soft, **but also not** too hard. They **also say** that if you are **more than** one hour from South Philly, you will not find an authentic sandwich!

TEXAS RED

Texans take chili **seriously**, and **as a result**, chili became the Texas State Dish in 1977. Chili **originated** in San Antonio in the 1880s. The **essential ingredients** are **ground beef**, **garlic**, **cumin**, and **chili peppers**. The **public environment** used **to celebrate** chili **is called** a "cook-off." At a cook-off, **thousands of people** gather **to create** their version of Texas Red. You can **attend** a cook-off **throughout** the year in Texas and **taste for yourself** some of the best chili in the United States.

are considered by some: são considerados por alguns
butcher: açougueiro
opened/to open: abriu/abrir
is credited for: lhe é atribuído
putting/to put: colocando/colocar
bun: pão
topping it/to top: cobri-lo/cobrir
reportedly: segundo se diz
instructed/to instruct: ordenou/ordenar
vendors: vendedores
to shout: gritassem
some people say: algumas pessoas dizem
tastes best: mais gostoso
reports that/to report: relataram que/relatar
will consume/to consume: consumirão/consumir
is home to: é o lar de
sandwich: sanduíche
long roll: pão largo
sliced pieces: rodelas cortadas
steak: bife
melted cheese: queijo derretido
comfort food: comida que conforta
it was invented/to invent: foi inventado/inventar
you cannot make: você não pode fazer
long and thin: compridos e finos
not fluffy: não fofos
but also not: mas também não
also say: também dizem
more than: a mais de
seriously: a sério
as a result: como resultado
originated/to originate: originou-se/originar
essential ingredients: ingredientes essenciais
ground beef: carne moída
garlic: alho
cumin: cominho
chili peppers: pimentas malagueta
public environment: arredores públicos
to celebrate: para celebrar
is called/to call: chamado/chamar
thousands of people: milhares de pessoas
to create: para criar
attend/to attend: assistir
throughout: ao longo do
taste for yourself: provar por si mesmo

gastronomy 187

Blue Plate Special

American diners are popular **neighborhood restaurants** that attract a **cross-section** of America, from **factory workers** to Wall Street **executives** and from **senior citizens** to **teenagers**. Americans of **all walks of life** and all ages love diners! The function of the diner **has always been to provide** a delicious and **inexpensive**, **home-style meal** in a **comfortable atmosphere**.

Diners **first evolved** from **mobile lunch wagons**. The first dining wagons with **seating** appeared in the late 19th century. The dining wagon **owners** were **able to serve** busy locations **without** buying expensive **real estate**. As the lunch wagons became more popular and more **customer** seating was needed, the diners were **converted** to buildings. The same **manufacturers** who had made the wagons **constructed** the **buildings**. Like the lunch wagon, these diners allowed owners to set up a **food service** business quickly using the **preassembled equipment**.

By the early 1900s, the downtown centers of New England became so **crowded** with mobile lunch wagons that **city ordinances** began **limiting** their service to only **daylight hours**. However, owners **worked around** this **ruling**. They would find a busy location **by the side of the road**, take off the wheels, **hook up to** power, and **set up** business in a permanent location.

The term "diner" **originated** with Patrick J. Tierney, who called his pre-fabricated restaurants "dining cars." His salespersons later **shortened it** to "diners." A common **myth** was that diners were **converted railroad cars**. In reality, the **streamlined locomotives** of the 1930s inspired manufacturers **to copy** their **sleek** appearance.

---

neighborhood restaurants: restaurantes do bairro
cross-section: grupo representativo
factory workers: operários
executives: executivos
senior citizens: cidadãos da terceira idade
teenagers: adolescentes
all walks of life: de todas as profissões ou classes sociais
has always been: sempre foi
to provide: fornecer
inexpensive: econômica
home-style meal: comida caseira
comfortable atmosphere: atmosfera confortável
first evolved: evoluíram primeiramente
mobile: móveis
lunch wagons: vagões de almoço
seating: assentos
owners: donos
able to serve: capazes de servir
without: sem
real estate: bens imobiliários
customer: clientes
converted/to convert: convertidos/converter
manufacturers: fabricantes
constructed/to construct: construíram/construir
buildings: edifícios
food service: serviço de alimentação
preassembled equipment: equipamento pré-montado
crowded: lotados
city ordinances: regulamentações municipais
limiting/to limit: limitando/limitar
daylight hours: horas diurnas
worked around: esquivavam-se
ruling: regras
by the side of the road: às margens das estradas
hook up to/to hook up to: conectavam/conectar
set up/to set up: montavam/montar
originated/to originate: originou-se/originar
shortened it/to shorten: encurtou/encurtar
myth: mito
converted railroad cars: vagões de trens convertidos
streamlined locomotives: locomotivas aerodinâmicas
to copy: a copiar
sleek: elegante
one million: um milhão

By 1937, **one million** people **ate at least** one meal a day at a diner. In the 1940s, there were almost 10,000 diners across the U.S. **Today, fewer than** 3,000 **remain**.

"Blue plate special" refers to a special **low-priced** meal. This meal **usually** changes daily. It **typically** consists of **meat** and three vegetables on a **single** plate. **During** the Depression, a manufacturer started making plates with **separate sections** for each part of a meal. For a reason **that has never been determined**, the plates were **only available** in the color blue. Because they were inexpensive and **saved on dishwashing**, diners began using them for their low-priced daily specials.

The **term** "blue plate special" was **very common** from the 1920s through the 1950s. As of 2007 there are **still** a few restaurants and diners **that offer** blue-plate specials **under that name**. **Sometimes** they offer the special on blue plates, but it is a **vanishing tradition**. **The phrase itself** is still a common American expression.

Do you have a **craving** for American diner food? Check out Diner City web site: www.dinercity.com. Here you will find diners **throughout** the United States and an interesting photo collection. Also, visit The Roadside at www.roadsidemagazine.com. This site is **dedicated** to the **preservation** of the American diner.

People who **frequent** diners know diner **lingo**. **Employees use it to name** meals. It is **truly** a **language unto its own**!

- "One on the city" (a **glass** of water)
- "Make it moo" (coffee with milk)
- "Bird seed" (a **bowl** of cereal)
- "Cockleberries" (**eggs**)
- "Breath" (**onions**)
- "Frog sticks" (**french fries**)
- "Shivering Liz" (**Jello**)
- "Bossy in a bowl" (beef **stew**)
- "Sweep the kitchen" (a **plate** of **hash**)
- "Skid grease" (**butter**)

ate/to eat: comeram/comer
at least: pelo menos
today: atualmente
fewer than: menos de
remain/to remain: permanecem/ permanecer
low-priced: baixo preço
usually: geralmente
typically: tipicamente
meat: carne
single: único
during: durante
separate sections: seções separadas
that has never been determined: que nunca foi determinada
only available: apenas disponíveis
saved on/to save on: economizavam/ economizar
dishwashing: lavagem de pratos
term: termo
very common: muito comum
still: ainda
that offer: que oferecem
under that name: com este nome
sometimes: às vezes
vanishing tradition: tradição que está desaparecendo
the phrase itself: a frase por si só
craving: desejo
throughout: através de
dedicated/to dedicate: dedicado/ dedicar
preservation: conservação
frequent/to frequent: frequentam/ frequentar
lingo: jargões, gírias
employees: empregados
use it/to use: o usam/usar
to name: nomear
truly: verdadeiramente
language: linguagem
unto its own: em si mesma
glass: copo
bowl: tigela
eggs: ovos
onions: cebolas
french fries: batatas fritas
Jello: gelatina
stew: cozido
plate: prato
hash: prato feito de carne moída misturada com batata assada ou frita
butter: manteiga

gastronomy

Chocolate Chip Cookies

It **may be hard** for **cookie aficionados to believe**, but **before** the 1930s, **no one had ever had** the **culinary pleasure** of **biting** into a chocolate chip cookie. Why? This chocolate delight **had not yet been** invented.

Ruth Wakefield is the woman **responsible for creating** the chocolate chip cookie. In 1930, Ruth and her husband Kenneth **purchased** a Cape Cod-style **tollhouse** located between Boston and New Bedford, Massachusetts. The house had originally **served as** a **haven** for travelers. **Tired passengers** stopped here **to pay tolls** and eat **home-cooked** meals.

The Wakefields decided **to revive** and continue the house's tradition. They **turned their home** into a hotel and called it the Toll House Inn. Ruth **cooked homemade** meals and **baked** for guests of the inn. Her incredible **desserts began attracting** people from all over New England.

Ruth's **favorite recipe** was Butter Drop Do cookies. As she prepared the batter one day **she realized** she **had run out of** baker's chocolate. She decided to use the chocolate she **had on hand**, a **semi-sweet** chocolate bar, **given to her** by Andrew Nestle. She cut it into **tiny bits** and **added them** to the dough. She **expected** the chocolate bits **to melt** as the cookies baked in the **oven**. However, the chocolate did not melt. **Instead**, it held its shape and softened to a **creamy texture**. **As you can imagine**, the cookies Ruth had created became very popular with guests at the inn. Her recipe **was published** in a Boston **newspaper**, **as well as** other papers in the New England area.

Meanwhile, Nestle saw **sales** of its Semi-Sweet Chocolate Bar

jump dramatically because so many people were using the bits of chocolate in Ruth's recipe. Ruth and Nestle **agreed** that Nestle **would print** the "Toll House Cookie" recipe on its **packaging**. Part of this agreement included **supplying** Ruth with all of the chocolate she could use for the rest of her life.

Nestle began to package their chocolate bars with a **special chopper** designed to **easily cut** the chocolate into **small morsels**. **Eventually,** Nestle **came up with** a better idea, and began **offering** Nestlé Toll House Real Semi-Sweet Chocolate Morsels.

The rest is "chocolate-chip" **history**. Ruth continued to cook and published a series of **cookbooks**. In 1966, she sold the Toll House Inn to a family that tried to **turn it into** a nightclub. The Saccone family, who restored its original form, bought it in 1970. **Sadly,** fourteen years later, the Toll House **burned down** on New Years Eve.

Ruth Wakefield **passed away** in 1977 but her **legacy** lives on, enjoyed by millions of people nationwide. **Still, to this day**, you can find her Toll House recipe **on the back of** Nestlé's chocolate chip cookie packages.

meanwhile: enquanto isso
sales: vendas
jump/to jump: dispararem/disparar
agreed/to agree: concordaram/concordar
would print/to print: imprimiria/imprimir
packaging: embalagem
supplying/to supply: abastecendo/abastecer
special chopper: cortador especial
easily: facilmente
cut: cortar
small morsels: pedacinhos pequenos
eventually: finalmente
came up with/to come up with: sugeriu/sugerir
offering: a oferecer
the rest is...history: o resto é... história
cookbooks: livros de receita
turn it into: a converteu em
sadly: lamentavelmente
burned down/to burn down: pegou fogo/pegar fogo
passed away/to pass away: faleceu/falecer
legacy: legado
still, to this day: ainda, até hoje
on the back of: na parte de trás de

COOKING VOCABULARY

aluminum foil: papel de alumínio
bake: assar
barbecue: churrasco
basil: manjericão
basting: pingar gordura na carne durante o cozimento
batter: massa de farinha com ovos e leite
bay leaf: folha de louro
blanch: escaldar
boiling point: ponto de ebulição
bread crumbs: migalhas de pão, farinha de rosca
broom: vassoura
broth: caldo, sopa de carne

curdle: coalhar
dash: pitada
diced: cortado em cubos
dining room: sala de jantar
dishwasher: lava-louças
drain: escorrer
freezer: refrigerador, geladeira
frozen: congelado
garnish: guarnição
ginger: gengibre
glaze: cobertura
grated: ralado
ground: moído
herb garden: herbário
herb: erva

juicy: suculento
kitchen sink: pia da cozinha
ladles: concha
mash: amassar, fazer purê
measuring cup: xícara de medida
nutmeg: noz moscada
quartered: cortado em quatro
rosemary: alecrim
sauté: levemente frito
scald: escaldar, ferver
season with salt: temperar com sal
stew: cozido
turn off: desligado
wedge: pedaço grande
whisk: bater, misturar

chicken: frango
wings: asas
deep-fried: fritas em muito óleo
coated: cobertas
spicy sauce: molho apimentado
named after: levam o nome de
originated/to originate: originaram-se/originar
tasty: saboroso
side dish: acompanhamento
first prepared: preparado pela primeira vez
owner: dona
brilliant idea: brilhante ideia
combining them/to combine: combiná-las/combinar
red-hot: picante
typically: tipicamente
thrown away/to throw away: jogadas fora/jogar fora
stock: caldo
sauced: com molho
served it/to serve: a serviu/servir
son: filhos
instant hit: sucesso instantâneo
are often called: são geralmente chamadas
local variations: variações locais
are most often found: são encontradas muitas vezes
bar menus: cardápio de bares
usually: normalmente
celery: aipo
carrot: cenouras
blue cheese: queijo azul
alternative: alternativa
truly authentic experience: experiência verdadeiramente autêntica
order/to order: peça/pedir
directly from: diretamente do

Buffalo Wings

Buffalo wings are **chicken wings deep-fried** and **coated** in a **spicy sauce**. Buffalo wings are **named after** the city of Buffalo, New York where they **originated**.

This **tasty** and popular **side dish** was created on October 3, 1964 and **first prepared** at the Anchor Bar in Buffalo, New York. Teressa Bellissimo, **owner** of the Anchor Bar with her husband Frank, had the **brilliant idea** of deep-frying chicken wings and **combining them** with her husband's spicy **red-hot** sauce. **Typically**, chicken wings were **thrown away** or used only for making **stock**.

Teressa created this deep-fried and **sauced** creation, **served it** to her **son** and his friends, and they were an **instant hit**.

In the Southern United States, wings **are often called** "hot wings" and come with many different sauces. There are **local variations** all over the United States in how they are prepared and served and they **are most often found** on **bar menus** as bar food.

Buffalo wings are **usually** served with **celery** sticks, **carrot** sticks and **blue cheese** dip. Some restaurants serve their wings with ranch dressing as an **alternative** to blue cheese.

For a **truly authentic experience**, **order** the original sauce **directly from** the Anchor Bar that made Buffalo chicken wings famous!

gastronomy

Saltwater Taffy

Taffy has been an American **beachside** tradition **for more than** 100 years. The exact history of how taffy **came to be** is still a mystery. Some **candy companies state** that David Bradley, a **shopkeeper** in Atlantic City, was the **first seller** of the candy. In 1883, a **huge** storm **hit the beaches**. Bradley's store **was filled with** the ocean water and his **entire stock** of taffy **was soaked**. A young girl asked if the store **still had** taffy **for sale**. **As a joke**, Bradley told the girl **to grab some** "saltwater taffy." **This is believed to be** the first reference to "saltwater taffy."

Joseph Fralinger is recognized **as the person who** made saltwater taffy popular. Fralinger observed **sunbathers** and **visitors** and **came up with the idea to package** saltwater taffy as a **treat** for **beachgoers** to take home with them. He thought tourists would want a reminder or **souvenir** of their vacation in Atlantic City. As an experiment, Fralinger **boxed the candy** and sold it one weekend. It was a huge **success**!

As Fralinger's success grew, competition **was sure to follow**. Shops **would compete** with new and different recipes **to entice** the visitors and **boost** their sales.

By the 1920s, everyone **was buying** and **enjoying** saltwater taffy after a day at the beach. Just as Fralinger **had predicted**, it was the perfect beach souvenir **to bring home** to family and friends.

Saltwater taffy **can be found** at boardwalks and in beach communities and is still a popular treat for people to bring home after visiting the beach. Traditional **flavors** include **peppermint**, **cinnamon** and chocolate. More adventurous **taste buds** can enjoy flavors like **rhubarb**, banana and marshmallow.

---

beachside: litoral
for more than: por mais de
came to be: originou-se
candy companies: empresas de doces
state/to state: declaram/declarar
shopkeeper: lojista
first seller: primeiro vendedor
huge: grande
hit/to hit: açoitou/açoitar
the beaches: as praias
was filled with/to fill: estava cheia/estar cheio
entire stock: todo o estoque
was soaked/to soak: ficou empapado/empapar
still had: ainda tinha
for sale: a venda
as a joke: como brincadeira
to grab: pegar
some: algumas
this is believed to be: acredita-se ser
as the person who: como a pessoa que
sunbathers: pessoas tomando banho de sol
visitors: visitantes
came up with the idea: teve a ideia de
to package: embalar
treat: delícia
beachgoers: banhistas
souvenir: lembrança
boxed the candy: colocou o doce em caixas
success: sucesso
was sure to follow: com certeza viria a seguir
would compete/to compete: apreciando/apreciar
to entice: para atrair
boost: aumentar
was buying/to buy: estava comprando/comprar
enjoying/to enjoy: apreciando/apreciar
had predicted/to predict: tinha previsto/prever
to bring home: trazer para casa
can be found: pode ser encontrado
flavors: sabores
peppermint: hortelã
cinnamon: canela
taste buds: papilas gustativas
rhubarb: ruibarbo

gastronomy

was created/to create: foi criada/criar
not by...but by: não pelo... mas pelo
after serving: após servir
patrons: clientes
guests: hóspedes
instant success: sucesso instantâneo
original version: versão original
only: apenas
apples: maçãs
celery: aipo
mayonnaise: maionese
chopped: picadas
walnuts: nozes
later: depois
became/become: tornaram-se/tornar-se
common part: parte comum
dish: prato
is usually: é normalmente
on top of: em cima de
bed of lettuce: cama de alface
cup: xícara
sweet: doce
tart: azeda
combination: combinação
tablespoon: colher de sopa
lemon juice: suco de limão
raisins: uvas passas
sprinkle/to sprinkle: espalhe/espalhar
after: após
cut/to cut: cortadas/cortar
add/to add: adicione/adicionar
toss/to toss: mexa/mexer
coat: recobrir
meat: carne
popular choices: alternativas populares
strips of chicken breast: tiras de peito de frango
turkey: peru
cubed smoked pork loin: lombo de porco defumado em cubos
grilled salmon: salmão grelhado
layer/to layer: disponha em camadas/dispor em camadas
lightly toss: misture levemente
entree: entrada

Waldorf Salad

Waldorf salad **was created** at New York's Waldorf-Astoria Hotel in 1896 **not by** a chef, **but by** the maître d'hôtel, Oscar Tschirky. **After serving** the Waldorf Salad to **patrons** and **guests**, the Waldorf salad became an **instant success**.

The **original version** of this salad contained **only apples**, **celery** and **mayonnaise**. **Chopped walnuts later became** a **common part** of the **dish**. Waldorf salad **is usually** served **on top of** a bed of lettuce.

CLASSIC WALDORF SALAD

Ingredients:

1 **cup** apples, chopped (Granny Smith or a **sweet tart** apple or a **combination** of different tart apples)
1 **tablespoon lemon juice**
1 cup celery, chopped
¼ cup mayonnaise
¼ cup **raisins** (optional)
¼ cup walnuts (optional)

Sprinkle apples with lemon juice **after** they are **cut**.
Add all other ingredients.

Toss to **coat** all pieces with mayonnaise.

Another option for a modern Waldorf salad is to add **meat** to the recipe. Some **popular choices** include **strips of chicken breast**, **turkey**, **cubed smoked pork loin**, or **grilled salmon**. **Layer** the meat on top of the Waldorf salad, or **lightly toss** to make a delicious **entree**.

Clam Chowder

Clam Chowder is a popular **soup containing clams** and **broth**. **In addition to** the clams, the chowder may contain **potato** chunks or **onions**. Small **carrot** strips **might occasionally be added** for color.

Chowder **has its roots** in the **Latin word** "calderia," which **originally meant** a **place** for **warming** things, and **later came to mean cooking pot**.

New England clam chowder is white and contains milk or cream. **Some people say that** New England clam chowder has become creamier **over the years as a result of** tourism. **Allegedly**, tourists visiting New England, **squeamish** of clams and seafood, prefer the creamier chowder. **At one time**, some restaurants served **clear** chowder, and let customers add cream to taste.

Manhattan clam chowder has clear broth and lots of fresh tomato for red color and flavor. This **tomato-based** clam chowder **started with** the **increased popularity** of the tomato in the mid-1800s and the large population of Italians in New York. **Originally**, this chowder was called "Coney Island clam chowder," **most likely** because of the many restaurants on Coney Island that served it. By the 1930s the popular **name became** "Manhattan clam chowder."

Clam chowder **is usually** served with saltine or oyster **crackers**. Throughout the United States, creamy New England-style clam chowder is served in **sourdough bread bowls**. **You will find** warm chowder in **fresh** sourdough bread bowls all over San Francisco, where sourdough is popular with tourists and has been considered a **signature dish** since 1849.

soup: sopa
containing/to contain: contendo/conter
clams: moluscos
broth: caldo, sopa de carne
in addition to: além de
potato: batata
onions: cebolas
carrot: cenoura
might occasionally be added: podem ser ocasionalmente adicionadas
has its roots: tem suas raízes
Latin word: palavra latina
originally: originalmente
meant/to mean: significava/significar
place: lugar
warming: esquentar
later came to mean: passou a significar
cooking pot: panela
some people say that: algumas pessoas dizem
over the years: com o passar dos anos
as a result of: como resultado de
allegedly: supostamente
squeamish: melindrosos
at one time: numa época
clear: claro
tomato-based: a base de tomate
started with/to start with: começou com/começar com
increased popularity: aumentada popularidade
originally: originalmente
most likely: provavelmente
name: nome
became/to become: tornou-se/tornar-se
is usually: é geralmente
crackers: biscoito fino bem torrado
sourdough bread bowls: tigela feita de pão fermentado
you will find: encontrará/encontrar
fresh: fresco
signature dish: prato que é marca registrada

farmers' markets: mercados dos fazendeiros
modeled after: tinham como modelo
rolled into town: entravam *(rolando)* na cidade
goods: mercadorias
city folk: cidadãos
took place/to take place: ocorreram/ocorrer
empty lots: terrenos vazios
major street: rua principal
term: termo
the city: a cidade
built/to build: construiu/construir
wooden building: edifício de madeira
best-designed: melhores projetos
city plan: plano de cidade
main artery: via principal
opened/to open: abria/abrir
twice a week: duas vezes por semana
ringing of bells: toque de sinos
daily: diários
third-oldest: terceiro mais antigo
major attraction: atração principal
throw fish to each other: jogam peixes um para o outro
famous worldwide: famoso mundialmente
consumers: consumidores
gathering places: pontos de encontros
to bring: para trazer
shop/to shop: compram/comprar
as well as: assim como
can provide: podem abastecer
may not be available: podem não estar disponíveis
income: rendimento
community workers: trabalhadores da comunidade
employment: emprego
youth: jovens
nearly twice as many as: quase o dobro de
for many reasons: por muitos motivos
cannot find: não podem achar
eating seasonally: comer alimentos sazonais
smells: aromas
fresh herbs: ervas frescas
flowers: flores
to support: para apoiar
come together: unirem-se

196　gastronomy

Farmers' Markets

America's first **farmers' markets** were **modeled after** similar markets in Europe. Wagons filled with produce from local farms **rolled into town** ready to sell their **goods** to the **city folk**. Most markets **took place** in **empty lots** on a **major street**. This is where the **term** "market streets" came from.

The first market in the history of the United States was in Boston in 1634. Twenty-eight years later, **the city built** a **wooden building** for the market to create a more permanent presence.

Philadelphia had the **best-designed** and regulated markets. William Penn's **city plan** included a market along the **main artery**, High Street, later named Market Street. The market **opened twice a week** with the **ringing of bells**.

One of the most famous **daily** markets today is the Pike Place Market in Seattle, Washington. The market opened August 17, 1907 and is the **third-oldest** farmers' market in the country. The market's **major attraction** is the Pike Place Fish Market, where employees **throw fish to each other** rather than passing them by hand. The "flying fish" are **famous worldwide**.

Farmers' markets are good for **consumers**, farmers, and for the community. Markets create **gathering places to bring** customers downtown, where they **shop** at local businesses **as well as** at the market. Farmers **can provide** the community with food and produce that **may not be available** at other stores in the area. Farmers' markets can also provide extra **income** for **community workers** and possible **employment** for local **youth**.

There are 4500 markets in the U.S. today, **nearly twice as many as** a decade ago. People visit the farmers' markets **for many reasons**: for the wonderful produce they **cannot find** anywhere else; for the benefits of **eating seasonally**; for the beauty and **smells** of the **fresh herbs** and produce and **flowers**; and of course, **to support** their local farmers and to **come together** with their community.

Soul Food

Soul food is a **term associated with** food **created by** African-Americans of the Southern United States. In the mid-1960s, "soul" was a **familiar adjective** used **to describe** African-American culture.

African-Americans **working as slaves** would **make the most of** what ingredients they had **at hand**. The fresh vegetables they had used in Africa **were replaced** by the **throwaway** foods from the **plantation house**. Their vegetables were the **tops of turnips** and **beets** and **dandelions**. They were cooking with **greens** they had never tasted before: collards, kale, cress, mustard and pokeweed. African-American slaves developed **recipes** that used **discarded meat**, such as **pigs' feet** and **ears**, **beef tongue** or **tail**, tripe and **skin**. Cooks added onions and garden herbs such as garlic, thyme, and bay leaf **to enhance** the **flavors**.

The slave diet **began to change** when slaves started working in the plantation houses as cooks. They **had access to** a **wider variety** of food and started **to share** their favorite meals with the families they were cooking for. Fried chicken began **to appear** on the tables; sweet potatoes **accompanied** the white potato. Local foods like apples, peaches and berries **were transformed** into delicious puddings and pies.

Nothing was ever **wasted** in the African-American kitchen. Bread pudding was created out of **stale bread**, and each part of the pig had its own special **dish**. Even the liquid from the **boiled** vegetables was **made into gravy** or turned into a drink.

The slaves' cuisine **became known as** "good times" food. The evening meal was a time for families to come together **after long days and hours** of hard work. **Songs** and **stories** were shared and dinnertime became a meal for **both body and soul**.

Soul food originated in the South, but this cooking tradition **has since spread** all throughout the United States. Today, soul food restaurants exist in **nearly every** African-American community in the U.S.

---

term: termo
associated with/to associate with: associado com/associar com
created by/to create: criada por/criar
familiar adjective: adjetivo familiar
to describe: para descrever
working/to work: trabalhando/trabalhar
as slaves: como escravos
make the most of: aproveitar ao máximo
at hand: em mãos
were replaced/to replace: substituídos/substituir
throwaway: restos
plantation house: casa de plantio
tops of: folhas de
turnips: nabos
beets: beterrabas
dandelions: dente-de-leão
greens: verduras frescas
recipes: receitas
discarded meat: restos de carne
pigs' feet: pés de porco
ears: orelhas
beef tongue: língua de vaca
tail: rabo
skin: pele
to enhance: melhorar
flavors: sabores
began/to begin: começou/começar
to change: a mudar
had access to: tinham acesso a
wider variety: variedade maior
to share: a compartilhar
to appear: a aparecer
accompanied/to accompany: acompanhavam/acompanhar
were transformed/to transform: eram transformadas/transformar
wasted/to waste: desperdiçado/desperdiçar
stale bread: pão velho
dish: prato
boiled/to boil: fervidos/ferver
made into gravy: convertido em molho
became known as: ficou conhecida como
after long days and hours: após longos dias e horas
songs: músicas
stories: histórias
both body and soul: corpo e alma
has since spread: desde então tem se espalhado
nearly every: quase todas

gastronomy

great: grande
pastime: passatempo
barbecue festivals: festivais de churrasco
are popping up/to pop up: estão aparecendo/aparecer
statewide: estaduais
cook-offs: competições de cozinha
turning it into: tornando-se
sport: esporte
to gather with: reunir-se com
friends: amigos
backyard: quintal
to enjoy: para degustar
hot grill: grelhas quentes
state/to state: afirmam/afirmar
began/to begin: começou/começar
in the south: no sul
however: contudo
taste: gosto
sometimes: às vezes
method: método
may vary: podem variar
from state to state: de estado para estado
argue/to argue: defendem/defender
unknown: desconhecida
primary meat: carne principal
the way it is cut: a forma como é cortada
pulled/to pull: despedaçado/despedaçar
rather than: em vez de
chopped/to chop: picado/picar
covered with/to cover with: coberta com/cobrir com
ribs: costelas
coated/to coat: cobertas/cobrir
a mix: uma mistura
sharp spices: temperos fortes
pit cooking: cozinhar num buraco
hint: leve sabor
pepper: pimenta
molasses: melado
gets preference: são preferidos
pork: porco

American Barbecue

Barbecue is a **great** American tradition and **pastime**. It has become so popular that **barbecue festivals are popping up** all across the nation and **statewide cook-offs** are **turning it into** a **sport**!

The popular tradition of "barbecuing" is **to gather with** your **friends** in the **backyard to enjoy** food prepared over a **hot grill**.

Barbecue experts **state** that the tradition of barbecue **began in the south**. **However**, the **taste**, ingredients used, and **sometimes** even the **method** of cooking **may vary from state to state**; so some people **argue** that its history is **unknown**.

In the central South, the **primary meat** used in barbeque is pork and ribs, but **the way it is cut** differs. It is **pulled rather than chopped**. The meat is slow cooked, shredded by hand and **covered with** large amounts of sauce. The **ribs** are **coated** with sauce or covered with **a mix** of **sharp spices** before **pit cooking**.

The sauce is a sweet tomato sauce with a **hint** of **pepper** and **molasses**. It is traditionally served with coleslaw, French fries, baked beans and cornbread. In the western United States, beef **gets preference** over **pork**.

The East Coast **is true to its original beginnings** and uses pork and vinegar sauces. Common **side dishes** are **coleslaw** and hush puppies. The **main variations** are tasted in the vinegar sauces, such as **rich** tomato or **tangy** yellow **mustard-based** sauce.

The history and origin of how barbecue **came to** the United States is **under dispute**. The Barbecue Association states that barbecue first came to California with **Franciscan friars** who **brought** it from the Caribbean.

Another **theory** is that barbecue **originated** in the late 1800s during the **western cattle drives**. The cowboys would **slowly cook** the **tough meat** over a **fire**. This was a way **to tenderize** the meat and make it tastier. Some say **German butchers** brought barbecue to Texas in the mid-1800s. **What is certain** is that barbecuing has been an American pastime for hundreds of years. **Today** almost everyone barbecues **at one time or another**, whether it's a small grill on an **urban patio** or a **complete pig roast** in your own backyard. **As time marches on**, Americans **continue to perfect** this **culinary delight** and tradition.

is true to its original beginnings: é fiel às suas origens
side dishes: pratos de acompanhamento
coleslaw: salada de repolho
main variations: principais variações
rich: rico
tangy: com sabor forte
mustard-based: à base de mostarda
came to/to come to: chegou a/chegar a
under dispute: não se chegou a um acordo
Franciscan friars: monges Franciscanos
brought/to bring: o trouxeram/trazer
theory: teoria
originated/to originate: originou-se/ originar
western cattle drives: condução do gado para o oeste
slowly cook: cozinhar lentamente
tough meat: carne dura
fire: fogueira
to tenderize: amaciar
German butchers: açougueiros alemães
what is certain: o que é certo
today: atualmente
at one time or another: de vez em quando
urban patio: pátio urbano
complete pig roast: assado de porco completo
as time marches on: à medida que o tempo passa
continue/to continue: continuam/ continuar
to perfect/to perfect: aperfeiçoando/ aperfeiçoar
culinary delight: delicia culinária

gastronomy 199

Test Your Comprehension

American Apple Pie, page 184

1. Muitas pessoas consideram a torta de maçã o quê?

2. *"Big apple"* (A Grande Maçã) é o apelido de qual cidade norte-americana?

Taste of America, página 186

1. Qual é a verdura oficial de Massachussets?

2. Segundo muitas pessoas, onde há o cachorro-quente mais saboroso?

3. Quais são os ingredientes essenciais para o chili texano?

Blue Plate Special, page 188

1. Qual é a função do restaurante econômico?

2. O que significa *"blue plate special"*?

3. Se alguém pede *"frog sticks"* (palitos de rã) num restaurante econômico, está pedindo na verdade o quê?

Chocolate Chip Cookies, page 190

1. Quem criou o biscoito com pedacinhos de chocolates?

2. O que Ruth fez quando acabou o chocolate para assar?

Teste sua Compreensão

Buffalo Wings, page 192

1. O que são as *"buffalo wings"* (asas de búfalo)?

2. Por que são chamadas *"buffalo wings"*?

Saltwater Taffy, page 193

1. Quem popularizou o *"saltwater taffy"*?

2. Por que se achou que seria popular?

Clam Chowder, page 195

1. Descreva a sopa de molusco norte-americana.

2. Por que a sopa de molusco da Nova Inglaterra ficou mais cremosa com o passar dos anos?

Farmers' Markets, page 196

1. Quando e onde foi o primeiro mercado de fazendeiros nos Estados Unidos?

2. O que é famoso mundialmente no mercado de *Pike Place*?

American Barbecue, page 198

1. Onde os especialistas afirmam ter começado a tradição do churrasco?

2. Qual é a carne usada principalmente no centro-sul e como é cozinhada?

3. Quais são as três teorias sobre como o churrasco chegou aos Estados Unidos?

Answers

Culture

The American Dream página 4 1. Imigração – o sonho de prosperidade e liberdade. 2. Criou milhares de trabalhos e melhorou o padrão de vida. 3. Viver uma vida satisfatória. **A Melting Pot página 5** 1. Pessoas de culturas e raças diferentes vivendo juntas. 2. A região Oeste. 3. Os nativos e os espanhóis **The American Cowboy página 6** 1. Tradição hispânica, originada no México Central, conhecido como "charro". 2. São responsáveis por alimentar os animais, marcar o gado e cavalos, cuidar dos ferimentos, mudar o gado para diferentes pastos, etc. 3. No Museu Nacional e Galeria da Fama da Vaqueira **American Jazz página 8** 1. Nova Orleans, Louisiana 2. Os afro-americanos desenvolveram novas formas de música por volta de 1880. **Early American Literature página 14** 1. Mark Twain, que nasceu em Missouri. 2. John Steinbeck escreveu *The Grapes of Wrath* (*As vinhas da ira*), sua obra-prima. **Artistic Expression página 15** 1. Liberdade de querer, liberdade de expressão, liberdade de crença e liberdade do medo. 2. pop art **The Birthplace of Broadway página 16** 1. Na cidade de Nova York. 2. A comunidade da Broadway foi especialmente ativa apoiando o esforço de guerra. **Cultural Values página 18** 1. Liberdade individual. 2. Educação.

Travel

Camping Trips página 24 1. Acampamento com carro, acampamentos com serviços completos e acampamento na natureza selvagem. 2. Pesquisar e perguntar sobre os alojamentos. 3. Responsabilidade ao acampar para preservar a beleza da natureza. **Rafting the Grand Canyon página 25** 1. Rio Colorado. 2. Excursões sobre história, geologia e fotografia. **Down by the Boardwalk página 26** 1. Final de 1800 em Nova Jersey. 2. Atlantic City em Nova Jersey 3. Pavilhão de vidro para borboletas. **Treasure Islands página 28** 1. Oahu, a cidade é Honolulu. 2. Kauai. 3. Selvas tropicais, maciços de lava inóspitos, praias e montanhas altas com elevadores para esquiar. **The First National Park página 30** 1. O parque nacional Yosemite na Califórnia. 2. Abraham Lincoln 3. Half Dome e El Capitán. **A Walking Tour of D.C. página 32** 1. 555 pés. 2. O segundo discurso inaugural de Lincoln e o discurso de Gettysburg. 3. Unidade, sacrifício, vitória e liberdade. **Made in the USA página 36** 1. Pipoca amanteigada ao jalapeño (tipo de pimenta mexicana). 2. Ao Departamento do Tesouro dos Estados Unidos em Washington DC ou ao Fort Worth no Texas **San Juan Orcas página 38** 1. O estado de Washington. 2. Da primavera ao outono. 3. Pode andar de caiaque pelas Ilhas de San Juan.

Tradition

Choices in Education página 44 1. 16-18. 2. Elementary (Fundamental I segmento), Junior High (Fundamental II segmento) e Senior High (Ensino Médio). 3. 4 ou mais. **Traditions for the New Year página 46** 1. 31 de dezembro. 2. A cidade de Nova York. 3. O Rose Bowl. **April Fool's! página 49** 1. Primeiro de abril. 2. Na França no final de 1500. 3. É tempo de brincadeiras. **An American Christmas página 50** 1. Inglaterra, Alemanha, Holanda 2. eggnog **Giving Thanks página 52** 1. Na quarta quinta-feira de novembro. 2. Os nativos norte-americanos e os colonos, que foram os primeiros imigrantes a chegarem aos Estados Unidos. **America's Favorite Sport página 54** 1. A partida do Rose Bowl 2. Canton, Ohio 3. As animadoras dos Dallas Cowboys **The National Pastime página 56** 1. comer cachorros-quentes, amendoins e Cracker Jacks, cantar e torcer nos estádios, colecionar autógrafos, tornar-se membro dos fãs-clubes. 2. Babe Ruth **The American Flag página 58** 1. liberdade e orgulho. 2. Francis Bellamy **Remembrance and Honor página 61** 1. Dia da Decoração. 2. Para honrar aqueles que deram suas vidas pelo país.

Respostas

Celebration

Luck of the Irish página 66 1. 1737 em Boston, Massachusetts 2. são beliscadas. **Powwows página 68** 1. Reunião entre o curandeiro e os líderes espirituais. 2. Pessoas se reunindo para banquetear, dançar, cantar e tocar tambor. 3. falso. **Seasonal Celebrations página 70** 1. Dar as boas-vindas ao outono e a mudança de cor das folhas. 2. Melhor escultura de gelo. 3. Capturando cobras em Rattlesnake Roundup. **Flavor of America página 72** 1. São montados e emoldurados para a posteridade. 2. Las Cruces, Novo México 3. dois bilhões de libras, ou 25% do queijo do país por ano. **Parents Appreciation Day página 75** 1. Cravo vermelho. 2. Não está clara. Alguns dizem que começou num serviço religioso em Virginia do Oeste ou em Vancouver, Washington. **Celebrating the Worker página 79** 1. Primeira segunda-feira de Setembro. 2. Na cidade de Nova York em 1882; 1894. 3. Encerramento da temporada de verão. **Shakespeare Festivals página 80** Um poeta e dramaturgo inglês. 2. Um festival gratuito celebrado em São Francisco. 3. Através de doações daqueles que apoiam a beleza da obra de William Shakespeare.

People

Trail of Discovery página 88 1. Para explorar o oeste norte-americano. 2. Sacagawea. 3. Por ser uma mulher, ajudou a dissipar a ideia de que o grupo era um destacamento de guerra. **Mother of Civil Rights página 89** 1. Ceder seu lugar a um passageiro branco no ônibus municipal. 2. 1956 **The Founding Fathers página 90** 1. Os líderes políticos que assinaram a Declaração da Independência ou a Constituição dos Estados Unidos e que foram ativos na Revolução Americana. 2. George Washington 3. Thomas Jefferson 4. A experiência com a pipa, em que foi comprovada a natureza da eletricidade. **Frank Lloyd Wright página 94** 1. Casas da pradaria. 2. Tetos inclinados, linhas horizontais bem definidas, linhas estendidas que se confundem com a paisagem. **Rags to Riches página 95** 1. As pessoas ricas eram obrigadas moralmente a devolver seu dinheiro para outras pessoas na sociedade. 2. Quando Carnegie era jovem, o coronel James Anderson, um homem rico, permitiu-lhe usar sua biblioteca pessoal gratuitamente. 3. Mais de US$ 350 milhões. **America Takes Flight página 96** 1. Com os lucros de seu negócio de bicicletas puderam pagar as construções dos aviões. 2. Era uma área que tinha ventos constantes. Podiam planar e aterrissar com segurança nas dunas da área. 3. Em 1928 foi a primeira mulher a voar sobre o Oceano Atlântico como passageira. Em 1932 tornou-se a primeira mulher a voar sobre o Oceano Atlântico. **Dr. Jonas Salk página 99** 1. A vacina contra a pólio. 2. Que a vacina fosse distribuída o máximo possível, para tantas pessoas quanto fosse possível. **Angel of the Battlefield página 100** 1. Por causa do seu trabalho compassivo durante a guerra civil, ajudou a muitos soldados feridos no campo de batalha. 2. Ajudou ao governo a buscar informações sobre os soldados desaparecidos.

Business

Introduction to Taxes página 108 1. O Serviço da Receita Federal. 2. Ao Tesouro dos Estados Unidos, que paga vários gastos governamentais. 3. O governo lhe cobrará juros e multas. **Entrepreneurship página 110** 1. Linguagem, habilidades nos negócios e capital inicial. 2. Bancos. 3. Montar um negócio que não precisa de muito dinheiro para ser montado. **Banking in America página 112** 1. Porque não têm documento de identificação para abrir uma conta bancária, diferenças culturais. 2. Os agentes da lei dizem que os criminosos veem os hispânicos como alvos fáceis, pois são conhecidos por carregarem frequentemente dinheiro vivo. 3. A finalidade do cartão é introduzir seus clientes no setor bancário e ajudar a criar um histórico de crédito. **Negotiating Your Salary página 114** 1. 20 por cento a mais. 2. Fique calado. 3. Ter tudo por escrito. **Retirement Plans página 116** 1. Um plano de aposentadoria qualificado patrocinado por uma empresa para os empregados. 2. Impostos de renda e a maioria dos impostos estatais. 3. 401k. **Mastering the Interview página 118** 1. Falso. 2. Confiança. 3. Faz com que seja visto com distinção e comprometido ou interessado na entrevista. 4. Usted. 5. Estão proibidas.

Answers

Empowerment

Citizenship página 124 1. As pessoas que saíram de um país estrangeiro para viver nos Estados Unidos. Têm algumas das mesmas liberdades e direitos legais dos cidadãos norte-americanos, mas não podem votar nas eleições. 2. Nativos das áreas territoriais dos Estados Unidos. Têm todas as proteções legais que têm os cidadãos, mas não têm todos os direitos políticos dos cidadãos dos Estados Unidos. **Empowerment with Education página 126** 1. Hispânicos. 2. Escolher algumas escolas e entrar em contato com seus escritórios de auxílio financeiro. 3. Mais de 78 mil. **Community Colleges página 128** 1. Mais de 1.200. 2. Um certificado de dois anos. 3. Enfermeira diplomada, aplicação da lei, auxiliar de enfermagem, radiologia e tecnologias da computação. **Helping Children Succeed página 130** 1. Verdadeiro. 2. Os alunos aprendem mais e os pais e professores sentem-se mais apoiados. 3. Passar um tempo na escola, procurar alguém que fale seu idioma, perguntar sobre aulas de idiomas, trabalhar como voluntário. **Bilingual Resources página 132** 1. Indústrias de serviço ao consumidor, venda, comunicações e setor bancário. 2. Muitos dos recrutadores testam os candidatos durante o processo de entrevista. 3. Falar inglês, ter experiência prévia de trabalho. **Legal Resources página 134** 1. Um advogado que estudou as leis de imigração dos Estados Unidos e formou-se numa faculdade de direito. 2. Podem ajudar a obter a situação legal do Departamento de Segurança Nacional ou representação perante o Tribunal de Imigração. **Owning Your Own Home página 136** 1. 46%. 2. Conseguir segurança econômica e ajudar as comunidades a conseguir maior estabilidade. **You and Your Community página 138** 1. Conhecer os vizinhos, integrar-se à vizinhança, ajudar a identificar e usar os recursos disponíveis. 2. Programas para adultos e crianças, cuidado infantil, programas de verão, concertos e festivais locais. 3. Trabalhar como voluntário.

History

Independence Day página 146 1. 50 estados. 2. O dia da independência. **Stars and Stripes página 147** 1. Vermelho, branco e azul. 2. Uma para cada estado. 3. 50 estrelas. 4. 13 listras, vermelhas e brancas. 5. Os treze primeiros estados. **Electoral College página 148** 1. O colégio eleitoral. 2. O vice-presidente. **Supreme Law of the Land página 149** 1. A Lei Suprema do país. 2. Emendas. **Divisions of Power página 150** 1. Executivo, judiciário e legislativo. 2. O Congresso. 3. O Congresso. 4. As pessoas de cada distrito votam num deputado e as pessoas de cada estado votam em dois senadores. 5. Há 100 senadores no Congresso, 2 de cada estado. **Bill of Rights página 153** 1. Do Bill of Rights (da Declaração de Direitos). 2. As 10 primeiras emendas da Constituição dos Estados Unidos. 3. Todas as pessoas que vivem nos Estados Unidos. **United States Presidency página 154** 1. George Washington. 2. Quatro anos. 3. Ser norte-americano nato, não ser naturalizado, ter pelo menos 35 anos de idade e morar nos Estados Unidos há pelo menos 14 anos. 4. Dois mandatos completos.

Respostas

Geography

World Heritage Sites página 166 11. Conservar os locais de importância cultural ou natural e preservar cada lugar para as gerações futuras. 2. No Parque Nacional das Cavernas de Carlsbad. 3. Peixes cegos e aranhas incolores. 4. Os seres vivos mais altos do planeta, árvores sempre-vivas que crescem até 350 pés. **Majestic Mountains página 168** 1. O Monte McKinley ou Denali no Alasca 2. O Parque da Montanha de Pedra, é o maior pedaço de granito exposto solto conhecido no mundo. **North American Deserts página 170** 1. Um deserto com temperaturas diurnas abaixo de zero durante parte do ano. 2. O deserto de Sonora. 3. O Vale da Morte. 4. Para ficarem em contato com os outros coiotes da área. **The Great Lakes página 172** 1. A praia arenosa. 2. São parte da imigração de patos e gansos, e fornecem comida, paradas de descanso e habitats. 3. Impactos humanos, como a construção de casas, turismo e erosão. **Land of Waterfalls página 174** 1. Uma fonte valiosa de energia hidroelétrica para Ontário e Nova York. 2. Yosemite Falls, na Califórnia. 3. Shoshone Falls, em Idaho. **Tropical Rain Forests página 176** 1. Uma incrível diversidade de fungos, musgos, caracóis, pássaros e outras vidas selvagens. 2. No Havaí, no Monte Waialeale. 3. Os porcos selvagens, plantas e animais introduzidos, agricultura, derrubada de árvores, incêndios. **Temperate Rain Forests página 177** 1. As florestas pluviais temperadas são mais jovens, o solo das florestas temperadas contém mais nutrientes, as florestas temperadas são mais escassas. 2. O Parque Nacional Olympic 3. A Floresta Nacional Tongass no sudeste do Alasca. **Volcanoes in the United States página 178** 1. 18. 2. Mauna Loa 3. Um famoso templo havaiano de 700 anos, casas, estradas.

Gastronomy

American Apple Pie página 184 1. A comida que lhe faz sentir bem. 2. A cidade de Nova York. **Taste of America página 186** 1. Feijão branco. 2. Num jogo de beisebol. 3. Carne moída, alho, cominho e pimenta. **Blue Plate Special página 188** 1. Fornecer uma comida deliciosa e barata, de estilo caseiro, num ambiente confortável. 2. Um prato especialmente barato. 3. batatas fritas **Chocolate Chip Cookies página 190** 1. Ruth Wakefield. 2. Usou o chocolate que tinha em mãos – uma barra de chocolate meio amargo, que tinha recebido de Andrew Nestle. **Buffalo Wings página 192** 1. Asas de frango fritas e cobertas com um molho apimentado. 2. Porque se originou na cidade de Buffalo, em Nova York. **Saltwater Taffy página 193** 1. Joseph Fralinger 2. Pensou que os turistas poderiam querer algo delicioso para guardar de recordação de suas férias em Atlantic City. **Clam Chowder página 194** 1. Uma sopa popular que contém moluscos e caldo, e às vezes pedaços de batata, cebolas e palitos de cenoura. 2. Porque os turistas tinham medo de comer mariscos e preferiam uma sopa mais cremosa. **Farmers' Markets página 196** 1. Em 1634, em Boston. 2. O "peixe voador", em que os empregados jogam peixes uns aos outros em vez de passá-los de mão em mão. **American Barbecue página 198** 1. No sul. 2. Porco e costelas – a carne é despedaçada ao invés de picada, cozida lentamente, é despedaçada à mão e coberta com grande quantidade de molho. 3. Os monges Franciscanos trouxeram do Caribe; das conduções de gado, quando os vaqueiros cozinhavam a carne sobre o fogo; açougueiros alemães trouxeram o churrasco para o Texas por volta de 1800.

ROTAPLAN
GRÁFICA E EDITORA LTDA
Rua Álvaro Seixas, 165
Engenho Novo - Rio de Janeiro
Tels.: (21) 2201-2089 / 8898
E-mail: rotaplanrio@gmail.com